The Shakes

By the same authors

King Arthur – The True Story

We would like to thank Mark Booth, Lindsay Symons, Roderick Brown, Andrea Henry, Dennis Barker, Tracey Jennings, Cathy Schofield, Gilly Smith, Jenny Johnson, Dan and Susanna Shadrake, Annette and Tim Burkitt, Andrew Lownie, Alison Patrick, Steven Griffin and Malcolm Ordever for all their invaluable help.

THE SHAKESPEARE CONSPIRACY

Graham Phillips & Martin Keatman

ARROW

This edition published by Arrow Books Limited 1995

1 3 5 7 9 10 8 6 4 2

First published in the United Kingdom in 1994 by
Century
Random House UK Ltd, 20 Vauxhall Bridge Road, London SW1V 2SA

Arrow Books Ltd
Random House UK Ltd, 20 Vauxhall Bridge Road, London SW1V 2SA

Random House Australia (Pty) Limited
20 Alfred Street, Milsons Point, Sydney,
New South Wales 2061, Australia

Random House New Zealand Limited
18 Poland Road, Glenfield
Auckland 10, New Zealand

Random House South Africa (Pty) Limited
PO Box 337, Bergvlei, South Africa

Random House UK Limited Reg. No. 954009

Papers used by Random House UK Limited
are natural, recyclable products made from wood grown in
sustainable forests. The manufacturing processes conform to
the environmental regulations of the country of origin.

A CIP catalogue record for this book
is available from the British Library

ISBN 0 09 930247 0

Printed and bound in Great Britain by
Cox & Wyman Ltd, Reading, Berkshire

Contents

List of Illustrations

Photographs

Title Page of the 1623 First Folio (British Library).
The Chandos Portrait (National Portrait Gallery).
The *Sir Thomas More* Insurrection Scene (British Library).
Sir Philip Sidney (National Portrait Gallery).
Christopher Marlowe (Corpus Christi, Cambridge).
Richard Burbage (Dulwich College Picture Library).
Ben Jonson (Dulwich College Picture Library).
William Cecil (National Portrait Gallery).
Robert Cecil (National Portrait Gallery).
Sir Francis Walsingham (National Portrait Gallery).
Sir Walter Ralegh and his son (National Portrait Gallery).
Lord Strange (Derby Collection).
Queen Elizabeth I (National Portrait Gallery).
The Shakespeare Memorial in Holy Trinity Church, Stratford.

Illustrations

Chapter 1

The Legend

What is the Shakespeare Conspiracy? According to the *Oxford English Dictionary*, a conspiracy involves a group plan devised to further some, usually corrupt, objective. This is arguably what has occurred to create the 'orthodox' life of William Shakespeare; myths and legends fashioned over the years to corrupt Shakespeare into something he was not. Many 'traditional' Shakespeare biographies are historically unfounded, spun from romantic mythology rather than surviving record. Even his imagined title – the Bard – is misleading. A Bard was a Celtic court poet, suggesting that Shakespeare was the court poet to Queen Elizabeth or James I. Although Shakespeare's plays were performed before these monarchs, we have no evidence that he ever wrote anything for either of them exclusively. Shakespeare was certainly never called the Bard in his lifetime.

The reason for so much Shakespearean mythology is that so little is known about the man himself. The life of William Shakespeare is shrouded in mystery. There is no record of him receiving an education, buying a book or writing a single letter, and no original manuscript of a Shakespeare play survives. There is no direct record of his conversations, and no one in his home town seems to have known that he was a successful playwright while he was alive. There is not even a contemporary portrait to reveal his true appearance. Although a number of mentions of William Shakespeare the poet-dramatist appear on record during the 1590s and early 1600s, they comment only briefly on his writings, telling us nothing about the man. Less is known about Shakespeare than almost any other playwright of his time.

This investigation aims to remove this cloak of secrecy and

1

solve the mysteries of William Shakespeare's life. From historical record we discover vital new evidence of another, more sinister, conspiracy in which Shakespeare was embroiled – a conspiracy which may ultimately have claimed his life.

Almost every nation on earth reads, studies and performs the works of William Shakespeare. No writer of any country, nor any age, has ever enjoyed such universal popularity. Besides religious or political leaders, it is difficult to bring to mind anyone re-nowned on such a colossal scale. Shakespeare has been published wider than any author in history; more than 50,000 separate publications of his works survive. In collections of quotations, Shakespeare is second to none. The *Oxford Dictionary of Quotations* contains 38 pages from the best selling book of all time, the Bible. It is only exceeded by one other source, the 70 pages of Shakespeare. Neither has any writer been so praised. As William Hazlitt observed, 'The striking peculiarity of Shakespeare's mind was its generic quality, its power of communication with all other minds.'

It is perhaps this quality that has earned Shakespeare the supreme accolade, that of lending his name to an era. Other than a monarch or an emperor, few can boast that a time or place is so exclusively theirs. As we talk of Napoleonic Europe or Victorian England, so we speak of Shakespearean London or the Age of Shakespeare. No other artist, let alone writer, has had their name inscribed on such a towering edifice. 'Thou in our wonder and astonishment, hast built thyself a long-live monument,' wrote Milton, in praise of Shakespeare.

Shakespeare is by far and without doubt the most popular and successful writer of all time. But what of the man himself? Who was William Shakespeare?

We begin with the 'orthodox' version of his life:

On 23 April 1564, in an upstairs room of a Stratford house in Warwickshire, a son was born to John and Mary Shakespeare; three days later the boy was baptised William at the local parish church.

For the first few years of his life, William Shakespeare lived at the family home in Henley Street, from where his father ran his business as a glover. Fortune smiled on the Shakespeare family; in 1565 John was elected alderman, and three years later he became chief magistrate, the highest civic office in the town.

Aged five, William began his education at the local grammar school, learning to read and write, before entering the middle school two years later. At seven he mastered Latin, received weekly lessons in practical drama, and at Whitsun took part in the school's annual play. Before leaving in his early teens, he had moved into the upper school where he studied logic, poetry and history.

William displayed a keen interest in drama, often visiting nearby Coventry to watch its famous Mystery Plays. Then in 1575, at the age of eleven, he was to witness a spectacular event which shaped his future career. At Kenilworth, twelve miles from Stratford, a theatrical pageant was staged before the Queen during her nineteen-day stay with the Earl of Leicester. Shakespeare was transfixed, there and then deciding that his vocation lay in drama. However, any hope of joining the theatre would have to wait; in 1576 John Shakespeare found himself in financial difficulties, and William was forced to enter his father's business as a glover.

William Shakespeare started his own family young. In November 1582, at eighteen, he married Anne Hathaway from nearby Shottery, and by twenty-one he had fathered three children: twins, Hamnet and Judith, and their older sister Susanna. Anne's father Richard had been a wealthy farmer, but he had died before the wedding and her family were also on hard times. The young couple were therefore obliged to live in Henley Street with William's parents.

With John Shakespeare facing bankruptcy, and having lost his position as alderman of the town, William was forced to take drastic measures to feed his family and became a poacher. Before long, he was caught killing deer on the nearby Charlecote Estate, and was hauled before Sir Thomas Lucy, the landowner and district magistrate. But the Shakespeares were well-respected and Lucy was lenient. William's only penance was that he promise to keep the peace thereafter, a promise he was to honour for the rest of his life.

Fortunes changed for William in 1587 when, at the age of

twenty-three, the premier company of actors, The Queen's Men, visited Stratford. Just before their performance on 13 June William Knell, one of the players, died, offering Shakespeare the chance of a lifetime. He stood in for Knell, so impressing the players with his natural talent that he was offered a permanent place in the troupe. Recognising a unique opportunity to provide for his family, William accepted the position. The journey from Stratford to London took three days on horseback, but the impoverished William was forced to leave his wife and children at home and make the journey on foot.

Shakespeare began his new career at James Burbage's Theatre in Shoreditch. However, acting alone failed to cover his board and keep, and so he found extra work as a theatre valet, looking after the patrons' horses. Something about the polite and smart young man gained the attention of the wealthy visitors, and before long he was noticed by the Earl of Southampton, who used his influence to make Shakespeare a full-time actor.

Shakespeare was not only well-mannered, he was also handsome. Everyone he met liked him instantly and deep affection often followed. He was gentle, unassuming and thoughtful; although extremely witty, he displayed not a trace of malice or cynicism in his wit.

By 1592 Shakespeare had begun his writing career, and playwright Robert Greene warned the country's most distinguished dramatists that Shakespeare was potentially their greatest rival. But Shakespeare's charm and charisma made him no enemies. In 1593, when Shakespeare joined the performing company of Lord Strange, the printer Henry Chettle wrote that Shakespeare was 'a civil playwright, excellent and uprighteous, honest and graceful in his writing'.

On 18 April 1593 Shakespeare's first poem, *Venus and Adonis*, was patronised by Lord Southampton, and over the next few years he was to write well over 150 published poems.

In the spring of 1594 Lord Strange died and Lord Hunsdon, the Queen's Chamberlain, offered to patronise the players. As Chamberlain, Lord Hunsdon was chief authority overseeing all royal entertainments, and so ensured that Shakespeare's company were billed to appear at court.

By 1595 Shakespeare was one of the most accomplished dramatists of his day, and in March of that year his plays were performed before the Queen herself. There was no stopping Shakespeare, and over the next twenty years he wrote no fewer than thirty-seven plays.

Shakespeare was not only a literary genius, he also had a firm head for business. By the late 1590s he acquired a financial investment in the company, and in 1599 bought shares in the newly built Globe Theatre in Southwark. His financial acumen had already reaped rewards. As early as 1597 Shakespeare returned to Stratford to buy New Place, the second largest house in the town. Thereafter his wife and family lived prosperously, and William helped discharge his father from bankruptcy.

Although busy in London, Shakespeare always made time each year for a special vacation to spend alone with his family. Although much of his time was spent writing, he often managed a small role in each of his plays; for example, playing the Ghost in his first staging of *Hamlet*. He even helped his friend, the playwright Ben Jonson, by acting for him. Indeed Jonson greatly admired Shakespeare's ability as a playwright who, in his opinion, 'never blotted a line' when he wrote.

By now Shakespeare was hailed as the greatest living playwright, and in 1598 the distinguished writer Francis Meres listed him as one of 'the most passionate amongst us to bewail and bemoan the perplexities of love'.

In May 1599 Shakespeare's company moved to the Globe Theatre in Southwark, heralding his finest hour. To add to his riches, in 1603 his company received the highest honour; the new king, James I, lent his name to the company, thereafter called The King's Men.

Unfortunately, on 29 June 1613 the Globe was gutted by fire, and although it was reopened the following year, Shakespeare retired to Stratford. He led a peaceful retirement, occasionally returning to London to drink and discuss literature with his poet friends Ben Jonson, John Donne and Francis Beaumont at the Mermaid Tavern in Bread Street, behind St Paul's Cathedral.

Sadly, on his birthday in 1616, Shakespeare contracted a fever and died in his sleep, aged fifty-two. He was buried a few days later in a tomb at Stratford's Holy Trinity Church.

This, in essence, is the life of William Shakespeare as related in many of his biographies, and outlined in the myriad guide books to Stratford-upon-Avon. It is Shakespeare's 'orthodox' biography, the story heard by tourists, theatre-goers and school children the world over. Amongst history's other great artistic luminaries – so often alcoholics, drug addicts, or down-and-outs – Shakespeare stands almost alone as a character beyond reproach.

According to this orthodox version of Shakespeare's life, the Bard is industrious, upstanding, charismatic and loved by all. He mixes freely with royalty and commoner alike, he never looks down on anyone, and makes no enemies. He is a self-made man, a devoted husband and a kindly father. He has one brush with the law, born of necessity, learns his lesson and becomes a paragon of virtue for the rest of his days. Not only is his literary genius second to none, he is also a superb, level-headed businessman, one of Stratford's most respected citizens.

Whether writers, musicians or painters, great artists seldom fit well into their contemporary society, usually not being recognised until after their deaths. They are often moody, manic or reclusive, and unless born into wealth, few succeed financially. Often, such is the price of genius. So why is William Shakespeare so different? Is this traditional story of his exemplary life really true?

Shakespeare has become something akin to the patron saint of English literature. Representing the very soul of the written word, he is almost a god to the world of theatre. Moreover, throughout the English-speaking world, millions culturally identify themselves with the great Bard, claiming they 'speak the language of Shakespeare'. Whether this image of William Shakespeare has been created deliberately or unconsciously, common sense would suggest that Shakespeare's life has to *some* extent been mythologised over the years. However, when we disentangle the historical Shakespeare from the literary legend, the extent of the mythologising is phenomenal. Almost *everything* in the orthodox life of William Shakespeare is fictitious.

The true history of William Shakespeare has remained virtually untold for four centuries, historians risking academic isolation if they dare to question a romance told for so long that it has become accepted 'fact'. This investigation focuses on the real

William Shakespeare – the man, not the legend – the poet-dramatist, not the patron saint of English literature.

Summary

According to the 'orthodox' version of Shakespeare's life, the Bard is industrious, upstanding, charismatic and loved by all. This, in essence, is the *legend* of William Shakespeare:

1. William Shakespeare was born in Stratford on 23 April 1564, in an upstairs room of a house in Henley Street, where his father John ran his business as a glover. Aged five, William began his education at the local grammar school, learning to read and write before entering the middle school two years later. At the age of seven he mastered Latin, received weekly lessons in practical drama, and each Whitsun took part in the school's annual play. By his early teens he had moved into the upper school where he studied logic, poetry and history.

2. In November 1582, at eighteen, he married Anne Hathaway from nearby Shottery, and by twenty-one he had fathered three children: twins, Hamnet and Judith, and their older sister Susanna. In 1587, when Shakespeare was twenty-three, the premier acting company The Queen's Men visited Stratford. Just before their performance on 13 June one of the players died and Shakespeare stood in. His natural talent so impressed the players that he was offered a permanent place in the troupe.

3. Shakespeare began his new career at James Burbage's Theatre in London, where he made extra money looking after the patrons' horses. Before long his writing potential was noticed by the Earl of Southampton, who used his influence to make Shakespeare a full-time actor and eventually a dramatist. In 1592 the playwright Robert Greene warned the country's most distinguished dramatists that Shakespeare was their greatest potential rival.

4. On 18 April 1593 Shakespeare's first poem, *Venus and Adonis*, was patronised by Lord Southampton, and over the next few years he wrote well over 150 published poems. By 1595 Shakespeare was one of the most accomplished dramatists of his day; in

March of that year two of his plays were performed before the Queen herself. Over the next twenty years he wrote no fewer than thirty-seven plays.

5. By the late 1590s Shakespeare had acquired a financial investment in the Burbage company, and in 1599 bought shares in the newly built Globe Theatre in Southwark. His financial acumen had already reaped rewards; as early as 1597 Shakespeare returned to buy New Place, the second largest house in the town of Stratford.

6. In May 1599 Shakespeare's company moved to the Globe, heralding his finest hour. In 1603 his company earned the highest accolade of all; the new King, James I, honoured the company with the title The King's Men. Unfortunately, on 29 June 1613 the Globe burned to the ground, and although it was rebuilt the following year, Shakespeare retired to Stratford.

7. Shakespeare led a peaceful retirement, often returning to London to drink and discuss literature with his poet friends Ben Jonson, John Donne and Francis Beaumont at the Mermaid Tavern in Bread Street, behind St Paul's Cathedral. Sadly, on his birthday in 1616, Shakespeare contracted a fever and died in his sleep, aged fifty-two. He was buried a few days later in a tomb at Stratford's Holy Trinity Church.

8. Shakespeare mixes freely with royalty and commoner alike. He never looks down on anyone and makes no enemies. He is a self-made man, a devoted husband and a kindly father. Not only is his literary genius second to none, he is also a superb, level-headed businessman, one of Stratford's most respected citizens.

Chapter 2

Myth and Reality

Every year over a million tourists visit the Warwickshire town of Stratford-upon-Avon, paying homage to the man who is arguably history's greatest literary genius, William Shakespeare. Yet the dramatist who penned the great works may not be all the Stratford tourist industry would have us believe. Many aspects of his life are more a matter of legend than historical fact.

Shakespeare is said to have been born in the so-called 'Birthplace' in Henley Street, a building now owned by the Birthplace Trust. Although Shakespeare's father John owned the property in Henley Street, there is no historical record to indicate that William Shakespeare was actually born there.

It is not even certain when Shakespeare was born. Although each year on 23 April a parade is held in the town, attracting sightseers and literary pilgrims from around the world, all that is known for sure is that he was christened on 26 April. The parish records show that he was baptised in Stratford-upon-Avon on 26 April 1564 as 'Gulielmus Shaksper', the son of John Shakespeare, a glover and wool-dealer. The same man, under the names 'William Shaksper' or 'Will Shakspere', appears in a number of town records; he married at eighteen, sired three children and was buried in Holy Trinity Church in 1616. Although he may, or may not, have been born on 23 April, it has been considered fitting, and gone virtually unquestioned, that the 'father of modern English' should have been born on St George's day, the feast of England's patron saint.

Following his christening, there is not one historical record of William Shakespeare until his marriage to Anne Hathaway in 1582, rendering all notions of his education complete guesswork.

9

Shakespeare's family tree.

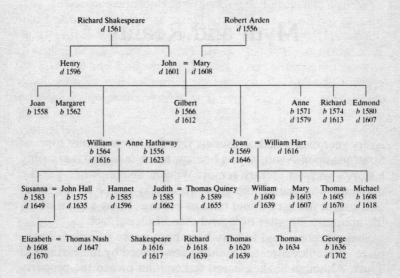

He *might* have attended the grammar school, the New King's School, but there is no evidence. As the son of an alderman, William would have been entitled to his education here. Nevertheless, this would depend on whether or not his father wished it. Unlike the aristocracy, few middle-class families of the time would have considered it necessary to provide their sons with a classical education. As a trader, it is more likely that John Shakespeare would have expected his son to follow in the family business; a glover's apprenticeship would seem more appropriate. He may have been taught to read and write, but that was probably all; the stories about Latin, classical poetry and acting lessons are pure fantasy. In fact, even mythologiser John Aubrey says that Shakespeare's contemporary playwright Ben Jonson said that Shakespeare 'had but little Latin and less Greek'. (See below.)

In 1565 John Shakespeare did become an alderman, and he

was in financial difficulties a decade later, but nothing is known of William. He *probably* worked in his father's business, but there is no way of proving it.

Well-worn tales of the young William Shakespeare regularly visiting the Coventry Mystery Plays, and his awe-struck attendance at the theatrical spectacular for Queen Elizabeth in Kenilworth, are also guesswork. The Queen did visit Kenilworth to be entertained by actors in 1575, and the craft guilds of Coventry did give their annual performances of the Mystery Plays during that period, but there is no evidence that Shakespeare or any of his family attended these events. The notion is an eighteenth-century 'maybe', becoming a nineteenth-century 'probably', and finally a twentieth-century 'certainly'.

The same mythological status applies to the legendary love-bond between Shakespeare and his wife Anne Hathaway, who is said to have been brought up in the famous cottage in Shottery on the outskirts of Stratford. In his will Shakespeare left her only his 'second best bed'. Why Shakespeare seemingly insulted his wife, and apparently failed to provide for her in her twilight years, is a question ill-received by Stratford's tourist industry, who often promote the ideal, family-man image. Even if it is accepted that Shakespeare left nothing to his wife because, as the orthodox biographers point out, she may have been provided for under English law regardless, why leave her the *second* best bed? The clear implication is that the *first* best bed was intended for someone else. Even if the 'second best bed' did not constitute an insult, there is still not one letter, poem or surviving document that contains a single word of affection between Shakespeare and his wife. If Shakespeare's love-life was as the orthodox biographers would have us believe, it is strange indeed that the man of whom Francis Meres wrote 'the most passionate amongst us to bewail and bemoan the perplexities of love' did not write a single thing for, or about, his beloved wife; this is the poet who not only wrote the greatest love sonnets ever published, but also *Romeo and Juliet*, the world's most famous love story.

The known circumstances of Shakespeare's marriage suggest that he was obliged to marry Anne. A licence for William Shakespeare's marriage was first issued in Worcester on 27 November 1582, not to Anne Hathaway but to a mysterious Anne Whately of Temple Grafton. Next day, the name was changed to Anne Hathaway of Stratford. Although this could have been a clerical error, it is equally possible that the prospective marriage to the Whately girl was cancelled by an irate Hathaway family, insisting that Shakespeare marry their pregnant daughter – Shakespeare's marriage was only six months old when his first child Susanna was baptised.

From the only known facts pertaining to the relationship between Anne and William, it seems far from ideal. Shakespeare evidently wanted to marry someone else, he married a woman who was already with child, and all he left her was his 'second best bed'. Romanticism aside, logic suggests that the Shakespeares had a difficult marriage, perhaps only saved by William's prolonged periods of absence in London.

It is not known where the Shakespeares lived before the purchase of New Place in 1597. Although there is no record of them owning or renting their own home in the 1580s, it is pure conjecture that they lived with Shakespeare's family. They may not have lived in Stratford at all, but if they did live with Shakespeare's family, times would probably have been hard; the town records show that Shakespeare's family was by now in financial trouble. As for the brave William supporting his family by poaching, this is yet another doubtful legend.

The story of the deer poaching at Charlecote Park first appeared in 1709, in an attempted Shakespeare biography by the playwright Nicholas Rowe. He names his source as the actor Thomas Betterton, who had made 'a journey into Warwickshire on the purpose of gathering up what remains' to be known of Shakespeare's life. All that is known for sure, therefore, is that a century after Shakespeare's youth the story was told. Historically, it is impossible for Shakespeare to have been poaching on Sir Thomas Lucy's deer park, since the records of the Charlecote Estate clearly show that Sir Thomas did not have a deer park at the time in question.

The story that Shakespeare thereafter led a spotless, law-abiding life is certainly not true. In late 1596 it was recorded by the Court of the Queen's Bench in Southwark that a William Wayte craved sureties of the peace against William Shakespeare 'for fear of death and so forth'. In other words Shakespeare had threatened his life. In November the following year tax collectors of the Ward of Bishopsgate recorded that they could not collect a tax from Shakespeare as he had fled the area. In October 1598 he was again listed as a 'tax delinquent', this time in the London parish of St Helen's; once more, he appears to have fled. The tax was still owing in 1599, as Shakespeare is again sought by the parish authorities.

Any theories concerning how Shakespeare joined the theatre, or how he first began writing, are simply that – theories. The only record of Shakespeare from his marriage at eighteen, until around his thirtieth year, are the births of his children, and his name on a legal document relating to his mother. The idea that he first became an actor by joining The Queen's Men during their Stratford tour in 1587 is mere supposition. A few days before the Stratford performance on 13 June William Knell did indeed die, fighting a duel with fellow actor John Towne at Thame in Oxfordshire. Knell had been an accomplished actor and his widow married another actor, John Heminge, who later became Shakespeare's associate. Whether or not this really gave Shakespeare his break is historically unknown. There is no surviving record pertaining to Shakespeare's first involvement with the theatre. Although many theories have been postulated to account for these important missing years, this formative period remains a total mystery.

Shakespeare's employment as a theatre valet is an even later legend. The account first appeared in the mid eighteenth century, well after the two earliest Shakespeare biographers, Nicholas Rowe (1709) and Alexander Pope (1725), fail to mention the episode. Nor is it historically known how Shakespeare came to be patronised by the Earl of Southampton. Even Rowe admits that he attempted to find out, but that he failed.

This body of legend and fable surrounding Shakespeare's life appears tame in comparison to the most baseless mythologising of all, the descriptions of the man's personality and appearance. The earliest eighteenth-century biographers, such as Rowe and Pope, simply refer to Shakespeare as a man of good wit, and even this was after a century of hearsay. By the nineteenth century scores of preposterous biographies appeared, each including new, imaginary descriptions of the playwright. The crescendo came this century, with the publication of H. Pearson's *A Life of Shakespeare* in the 1940s. Pearson appears to have incorporated every adjective given by his predecessors, stringing them together in lines of unfounded adoration. According to Pearson, Shakespeare was 'friendly, gentle, obliging, kindly, unassuming, engaging, sweet-natured and good-mannered'. Pearson fails to explain that his list of superlatives is historically ungrounded.

A Life of Shakespeare marked the pinnacle of Shakespearean mythologising, Pearson himself being one of the most accomplished mythologisers of all. Regrettably, he has been quoted and requoted in numerous Shakespearean guide books, and his invented Shakespearean fables have been published over and over again. Pearson may have written *A* life of Shakespeare, but he certainly did not write *The* life of Shakespeare. Virtually no historical evidence exists that gives insight into Shakespeare's character.

Regarding Shakespeare's physical appearance, no authenticated portrait exists. The Chandos portrait in the National Gallery is believed to be of William Shakespeare as, according to its late seventeenth-century provenance, it was originally owned by the poet Sir William Davenant, then by actor Thomas Betterton, both theatrical characters. However, even if it had first belonged to Davenant, the fact that he was only ten when Shakespeare died seems to exclude it as a life portrait. Other supposed portraits, such as the famous Flowers portraits, often found on pub signs and the covers of text books, were much later representations. Although the debate continues, no authenticated portrait of William Shakespeare has yet been discovered.

The only picture in existence with any valid claim to being an authentic likeness of Shakespeare is the cover engraving of the oldest surviving edition of his plays printed in 1623. Now called the First Folio, it was actually entitled *Mr William Shakespeare's Comedies, Histories, and Tragedies*, and contained thirty-six plays. In the introduction we learn that Shakespeare is dead, but not when or how he died. The crude 'portrait' of Shakespeare that appeared on the frontispiece is the oldest surviving representation, and shows the bald-headed, round-faced man the world has come to know. However, inconsistencies in the depiction – two left eyes, hair longer on one side than the other, a huge head on a diminutive torso – suggest a caricature rather than a contemporary portrait.

Returning to his career, the first record of William Shakespeare as a poet or dramatist is in the spring of 1593, when his poem *Venus and Adonis* was published in London, accompanied by a dedication to his patron, the Earl of Southampton. This was the first published work of the man who was destined to become the most famous poet in history. Thereafter, throughout the 1590s, more of Shakespeare's works were published and his plays performed.

Besides his name appearing on various legal documents, such as court proceedings, house deeds and so forth, all that is known about Shakespeare's life can be summarised in a few paragraphs:

He may have begun his career at James Burbage's Theatre in Shoreditch. Erected in 1576, this was the first purpose-built theatre in England since Roman times. In 1593 Shakespeare seems to have been working in the theatre as an actor, employed by Lord Strange's company. When *Titus Andronicus* was published the following year, its title page proclaimed it had first been played for Lord Strange (who later became the Earl of Derby). In 1594, when Lord Strange died, Lord Hunsdon, the Queen's Chamberlain, offered to patronise the players and in December of that year Shakespeare was paid a share of £20 for 'several comedies' acted before Queen Elizabeth herself.

In 1599 Shakespeare purchased a minor shareholding in the Globe, along with fellow actors including John Heminge and Henry Condell. After the death of Queen Elizabeth in 1603, the players were granted a licence to perform their plays for the new King, James I, and in 1608 Shakespeare was one of seven actors who acquired a shareholding in the new Blackfriars Theatre. Although the theatre shares indicate Shakespeare's financial stability by this time, they do not account for his earlier wealth; he had already bought New Place in 1597. Moreover, surviving records from Stratford show that he made most of his money in the grain market and from property deals.

Although a few passing mentions of William Shakespeare the poet-dramatist appear on record during the 1590s and early 1600s, they comment only briefly on his writings and tell us nothing about the man. Of all his contemporary poets and dramatists – such as Christopher Marlowe, Edmund Spenser, Gabriel Harvey, Thomas Nashe, John Donne, John Fletcher, Thomas Lodge, Robert Greene, Philip Sidney, George Chapman, Thomas Heywood, Francis Beaumont, John Lyly, Ben Jonson, Thomas Kyd, George Peele, Thomas Dekker, Thomas Middleton and John Webster – Webster is the only playwright of whom we know less, but, unlike Shakespeare, Webster was not recognised in his day.

Although the orthodox biographers argue that plenty is known about Shakespeare's life, the assertion is true but misleading. Decades of research have accumulated considerable documentation regarding Shakespeare's business life, indeed far more than to many other playwrights. But despite the years of searching, almost nothing regarding Shakespeare the poet-dramatist has surfaced, including no contemporary references to his education, the launch of his career, his personality, his views, his interests, any conversations with him or even his personal writings. All that exists is less than a dozen contemporary allusions to Shakespeare's work, and some of *these* may not be all they seem.

The first is the testimony of the dying poet Robert Greene, in the late summer of 1592. The document, known as the *Groat's-worth of Wit*, is purported to show that Shakespeare was recognised as both an actor and playwright as early as 1592. However, all Greene says, when addressing his fellow poets, is that someone described as an 'upstart crow' . . . 'supposes he is as well able to bombast out a blank verse [write plays or poems] as the best of you'.

Shakespeare has been linked to the 'upstart crow' because, according to Greene, the 'upstart crow' thinks himself the only 'shake-scene' in the country. The term 'shake-scene' – presumably one who can make the stage tremble with his presence – is believed to be a pun on Shakespeare's name. This is possible, as Greene refers to the 'upstart crow' as having a 'tiger's heart wrapped in a player's hide', a play on 'tiger's heart wrapped in a woman's hide' from *Henry VI: Part III*. But even if the 'upstart crow' *is* Shakespeare, the passing allusion hardly constitutes evidence that Shakespeare was considered a great poet and dramatist respected by all. All it means is that Shakespeare *thinks* he is and that Greene, for one, *does not*.

In 1593 the printer Henry Chettle supposedly wrote that Shakespeare was 'a civil playwright, excellent and uprighteous, honest and graceful in his writing'. Although Shakespeare's biographers often give this precise quote, what Chettle actually said is very different, and may not even be alluding to Shakespeare. Chettle said simply that he disagrees with the testimony of Robert Greene in his *Groat's-worth of Wit*. He complains that Greene's writing had offended a number a playwrights, and writes of one whom he does not name:

> . . . his demeanour [is] no less civil than he [is] excellent in the quality he professes: Besides divers of worship have reported his uprightness of dealing, which argues his honesty, and his facetious grace in writing, that approves his art.

There is no way of knowing whether this playwright was Greene's 'upstart crow'. The belief that Chettle praised Shakespeare relies on two important *ifs*: *if* the upright playwright is the 'upstart crow', and *if* the 'upstart crow' is Shakespeare. Although the evidence for these two early appraisals referring to Shakespeare is tenuous, writers down the centuries have often quoted them in reference to Shakespeare, out of context and without the all-important explanatory detail.

The notion that by 1598 Shakespeare was hailed as the greatest living playwright derives from the accolade, 'the most passionate amongst us to bewail and bemoan the perplexities of love', by the writer Francis Meres in his *Palladis Tamia*, registered for publication in September that year. It is true that Meres also considered Shakespeare was among 'the most excellent' English playwrights, but only a handful of others seem to have shared his opinion at this early stage.

Shakespeare was certainly making some impression by the time he had reached his forties. William Camden, antiquary and headmaster of Westminster School, in his *Remaines* of 1605, called Shakespeare one of the 'most pregnant wits of our times'. His contemporary playwrights also began praising him. In 1612 John Webster writes in complimentary terms about seven fellow dramatists, including Shakespeare, hoping that, 'What I write may be read by their light'.

There are a few other passing references to Shakespeare's works by other contemporary dramatists, such as Thomas Heywood in 1612, and Francis Beaumont who wrote a poetical letter to Ben Jonson in 1615 saying, 'And from all learning keep these lines as clear as Shakespeare's are'. Brief allusions such as these, however, are the only literary comments known to have been made about Shakespeare during his lifetime, and do not constitute proof that Shakespeare was widely recognised in his day. As far as is known, very few of his other contemporaries ever mentioned the name William Shakespeare.

At a time when numerous tributes from fellow poets usually accompanied the passing of one of their number, when Shakespeare died no one seemed to have noticed. Francis Beaumont's death, a few weeks before Shakespeare's, was accompanied by scores of verses in his honour, and when Ben Jonson died an entire book of eulogies was compiled by some of England's greatest poets. Even when Shakespeare's lesser-known colleague Richard Burbage died, playwright Thomas Middleton wrote, 'In London is not one eye dry'. It was seven years after his death before anyone is known to have shed a tear for Shakespeare.

One of the first of the belated tributes came from fellow dramatist Ben Jonson. Jonson seems to have admired Shakespeare, but as the Jonson eulogy did not appear until 1623, it may not have been until late in his life that Shakespeare had acquired such respect. His company was certainly doing well by 1603 when it became The King's Men, and his plays were performed before the new monarch, but virtually nothing else is known about Shakespeare the man – his personality, his standing – until at least seven years after his death.

There is, in fact, only one fragment of contemporary evidence pertaining to Shakespeare's personality, a reference to a joke he seems to have made. On 13 March 1602 John Manningham, a barrister of Middle Temple wrote in his diary:

> Upon a time when Burbage played Richard III there was a citizen grew so far in liking with him that before she went from the play she appointed him to come that night unto her by the name of Richard the Third. Shakespeare, overhearing their conclusion, went before, was entertained, and at his game ere Burbage came. The message

being brought that Richard the Third was at the door, Shakespeare caused return to be made that William the Conqueror was before Richard the Third. Shakespeare's name William.

It is not known if Manningham knew Shakespeare personally, although the passage appears to imply that he did not. It is interesting that Manningham should have to remind himself that Shakespeare's name was William, when he did not need to recall that Burbage's name was Richard. Moreover, in his diary Manningham records seeing a number of Shakespeare plays, but not once does he mention the author's name. If Manningham's diary is any indication, the playwright was not widely known in 1602.

Few records pertain to Shakespeare's acting career. His fellow shareholders Heminge and Condell placed him at the head of a list of 'principal actors' in the plays in the First Folio, and Ben Jonson lists him as an actor in a couple of *his* plays, the first *Every Man in his Humour* of 1598. But any details, such as the notion of Shakespeare always playing a role in his plays, are simply legends based on unreliable eighteenth-century reports. There *may*, however, be truth in the story that Shakespeare played the Ghost in *Hamlet*.

A minor poet, John Davies of Hereford, refers to Shakespeare's stage presence. In 1610 he compares Shakespeare to the classical Roman playwright Terence, introducing a short epigram:

To our English Terence, Mr Will Shake-speare

Say some (good Will), which I, in sport do sing
hadst thou not played some kingly parts in sport
Thou hadst been a companion for a king
And been a king amongst the meaner sort.
Some others rail, but rail as they think fit
Thou hast no railing, but a reigning wit
And honesty thou sowst, which they do reap
So, to increase their stock which they do keep.

The assumption is that Davies is telling us that Shakespeare has

The list of principal actors from the First Folio of 1623.
Shakespeare's name heads the list.

The Workes of William Shakespeare,

containing all his Comedies, Histories, and
Tragedies : Truely set forth, according to their first
ORIGINALL.

The Names of the Principall Actors
in all these Playes.

William Shakespeare.	Samuel Gilburne.
Richard Burbadge.	Robert Armin.
John Hemmings.	William Ostler.
Augustine Phillips.	Nathan Field.
William Kempt.	John Underwood.
Thomas Poope.	Nicholas Tooley.
George Bryan.	William Ecclestone.
Henry Condell.	Joseph Taylor.
William Slye.	Robert Benfield.
Richard Cowly.	Robert Goughe.
John Lowine.	Richard Robinson.
Samuell Crosse.	Iohn Shancke.
Alexander Cooke.	Iohn Rice.

acted in the part of a king, that he has performed for the King, and amongst other dramatists he is himself a king. Unfortunately, this tells us next to nothing. Which plays did he perform in? Was his a lead role? Many Elizabethan plays included kings as periphery characters, the Ghost in *Hamlet* for instance. As the only contemporary reference to Shakespeare's acting skills, Davies's verse is infuriatingly brief.

Of Shakespeare's personal life even less is known. From surviving property deeds it is clear that he was sufficiently successful by 1597 to buy the second largest house in Stratford, but the idea that he loyally visited his family once a year seems to have originated with the self-styled antiquarian John Aubrey in the 1680s, over half a century after Shakespeare's death. Aubrey wrote the *Minutes of Lives*, an abysmal attempt to condense into a few pages the biographies of many historical characters. Aubrey was frequently inaccurate in his other biographies and cannot be considered seriously as a source on Shakespeare. Often quoted by Shakespeare's orthodox biographers, Aubrey was described by his employer, the Oxford scholar Anthony Wood, as 'a shiftless person, roving, and maggoty headed, and sometimes little better than crazed'. Wood goes on to say that Aubrey 'thought little, believed much, and confused everything'.

Shakespeare seems to have written no further plays after the Globe burned down in 1613, and he may have retired to Stratford. But his retirement is simply a matter of legend. The regular discourses in the Mermaid Tavern are nineteenth-century fiction, as are many other speculations regarding Shakespeare's withdrawal to Stratford. There may be truth in the account of his death, from a fever contracted after an evening's drinking, as it was based on a report by the Stratford vicar John Ward in the 1660s, within living memory of the event. However, it is not known for sure that he died on his birthday. All that is known is that Shakespeare was buried at Holy Trinity Church in Stratford on 25 April 1616.

Summary

Most traditional biographies of William Shakespeare are historically unfounded, spun from romantic mythology rather than surviving records. Many aspects of Shakespeare's life are more a matter of legend than historical fact.

1. Although Shakespeare's father John owned property in Henley Street, there is no historical record to indicate that William Shakespeare was born in the so-called Birthplace. It is not even certain when Shakespeare was born. All that is known for sure is that he was christened on 26 April 1564. Following his christening, there is not one single historical record of William Shakespeare until his marriage to Anne Hathaway in 1582, making all notions of his schooling complete guesswork.

2. The same mythological status applies to the legendary love-bond between Shakespeare and his wife Anne Hathaway. In his

will, Shakespeare left her only his 'second best bed'. Why Shakespeare seemingly insulted his wife, and apparently failed to provide for her in her twilight years, is a question ill-received by Stratford's tourist industry, who often promote the ideal, family-man image.

3. The story that Shakespeare led a spotless, law-abiding life is certainly not true. In late 1596 it was recorded in the rolls of the Court of the Queen's Bench in London that a William Wayte craved sureties of the peace against William Shakespeare for fear of his life. Also, on at least three occasions Shakespeare is listed as a 'tax delinquent' in London.

4. Although the orthodox biographers argue that we know much about Shakespeare's life, the assertion is misleading. Considerable documentation regarding Shakespeare's business life has been uncovered; but despite years of searching, almost nothing regarding Shakespeare the poet-dramatist has surfaced, including no contemporary references to his education, the launch of his career, his personality, his views, his interests, any conversations with him or even his personal writings.

5. All descriptions of Shakespeare's personality and appearance are at best guesswork. The earliest biographies simply refer to Shakespeare as a man of good wit, and even this was after a century of hearsay. There is virtually no historical evidence to tell us what Shakespeare was like. As for Shakespeare's physical appearance, no authenticated contemporary portrait survives.

6. There is no evidence of how Shakespeare became involved in the London theatre. The only record of Shakespeare from his marriage at eighteen until around his thirtieth year are the births of his children, and his name on a legal document relating to his mother. The idea that he first became an actor by joining The Queen's Men when they visited Stratford in 1587, and his work as a theatre valet, are simply legends.

7. Nor is there anything regarding Shakespeare's acting career. His fellow shareholders Heminge and Condell placed him at the

head of a list of 'principal actors' in the First Folio of Shakespeare's plays in 1623, and Ben Jonson lists him as an actor in a couple of *his* plays. But any further details are simply legends based on unreliable eighteenth-century reports.

8. Very little is known about Shakespeare's literary standing during his lifetime. There are only a few brief allusions to Shakespeare's work while he was alive, which do not constitute proof that he was widely recognised as a genius in his day. As far as is known, very few contemporary playwrights ever mentioned the name William Shakespeare.

9. The closing years of Shakespeare's life remain a complete mystery. However, the report of his death from a fever contracted during an evening's drinking the night before his birthday may be trustworthy, as it was recorded by the Stratford vicar John Ward in the 1660s, within living memory of the event. All that is known for certain is that Shakespeare was buried at Holy Trinity Church in Stratford on 25 April 1616.

Chapter 3

Historical Evidence

We must now examine the historical evidence relating to Shakespeare that still survives from the period he was alive. From fragmentary records, such as legal documents, parish registers, contemporary letters and diary extracts, a rough outline of Shakespeare's life has gradually emerged over the centuries since his death. However, it amounts to very little. Apart from a few further literary references, this is all that is known for certain about the life of William Shakespeare:

1564. 26 April: Shakespeare is baptised 'Gulielmus filius Johannes Shakspere', William son of John Shakespeare. His mother is Mary, maiden name Arden, formally of Wilmcote near Stratford.

1582. 27 November: A licence is issued for William Shakespeare to marry an Anne Whately of Temple Grafton.
    28 November: Marriage of William Shakespeare to Anne Hathaway of Stratford.

1583. 26 May: Baptism of Shakespeare's daughter Susanna.

1585. 2 February: Baptism of Shakespeare's twins Hamnet and Judith.

1589. William Shakespeare named in legal proceedings regarding an unpaid mortgage on his mother's property in Wilmcote.

1592. Greene's *Groat's-worth of Wit* warns other writers about the arrogant 'upstart crow', possibly referring to William Shakespeare.

1593   The printer Henry Chettle takes offence at Greene for his criticism of various writers, one of whom may be the 'upstart crow'.

18 April: *Venus and Adonis* registered in the Stationers' Register (the nearest equivalent to modern copyright) and published later in the year. It is dedicated by the author William Shakespeare to the Earl of Southampton.

1594.   19 May: Registration of William Shakespeare's second published work, the poem *The Rape of Lucrece*, also dedicated to Lord Southampton.

December: 'Will Kempe, Will Shakespeare, and Richard Burbage, servants to the Lord Chamberlain' are paid £20 for 'several comedies' acted before the Queen.

1594–98.   *Henry VI* (Parts I & II), *Richard III, Titus Andronicus, Romeo and Juliet* and *Richard II* are anonymously published in London.

1596.   August: Shakespeare's son Hamnet dies and is buried in Stratford.

29 November: Rolls of the Queen's Bench in London record that a William Wayte craves sureties of the peace against William Shakespeare 'for fear of death and so forth'.

1597.   4 May: Shakespeare buys New Place, the second largest house in Stratford, for £60.

November: Tax collectors for the ward of Bishopsgate in London list Shakespeare as failing to pay a tax of five shillings (25p) before leaving the area.

1598.   Francis Meres in his *Palladis Tamia* considers Shakespeare to be among 'the most excellent' English playwrights. Meres also praises Shakespeare's poems and names twelve of Shakespeare's plays. This list, coupled with the known existence of the six already printed (four of which are included in Meres's list), brings the total number of known Shakespeare plays to fourteen by this year.

24 January: Abraham Sturley of Stratford writes to a Richard Quiney, saying that Shakespeare may decide 'to deal in the matter of our tithes' (a tax on agricultural produce).

4 February: Shakespeare is listed in Stratford as holding 80 bushels of grain.

1 October: Shakespeare wanted for tax evasion in the London parish of St Helen's in Bishopsgate.

25 October: Richard Quiney of Stratford writes to Shakespeare asking him for a loan of £30. (This is the only known letter ever addressed to Shakespeare.)

A few days later, Richard's father Adrian writes to his son, 'If you bargain with Mr Shakespeare or receive money therefore, bring your money home if you may.'

A few days after, Abraham Sturley writes to Richard regarding his hope of a loan from Shakespeare saying, 'I will like of as I shall hear when, and where, and how.' ('I'll believe that when I see it.')

December: Stratford Civic Chamber records ten pence paid to Shakespeare for one load of stone.

1599. Printer William Jaggard publishes *The Passionate Pilgrim*, a collection of poems he attributes to Shakespeare. Included are two of the 154 *Sonnets* (138 & 144) published in full ten years later.

February: According to John Heminge and Henry Condell twenty years later, Shakespeare held a 10 per cent shareholding in the Globe Theatre built in that year. In 1635 Cuthbert Burbage (a 50 per cent shareholder) also records that Shakespeare had been a shareholder, along with Heminge, Condell, Augustine Phillips and 'other partners'.

May: An inventory of property belonging to Thomas Brend (father of Nicholas Brend, the leaseholder of the land on which the Globe stood) lists Shakespeare as occupying a new house in St Saviour's Parish.

6 October: Shakespeare again wanted for tax evasion in London's St Helen's parish, and traced to Sussex by the authorities.

1600.   October: The tax owed by Shakespeare is referred to the Bishop of Winchester for collection. Later the bishop records that the sum is paid in full by unnamed persons referred to him by the sheriff.

c1601.   The students of St John's College, Cambridge, stage the play *Pilgrimage to Parnassus*, which includes a speech by the actor William Kempe. During his speech Kempe mentions his 'fellow' Shakespeare, suggesting that neither he (Shakespeare) nor Ben Jonson have respect for the plays written by university men. As this was probably a jibe aimed at the students, it is unlikely to give an accurate impression of Shakespeare's attitude. However, the reference does suggest that Shakespeare's work was at least as popular as Jonson's. In the play itself, Shakespeare is repeatedly referred to as 'Sweet Mr Shakespeare' and one of the characters says, 'O sweet Mr Shakespeare, I'll have his picture in my study at court . . . Let the duncified world esteem of Spenser and Chaucer, I'll worship sweet Mr Shakespeare and to honour him will lay his *Venus and Adonis* under my pillow'. As the play appears to be ridiculing the theatre, it is difficult to determine the true context of these lines.

September: Shakespeare's father dies and is buried at Holy Trinity Church.

1602.   Stratford legal proceedings regarding New Place use the words 'generous gentleman' when referring to Shakespeare.

13 March: John Manningham, a barrister of Middle Temple, writes in his diary of the joke between actor Richard Burbage and William Shakespeare.

1 May: Shakespeare pays William and John Combe £320 for 107 acres of land north of Stratford.

28 September: Shakespeare buys a cottage on 'Walkers Street alias Dead Lane' in Stratford for an undisclosed amount.

1603.   A lease for a property east of New Place mentions that it adjoins the land of Mr William Shakespeare.

19 May: Shakespeare's company is granted a king's licence to continue to perform. The licence names Lawrence Fletcher, William Shakespeare, Richard Burbage, Augustine Phillips,

John Heminge, Henry Condell, William Sly, Robert Armin, Richard Cowly 'and the rest of their associates'.

1604. March: The same company, with William Shakespeare now heading the list, is given red cloth to prepare for King James's tour of the city of London.

From the document of 1612, we learn that Shakespeare is lodging with Christopher Mountjoy, a maker of women's headdresses in Cripplegate.

July: Shakespeare takes legal action to collect a debt of £1.15s.10d (£1.80) from a Stratford apothecary, Philip Rogers. The money owed is for malt supplied to Rogers by Shakespeare the previous March.

1605. William Condell, antiquary and headmaster of Westminster School, in his *Remaines* calls Shakespeare one of the 'most pregnant wits of our times'.

May: Actor Augustine Phillips makes a will naming seven men of the company who are to receive between 20 and 30 shillings (£1 and £1.50) in gold. The first name on the list is William Shakespeare.

24 July: Shakespeare purchases half the corn and hay tithes (concessions) in three of Stratford's hamlets (Old Stratford, Welcome and Bishopton). The price paid is £440.

1607. 5 June: Marriage of Shakespeare's daughter Susanna to John Hall, a local physician.

1608. 9 August: The Blackfriars Theatre is leased by seven men, including Richard and Cuthbert Burbage, John Heminge, William Shakespeare and Henry Condell. (This is according to Heminge and Condell in 1619. However, although there is no contemporary record of the event, the lease purchase is also attested to by Cuthbert Burbage in 1635.)

December: Shakespeare sues John Addenbrooke of Stratford for a debt of £6 plus £1.15s (£1.75) costs. Addenbrooke is arrested.

1609. Printer Thomas Thorpe publishes the 154 *Shake-speare's*

Sonnets. Unlike Shakespeare's poems, there is no dedication by the author himself. There are also numerous misprints, making it unlikely that Shakespeare himself was directly involved in the publication.

1610.   Shakespeare involved in legal proceedings regarding New Place, and buys a further 20 acres of land.

8 October: John Davies's poem entered in the Stationers' Register. A few lines refer to Shakespeare as an actor, comparing him with the Roman playwright Terence and praising him as a dramatist.

1611.   Shakespeare involved in legal proceedings regarding his tithe holding.

September: Shakespeare's name appears on a list of Stratford citizens contributing to a fund to persuade parliament to pass a bill for the better repair of highways.

1612:   John Webster writes in complimentary terms about seven of his fellow playwrights, including Shakespeare. Webster hopes 'What I write may be read by their light'.

Playwright Thomas Heywood also refers to Shakespeare's works in passing.

11 May: Shakespeare's signature appears on a deposition (witness statement) regarding a legal suit being brought against Christopher Mountjoy.

1613.   28 January: John Combe, a Stratford pawnbroker, draws up a will in which he leaves Shakespeare £5.

10 March: William Shakespeare buys a house in Blackfriars near the Blackfriars Theatre for £140. The next day he mortgages the property back to its previous owner for £60. Both the deed and mortgage documents are signed by Shakespeare.

1614.   A number of Stratford landowners attempt to enclose land belonging to the town corporation. Shakespeare is involved as both the owner of 107 acres and as part-owner of tithes from adjoining land. On 17 November the Town Clerk writes in his diary that Shakespeare 'told me that they assured him they meant to enclose no further than a gospel bush'. He also writes memorandum regarding Shakespeare's opposition to the proposed enclosures, saying that Shakespeare had told a J. Greene that he was not able to 'bear the enclosing of [the hamlet of] Welcome'. Greene and Shakespeare eventually secure a deed from one of the landowners, William Combe, indemnifying them against any injury they might suffer from the enclosure.

1615. Francis Beaumont writes a poetical letter to Ben Jonson including the words, 'And from all learning keep these lines as clear as Shakespeare's are'.

May: Shakespeare is named in a suit involving the record of ownership of his Blackfriars property.

1616. 10 February: Shakespeare's daughter Judith marries Thomas Quiney.

25 March: Shakespeare makes his will (amended from January). Daughter Susanna gets most of the property, nearly all goods and household effects go to son-in-law John, daughter Judith receives a yearly allowance of around £150, and wife Anne gets the 'second best bed'.

The will, drawn up by Shakespeare's executor but signed by Shakespeare himself, contains nothing to link Shakespeare with any literary activities. There is no reference to books, manuscripts or even the shares in the Globe and Blackfriars theatres.

25 April: The burial register of Stratford's Holy Trinity Church records the burial of 'Will Shakspere gent'.

* * *

What can be deduced from this sketchy outline of Shakespeare's life?

Regarding his family, he married Anne Hathaway at the age of eighteen, a woman who was (from the inscription on her grave) eight years his senior. His first daughter Susanna was born some six months later and twins Judith and Hamnet were born two years after that. Hamnet died when he was eleven, Susanna married local physician John Hall, and Judith married Thomas Quiney (the son of Richard, the man who tried to borrow money from Shakespeare in 1598).

Of his acting and writing career, before the publication of *Venus and Adonis* at the age of twenty-nine nothing is known except that Shakespeare had somehow become acquainted with the wealthy Earl of Southampton. By the age of thirty, Shakespeare seems to have been a writer/actor attached to the Lord Chamberlain's Men, and his plays seem to have been performed before the Queen. But how Shakespeare came to be associated with such influential noblemen as Southampton and the Chamberlain Lord Hunsdon, or how and when he first became involved in London's theatre, has remained a mystery.

At thirty-four Shakespeare is a 10 per cent shareholder in the Globe theatre, he has written at least fourteen plays, Francis Meres considers him one of England's best playwrights, and he is sufficiently wealthy to purchase the second largest house in Stratford. At thirty-nine his company becomes The King's Men and his plays are performed before the new monarch, James I. At forty-four he is a part leaseholder in the Blackfriars Theatre and his *Sonnets* are published.

Until aged around forty-four, Shakespeare appears to have spent much of his time lodging in London, moving residence several times. Thereafter, apart from the purchase of a house in Blackfriars (in which he never seems to have lived) there is virtually no record of his presence in the capital.

The surviving documentation of Shakespeare's life in Stratford comes down to little more than business, legal and property transactions, showing merely that he became increasingly prosperous, seemingly dealing in land and grain. He was certainly a wealthy man by the turn of the century. New Place, for which he paid £60, would by today's standards be worth at least £250,000.

It is difficult to give a precise modern comparison for the value of money in Shakespeare's time. Property was relatively cheaper, and so £60 would not in all cases be 4,000 times its present value. At the other end of the scale, a pint of beer could be bought for less than a penny (240 to the pound), and so money was roughly worth around 500 times its present value in relation to food and drink.

The best idea of Shakespeare's wealth is to compare his £60 house and his hundreds of pounds-worth of land and tithes with the average £2 that a popular dramatist would receive for each play, with no further royalties. Around £100 is about the life's income Shakespeare might have expected from the sale of his plays alone. The majority of his wealth must therefore have come from his business interests in Stratford and his financial stake in the Burbage company and its theatres.

Shakespeare may have retired to Stratford sometime in his mid-to-late forties, but whether or not he continued to write is unknown. By his death at the age of fifty-two, however, he had written some thirty-seven plays, 154 sonnets and two poems that still survive. (There is also the collection of poems attributed to Shakespeare in William Jaggard's *The Passionate Pilgrim*.)

There are only a few literary criticisms of Shakespeare during his lifetime: Francis Meres, a respected writer who considered Shakespeare one of England's finest playwrights in 1598; William Camden, an antiquary who called Shakespeare one of the 'most pregnant wits of our times' in 1605; and playwrights John Webster, Thomas Heywood and Francis Beaumont, who briefly compliment Shakespeare in 1612 and 1615. There are also two further possibles: Robert Greene, the playwright who *may* have reprimanded Shakespeare for his arrogance during his early career, and Henry Chettle, a printer who *may* have admired Shakespeare in his younger days. Apart from John Davies in 1610, calling Shakespeare the 'English Terence', other surviving references tell us nothing of Shakespeare or his life, mainly being documents registering or recording performances of the plays themselves.

Taken together, these comments amount to a handful of lines. In Shakespeare's early thirties Thomas Greene did not appreciate him but Henry Chettle apparently did (if he is the 'upstart crow'). A few years later William Camden admired him and Francis Meres considered him one of the best playwrights, as did fellow poets John Webster, Thomas Heywood, Francis Beaumont and John Davies. But even these are merely literary observations on Shakespeare's work; there is no evidence that any of these writers actually met Shakespeare in person.

We do, however, have a substantial list of Shakespeare's associates:

Family: Anne Hathaway (wife), Susanna (daughter), Judith (daughter), Hamnet (son), John Hall (son-in-law) and Thomas Quiney (son-in-law).

London theatre associates: William Kempe, Richard Burbage, Cuthbert Burbage, John Heminge, Henry Condell, Augustine Phillips, Lawrence Fletcher, William Sly, Robert Armin and Richard Cowly.

Other London associates: Nicholas Brend (Globe leaseholder), John Manningham (lawyer), Thomas Brend (landlord), Christopher Mountjoy (landlord and headdress maker) and William Wayte (seemingly threatened by Shakespeare).

Patrons: The Earl of Southampton, Lord Hunsdon and Lord Strange.

Possible business associates in Stratford: J. Greene, Abraham Sturley, Richard Quiney, Adrian Quiney, William Combe, John Combe, Philip Rogers and John Addenbrooke.

Other Stratford associates: Thomas Greene (Stratford's Town Clerk), and Anne Whately (possible lover).

Setting aside Shakespeare's literary critics – Greene, Webster, Meres, Heywood, Camden, Beaumont, Chettle and Davies – and publishers Jaggard and Thorpe, who may not actually have met Shakespeare, there is a surviving list of at least thirty-five people in London and Stratford who seemingly knew Shakespeare personally. However, we learn virtually nothing from them about Shakespeare himself. There are, in fact, only two records of any conversations or meetings with Shakespeare: John Manningham's mention of Shakespeare's joke with Richard Burbage, and the Stratford Town Clerk recording Shakespeare's opinions regarding land enclosure.

All that remains from which to assess Shakespeare's character are Kempe's statement that Shakespeare did not like the plays of university men (which was probably a jibe); Abraham Sturley's opinion that Shakespeare was mean with his money, a Stratford legal document conversely describing him as a generous gentle-man; and William Wayte's apparent fear that Shakespeare might kill him. Other than the fact that although he was relatively wealthy he sought to evade tax, this is all we really know about William Shakespeare's personality from the contemporary evidence alone.

It was not until seven years after his death that the first substantial comments on Shakespeare and his works were made. It was from these that the myths of Shakespeare's life appear to have sprung.

Summary

From fragmentary records, such as legal documents, parish registers, contemporary letters and diary extracts, a rough outline of Shakespeare's life has gradually emerged over the centuries since his death. It amounts to very little, leaving us with no impression of Shakespeare the man.

1. Shakespeare married Anne Hathaway, a woman eight years his senior, at the age of eighteen. Their first daughter Susanna was born some six months later, and twins Judith and Hamnet were born two years after. Hamnet died when he was eleven, Susanna married local physician John Hall, and Judith married Stratford businessman Thomas Quiney.

2. Before the publication of *Venus and Adonis* when he was twenty-nine, we know nothing of Shakespeare's career except that he had somehow become acquainted with the wealthy Earl of Southampton. By the age of thirty, Shakespeare seems to have been a writer/actor attached to the Lord Chamberlain's Men, and his plays had been performed before the Queen. But just how Shakespeare came to be associated with such influential noblemen as Southampton and the Chamberlain Lord Hunsdon, or how and when he first became involved in London's theatre, has remained a mystery.

3. At thirty-four Shakespeare was a 10 per cent shareholder in the Globe Theatre and he had written at least fourteen plays. Writer Francis Meres considered him one of England's best playwrights,

and he was rich enough to buy the second largest house in Stratford. At thirty-nine his company became The King's Men and his plays were performed before James I. At forty-four he was a part shareholder in the Blackfriars Theatre and his *Sonnets* were published.

4. Until he was about forty-four, Shakespeare appears to have spent much of his time lodging in London, moving residence several times. Thereafter, apart from the purchase of a house in Blackfriars (in which he never seems to have lived), there is virtually no record of him in the capital.

5. The surviving documentation of Shakespeare's life in Stratford comes down to little more than business, legal and property transactions, showing merely that he became increasingly prosperous, seemingly dealing in land and grain. He was certainly a wealthy man by the turn of the century. New Place, for which he paid £60, would be worth at least £250,000 by today's standards. Around £100 is about the life's income Shakespeare might have expected from the sale of his plays alone. The majority of his wealth must therefore have come from his business interests in Stratford and his financial stake in the Burbage company and its theatres.

6. Shakespeare may have retired to Stratford sometime in his mid-to-late forties, but whether or not he continued to write is unknown. By his death at the age of fifty-two, however, he had written some thirty-seven plays, 154 sonnets and two poems that still survive.

7. There are only a few literary criticisms of Shakespeare during his lifetime: Francis Meres, a respected writer who considered Shakespeare one of England's finest playwrights in 1598; William Camden, an antiquary who called Shakespeare one of the 'most pregnant wits of our times' in 1605; John Davies, a poet who called Shakespeare the 'English Terence' in 1610; and playwrights John Webster, Thomas Heywood and Francis Beaumont, who briefly compliment Shakespeare in 1612 and 1615.

8. There are also two further possible critics: Robert Greene, the

playwright who *may* have reprimanded Shakespeare for his arrogance during his early career, and Henry Chettle, a printer who *may* have admired Shakespeare in his younger days. Other surviving references tell us nothing of Shakespeare nor of his life, mainly being documents registering or recording performances of the plays themselves.

9. All that remains from which to assess Shakespeare's character are actor William Kempe's statement that Shakespeare did not like the plays of university men, Stratfordian Abraham Sturley's opinion that Shakespeare was mean with his money, a Stratford legal document conversely describing him as a generous gentleman, and William Wayte's apparent fear that Shakespeare might kill him. Other than the fact that although he was relatively wealthy he sought to evade tax, this is all we really know about William Shakespeare's personality from the contemporary evidence alone.

Chapter 4

The Merchant of Stratford

Left with so sparse a record of William Shakespeare, we must turn to historical detective work. What can be deduced from an examination of the surviving details of Shakespeare's life? Although initially it appears unremarkable, even dull, a closer inspection reveals a series of mysterious discrepancies: Shakespeare appears to be leading two separate and very different lives.

In 1597, while Shakespeare is wealthy enough to buy the second largest house in Stratford, he is sought by tax collectors in London for a petty five shillings. The following year he owns a considerable store of grain in Stratford, while in London he is again seemingly unable to pay his taxes. In 1600, in Winchester, an unnamed benefactor pays Shakespeare's tax on his behalf, although in Stratford he continues to grow richer, within a couple of years buying a further 107 acres of land and a cottage.

In Stratford he is so often the plaintiff in legal suits, in London he is forever evading the courts. In Stratford he is described as a 'generous gentleman', in London he is the subject of a restraining order for threatening the life of William Wayte. In London he consistently rents accommodation (Bishopsgate 1597, St Helen's 1598, St Saviour's 1599 and Cripplegate 1604), while in Stratford he is constantly buying property.

Not only does Shakespeare apparently lead two very different life-styles in London and in Stratford, but the available evidence indicates that his associates in each location are completely unaware of his other life. In 1600, as he is traced by the tax collectors to Sussex, the authorities seem to have gone to some lengths to find him. Again we are confronted by mystery. If

Shakespeare's permanent residence and assets were in Stratford, why did the London tax authorities not take legal action there? We can only assume that it was not common knowledge in London that Shakespeare had any connection with Stratford-upon-Avon.

In Stratford, there is no record that anyone knew that Shakespeare had a writing or theatrical career. There is no evidence that he was ever, during his lifetime, known as an author of any kind; except for his wealth, no one seems to have regarded him as important in his home town. In the Stratford burial register his son-in-law John Hall is given the epitaph 'most skilful physician', whereas Shakespeare's reads simply 'gent'. Even Shakespeare's relatives give no recognisable indication that they are remotely aware of his literary activities. John Hall, for example, had his own books published, but never once does he mention Shakespeare. It is certainly odd that we find no indication whatsoever that anyone in the Stratford community was touched by the William Shakespeare whom Ben Jonson called the 'soul of the age'. That is, of course, unless this was not the same William Shakespeare.

The more we discover, the less likely it seems that the thespianic London tenant was the same man as the respected Stratford landlord. In 1616, the year he died, the Stratford Shakespeare wrote his will. Whereas the wills of Shakespeare's contemporary playwrights tend to be personal obituaries, the Stratfordian's will contains no personal feelings – it is nothing more than a legal text. There is no mention of the shares in the Globe or Blackfriars theatres; indeed, the shares fail to turn up in the records of any of Shakespeare's heirs. Also, there is not a single reference to books or manuscripts in the will.

There is not even evidence of Shakespeare's education, not in Stratford or anywhere else. No mystery concerns most other playwrights of the time: Christopher Marlowe studied at Cambridge, as did Edmund Spenser, Gabriel Harvey, Thomas Nashe and John Fletcher; Thomas Lodge studied at Oxford, as did Robert Greene, Philip Sidney, George Chapman, Thomas Heywood and Francis Beaumont; Ben Jonson attended Westminster School, and Thomas Kyd was educated at Merchant Taylors School in London. But where did William Shakespeare study?

There are no surviving records of his education at all, and no mention of it by any of his contemporaries.

In short, there is no evidence that the Stratford Shakespeare ever received a day's schooling in his life. Nothing associates him with literary or intellectual interests of any kind, and there is no record of him buying a single book; most intriguing of all, none of his letters have ever been found, nor any reference to them discovered. Dwelling for two decades in London, while conducting business and maintaining a family in Stratford, must surely have required writing hundreds, if not thousands, of letters over the years. Strangely, no letters, nor *any* correspondences from Shakespeare have been discovered, despite the fact that historians have spent at least two centuries searching for them. Papers of those with whom he did business *have* survived, so why the complete lack of Shakespeare's own communications? The natural assumption is that he wrote few letters. Nevertheless, it is peculiar that a successful Stratford landowner should apparently write so little; unless, of course, he was illiterate.

There is certainly a case to be answered regarding Shakespeare's literacy. The only certain specimens of Shakespeare's handwriting are six signatures; three on his will and one each on three other legal documents. But each of these documents was drawn up by someone else. It seems incongruous that not even his will was written personally. Furthermore, the signatures themselves suggest writing difficulty. Not only are they shaky and untidy, but each time they read differently: *Willm Shaksp, William Shakspe, W Shakspe, Wiliam Shakspere, Willm Shakspere*, and *William Shakspeare*. Surely an experienced writer would exhibit greater consistency in his signature.

In conclusion, there is nothing whatsoever to suggest that William Shakespeare of Stratford-upon-Avon was a writer of any kind, let alone the greatest literary genius of all time. In fact, from the Stratford records alone, there is every reason to attribute him with a very different profession entirely. The documentation clearly shows how he made his living. He buys sizeable tracts of land and corn tithes, he holds large stocks of grain and takes action to recover debts for the supply of malt. Leaving aside the London records and considering only his life in Stratford, the logical conclusion would be that William Shakespeare was merely a grain dealer. Is this Stratford grain dealer a

The six surviving Shakespeare signatures.

1. The Mountjoy Deposition, 1612 (Public Records Office).
2. The Blackfriars Conveyance, 1613 (Guildhall Library).
3. The Blackfriars Mortgage, 1613 (Guildhall Library).
4, 5, 6. Shakespeare's Will, 1616 (Public Records Office).

completely different man to the London playwright? Were there two William Shakespeares?

* * *

Although in the late sixteenth and early seventeenth centuries the playwright William Shakespeare was living and working in London, and at the same time a man with the same name was living in Stratford, a hundred miles to the north, how did they become linked together? In 1590 another William Shakespeare was working as a butcher in Cornwall. Why was he not considered to be the elusive London playwright?

In 1623 the first compilation of Shakespeare's plays was published. Now called the First Folio, it was entitled *Mr William Shakespeare's Comedies, Histories and Tragedies* and contained thirty-six plays, including eighteen never before printed. The works were introduced by a preface comprising a dedication by John Heminge and Henry Condell, and four poems praising the author by writers Ben Jonson, Hugh Holland, Leonard Digges and a mysterious I.M. At the time of the publication of the First Folio no one appears to have been interested in the location of Shakespeare's home town, and a decade passed before speculation began that it may have been Stratford-upon-Avon. The first was in 1634, when a Lieutenant Hammond visited Stratford, and finding the Shakespeare tomb in Holy Trinity Church suggested that this was the author of the increasingly popular plays in the First Folio.

The Stratford speculation seems to have originated from two references in the preface to the First Folio. One by Leonard Digges referred to 'thy Stratford monument', another by Ben Jonson called the author the 'Sweet Swan of Avon'. But an explanation other than the town of Stratford-upon-Avon could account for these lines. Stratford could have been the Stratford in East London, not far from where Shakespeare spent much of his career, and the Avon could have been a reference to the River Avon in Hampshire which passed through estates of the Earl of Southampton, not the Avon running through Warwickshire. The Digges reference may therefore refer to a London playhouse, rather than a tomb memorial, and Jonson's reference might concern Shakespeare's beloved patron Lord Southampton.

In 1662 John Ward became vicar of Stratford and developed a fascination for Shakespeare, the playwright who was said to have lived in his parish. In his diary Ward recorded all he could discover about the Stratford Shakespeare, which was very little. He therefore wrote a note reminding himself 'to pursue Shakespeare's plays and be versed in them, that I may not be ignorant of the matter'. He also decided to speak with one of the Stratford Shakespeare's surviving granddaughters, Lady Bernard of Abingdon. However, despite remaining vicar for nineteen years, in which time he completed a further sixteen diaries, he never again mentioned Shakespeare. It can only be inferred that he discovered nothing more about the Stratford Shakespeare as a playwright.

Around the same time, in 1663, the writer Thomas Fuller compiled a few lines on the Shakespeare of Stratford in his *Worthies of England*, but he too was unable to discover a scrap of information, other than hearsay, to couple the Stratfordian with the Shakespeare plays.

The final stage in associating Shakespeare the playwright with the Shakespeare of Stratford came in 1681, when antiquarian John Aubrey included William Shakespeare in his *Minutes of Lives*. Aubrey took it for granted that Shakespeare of Stratford was the famous playwright and the idea won general acceptance. After the fame that Shakspeare eventually brought to Stratford, few Stratfordians have questioned Aubrey to this day. It should not be forgotten that this first 'biography' of Shakespeare, which acted as the springboard for the later 'orthodox' Shakespeare biographies, was written half a century after the playwright's death.

But if the Stratford man was not William Shakespeare the playwright, why does the memorial beside his tomb in Holy Trinity Church show a figure similar to the portrait on the First Folio, and holding a quill? The memorial consists of a bust, topped by a square block bearing the family's coat of arms, a jawless skull and two cherubs, one holding a spade, the other an hourglass. The bust itself depicts a plump, bald, middle-aged man holding a pen in one hand and a sheet of paper under the other, both resting on a cushion (see plate 14).

The present bust was made by the theatrical manager John

William Dugdale's 1656 illustration of Shakespeare's original tomb memorial. The man honoured in the memorial is a dealer in bagged commodities.

Hall in 1748 when the original required restoration. Fortunately, two earlier drawings of the original monument have survived, both showing a figure very different from the one we know today. In an engraving in Sir William Dugdale's *Antiquities of Warwickshire* of 1656, and an illustration in Nicholas Rowe's biography of 1709, the Shakespeare bust clearly shows a different figure to the one depicted in the restored monument – the face is much thinner and the features are more angular. But, more importantly, in neither illustration is there a pen nor parchment. Instead the figure's hands are placed upon a sack.

Since it was accepted practice to depict the profession in an individual's monument, it would seem that Hall decided that in addition to giving the figure a facelift, in order to make it more resemble the picture in the First Folio, a pen and parchment were more appropriate for Shakespeare the playwright. However, thanks to Dugdale and Rowe, we now know that the man in the original monument was not honoured as a literary figure, but as a dealer in bagged commodities, which is precisely how the historical records show that the William Shakespeare of Stratford made much of his money – in malt and grain.

Even the simple epigraph on the tomb slab, a few feet from the bust, seemingly composed by the deceased himself, hardly echoes the work of history's most famous playwright:

> Good friend for Jesus sake forbear
> To dig the dust enclosed here
> Blessed be the man that spares these stones
> And cursed be he that moves my bones

The only remaining evidence suggesting that the William Shakespeare honoured in the monument was a writer comes from the part Latin, part English, wording on a stone plaque beneath the bust. The upper section reads:

IUDICIO PYLIUM, GENIO SOCRATEM, ARTE MARONEM: TERRA TEGIT, POPULUS MAERET, OLYMPUS HABET.

[A Nestor in wisdom, a Socrates in intellect, a Virgil in art: The earth encloses, the people mourn, Olympus holds.]

Underneath is the English inscription:

STAY PASSENGER, WHY GOEST THOU BY SO FAST? READ IF THOU CANST, WHOM ENVIOUS DEATH HAST PLAST

WITH IN THIS MONUMENT SHAKESPEARE: WITH WHOM
QUICK NATURED DIED: WHOSE NAME DOTH DECK THIS
TOMB. FAR MORE THAN COST. SEE ALL THAT HE HATH
WRIT. LEAVES LIVING ART, BUT PAGE TO SERVE HIS WIT.

This somewhat confusing epitaph indicates that the Shakespeare honoured is a wise, witty and intellectual writer. However, once again, someone (probably Hall in 1748) had added to the original text. Dugdale's illustration (1656) shows writing beneath the bust, beginning with the Latin words IUDICIO PYLIUM, although the rest is simply implied by a series of dashes. However, Nicholas Rowe's illustration (1709) shows the entire script that filled the plaque:

IUDICIO PYLIUM, GENIO SOCRATEM, ARTE MARONEM:
TERRA TEGIT, POPULUS MAERET, OLYMPUS HABET.

It seems that the passage in English, leaving no doubt that the profession of the deceased had been a writer, was not on the original. The Latin inscription that was on the original, 'A Nestor in wisdom, a Socrates in intellect, a Virgil in art: The earth encloses, the people mourn, Olympus holds', may not necessarily refer to the deceased, but may simply have been some sort of Shakespeare family motto.

The historical reality of the tomb seems consistent with the Stratford town records, which suggest that Shakespeare was a grain dealer with no literary associations. The solution to the Shakespeare enigma would therefore seem to be that the Shakespeare of Stratford was not the London playwright. The London playwright, like many other great writers, artists or composers, suffered financially, while the Stratford Shakespeare was a wealthy businessman. In the decades after both had lived they had been erroneously confused as one.

If only the mysterious Mr Shakespeare would relinquish his secrets so readily. The strange paradox of Shakespeare's double life is even more peculiar. Considering that the surviving records make it appear so unlikely that the Stratfordian was Shakespeare the playwright, the enigma is compounded by four items of evidence which seem to prove beyond doubt that the Stratford and

London Shakespeares *were* the same man. Indeed the only surviving evidence conclusively to link the two men together are the documents bearing Shakespeare's signatures.

The Stratford Shakespeare's will of 25 March 1616 is preserved in the Public Records Office in London. In it he leaves 26 shillings and 8 pence for the purchase of rings 'to my fellows John Heminge, Richard Burbage, and Henry Condell'. This reference firmly associates the Stratford man with the London playwright. Heminge, Burbage and Condell were the associates of the London Shakespeare and co-shareholders in the theatres. The fact that he calls them his 'fellows' is evidence not only that the Stratford Shakespeare knew them, but that they were also his colleagues.

In 1612 the London Shakespeare signed an affidavit regarding a legal suit being brought against his old landlord Christopher Mountjoy. Also in the Public Records Office, the document is signed 'Willm Shaksp of Stratford-upon-Avon'. Furthermore, in the Guild Library (London) is the 1613 conveyance for the Blackfriars property purchased by Shakespeare in London. It is also signed 'William Shakspe of Stratford-upon-Avon'. On both of these documents, and on the document mortgaging the Blackfriars property back to its previous owner (signed 'W Shakspe', and now in the British Library), the signature is in the same handwriting as the signatures on the Stratford will.

The mystery of William Shakespeare is thus exacerbated. If the Stratford Shakespeare *was* the great playwright, how did no one in his home town appear to know? No one writes about him or speaks of him as a dramatist, his tomb honours him merely as a grain dealer, and his epitaph reads simply 'gent'. Why is there no indication of his learning? There is no record of his education, he apparently buys no books, nor does he leave any in his will. What happened to his shares in the London theatres? None are included in his will, nor in the wills of his heirs. Why does he leave no writings? There are no letters, diaries or mere jottings that survive, or are ever referred to. What of his poems, plays or manuscripts? None have surfaced, nor are they ever mentioned in Elizabethan Stratford. Why does Shakespeare evidence writing difficulty? He only signs his name to documents drawn up by others, and his signature varies *every* time, even on the same document. Even the curse on his tomb seems infantile in comparison to the genius of Shakespeare.

This mystery, unknown or ignored by Stratford's thousands of visitors, has fuelled academic controversy for years, and has led to speculation that William Shakespeare was in fact a frontman for the works of someone else.

Summary

Although initially Shakespeare's life appears unremarkable, a closer examination of the surviving records reveals many mysterious discrepancies. Shakespeare seems to have led two separate and very different lives – one as a London dramatist, the other as a Stratford grain merchant.

1. In the late 1590s and early 1600s, while Shakespeare was wealthy enough to buy considerable property in Stratford, he was consistently sought by tax collectors in London for petty sums of money. Not only did Shakespeare apparently lead two very different lives in London and in Stratford, but the available evidence indicates that his associates in each location were completely unaware of his other life.

2. In Stratford he was often the plaintiff in legal suits, in London he was forever evading the courts. In Stratford he was described as a 'generous gentleman', in London he became the subject of a restraining order after threatening a man's life. In London he consistently rented accommodation, while in Stratford he constantly bought property.

3. In 1600, as he is traced by tax collectors to Sussex, the authorities seem to have gone to some lengths to locate him. But as Shakespeare had his permanent residence and assets in Stratford, why did the London tax collectors not take legal action there? It seems that it was not common knowledge in London that Shakespeare had any connection with Stratford-upon-Avon.

4. There is no record that anyone in Stratford knew that Shakespeare had a writing or theatrical career. Nor is there evidence that he was ever, during his lifetime, known in Stratford as an

author of any kind. Except for his wealth, no one seems to have regarded him as special in his home town.

5. No original Shakespeare manuscript survives and the only certain specimens of the Stratford Shakespeare's handwriting are six signatures; three on his will, and one each on three other legal documents. Astonishingly, the signatures suggest writing difficulty. Not only are they shaky and untidy, but each time they read differently.

6. There is no evidence that the Stratford Shakespeare ever received an education. There is no record of him buying a single book and none of his letters or writings have ever been found. From the Stratford records alone, Shakespeare does not appear to have been a poet-dramatist, but a merchant who made his money as a grain dealer.

7. Even the memorial beside Shakespeare's tomb, showing a figure holding a pen and parchment, is an eighteenth-century replacement. Two earlier drawings of the original monument have survived, and both show a figure very different from the one we know today. In an engraving in Sir William Dugdale's *Antiquities of Warwickshire* of 1656, and an illustration in Nicholas Rowe's biography of 1709, the hands of the bust do not hold a pen and parchment but are resting on a sack. As it was traditional to depict the profession in a person's monument, it would seem that Shakespeare was not honoured as a literary figure, but as a dealer in bagged commodities, which is exactly how the records show that the Shakespeare of Stratford made his money, in malt and grain.

8. Although the surviving records make it seem unlikely that the Stratford Shakespeare was the London playwright, other evidence appears to prove conclusively that the two men *were* the same. The Stratford Shakespeare's will names his 'fellows John Heminge, Richard Burbage, and Henry Condell'. This reference firmly associates the Stratford man with the London playwright. Heminge, Burbage and Condell were the playwright's associates

in the theatre. The fact that he calls them his 'fellows' is evidence not only that the Stratford Shakespeare knew them, but that they were also his colleagues. Furthermore, the surviving signatures of the London and Stratford Shakespeares are in the same handwriting.

Chapter 5

Francis Bacon

In 1781 the English clergyman Reverend Wilmot concluded that Shakespeare had not possessed the necessary education or experience to have written the plays accredited to him. Unlike previous doubters, Wilmot proposed an alternative candidate, someone who had used William Shakespeare as a cover to protect his own identity. Noticing certain similarities between the ideas expressed in Shakespeare's plays and the works of the Elizabethan lawyer and politician Francis Bacon, it occurred to Wilmot that Bacon might be the real playwright. Although Wilmot's notion was little more than an idle thought, others eventually came to the same conclusion, launching a more thorough campaign. As complex legal matters and terminology are included in the plays, they believed that the author possessed a profound knowledge of the law; accordingly, only a practising lawyer such as Bacon could have been the true dramatist.

In 1857, in his pamphlet *Bacon and Shakespeare*, William Henry Smith was the first to make a substantial claim for Bacon's authorship, and others soon uncovered additional evidence supporting his case. Consequently, Shakespeare's orthodox biographers and Stratford's rapidly expanding tourist industry presented their counter-arguments with equal vigour. The Shakespeare controversy had begun, the Bacon adherents becoming known as the Baconians, the traditional biographers as the Stratfordians.

Before considering the Baconian case, we must examine Bacon's life.

Francis Bacon was born in London on 22 January 1561. Educated at Cambridge, he studied law at Gray's Inn and became a

Francis Bacon. Did Bacon leave coded messages in the Shakespeare plays?

barrister. His political career began in earnest. He was elected for Parliament in 1584, sought position at court and was appointed Queen's Council. Bacon progressed steadily upwards. Knighted by James I in 1603, in 1607 he was appointed Solicitor General, and in 1613 he was made Attorney General. His political influence reached its height when he was appointed to the Privy Council in 1616, being made Lord Keeper and Lord Chancellor within two years.

Bacon's life ended in disgrace. In 1621, after being made Viscount St Albans, he was accused of accepting bribes. He was found guilty by the High Court, fined, imprisoned for a time and banned from holding public office for the rest of his life. He died five years later, on 9 April 1626, from an acute chest condition, having spent his last years writing.

Francis Bacon had already composed a number of influential published works. His first, in 1597, was a collection of ten essays on political behaviour. Then, in 1603, he published *The Advancement of Learning*, hoping to move the staunchly religious James I to support the development of physical science. He also examined ancient mythology in *On the Wisdom of the Ancients* of 1609, while *The Great Instauration* of 1620, which included an encyclopedia of natural phenomena, ultimately established Bacon's reputation as a leading scientific philosopher. During and after his imprisonment Bacon completed a considerable array of historical, scientific and philosophical works, including *The History of Henry VII*, *De Augmentis Scientiarum*, *The New Atlantis*, *Sylva Sylvarum* and a number of other, shorter pieces.

In the Baconian argument, Bacon was capable of writing the works attributed to Shakespeare. Whereas Shakespeare left no evidence of education or political expertise (in the Baconian opinion, both essential for authorship of the plays), Bacon was a leading politician, an historian and a philosopher. Most importantly, he *was* an accomplished writer, while Shakespeare evidently had no such background. Furthermore, there was direct evidence that Bacon was a dramatist who had once written a play under his own name. In 1592, on the anniversary of Elizabeth's coronation, Lord Essex presented a drama before the Queen, generally believed to have been composed by Francis Bacon.

A specific link to the plays of Shakespeare was that the writer who praised Shakespeare's works most loudly, Ben Jonson, was one of Bacon's closest friends. In 1621, just prior to the appearance of the First Folio, Jonson was guest of honour at Bacon's sixtieth birthday party at York House on the Strand in London. The fact that Jonson was so important an associate at the very pinnacle of Bacon's career (five days later the King made him Viscount St Albans) implies that the two men shared a close bond. According to the Baconians, this included the sharing of Bacon's secret.

In Baconian theory, Bacon never intended to become a lawyer, but was persuaded to do so by his parents. His true vocation as a poet-dramatist he was forced to conceal. For a politician like Bacon to have associated himself with the common theatre would have prejudiced his standing at court. As Bacon was undeniably ambitious, he had ample reason to separate his name from such works. But, more importantly, historical drama, such as the Shakespeare plays, could hardly avoid expressing political opinion. If these proved offensive or displeasing to the monarch or government of the day, the author might well find himself in serious trouble, and in danger of imprisonment or execution. Ben Jonson, for instance, had been imprisoned for libellous writings and narrowly escaped torture, as did playwrights George Chapman and John Marston.

Courtiers who did write seldom published dramatic or poetic works under their own names, preferring to use a pseudonym or, more usually, publish their works anonymously. But why should Shakespeare – in Baconian theory, the struggling actor – be used as a frontman? Why not simply remain anonymous? What reason would Bacon have for covering his tracks so profoundly?

The Baconian arguments centre mainly on the Essex rebellion of 1601, when the Earl of Essex led an abortive revolt against Queen Elizabeth. When the uprising was quashed, Essex was executed and the Privy Council investigated every aspect of the affair. They soon discovered that one of the rebels had arranged for the Lord Chamberlain's Men to perform *Richard II* (a play attributed to Shakespeare) on the eve of the insurrection, in the hope that the scene of the deposition of a king might arouse sympathy for the rebel cause. It certainly appears that the Queen was outraged by the performance, believing that the conspirators hoped to influence the London populace to favour the Essex rebellion. According to William Lambarde, keeper of the Tower records, she had complained 'I am Richard II, know ye not that?'

Ten days after the revolt Augustine Phillips, one of the players, was interrogated by the Privy Council, apparently admitting that the company had been paid by rebel sympathisers to stage the play. Fortunately for the actors, no evidence was found to implicate them directly with the rebellion, of which they had seemingly been ignorant. Southampton, however, was arrested and sentenced to death, later commuted to life imprisonment.

According to the Baconians, the Shakespeare plays had originally been published anonymously, but after the Essex revolt, fearing that Southampton's fate might befall him, Bacon decided to use a hapless frontman to claim authorship. William Shakespeare fitted the bill; he was already associated with the theatre (albeit as a humble actor), he was also a modestly successful poet and his works had already been patronised by the Earl of Southampton. Who better as the fall guy? The unwitting Shakespeare agreed to front the works and was well paid. However, upon the Queen's death soon after, Shakespeare's role was no longer necessary. When James I came to the throne, Southampton was released and the rebellion was assigned to history. But erring on the side of caution, in the event that the political tide again turned, Bacon continued to use Shakespeare as the supposed author.

Having established a feasible frontman scenario, the Baconians began their search for proof that Bacon was indeed a secret dramatist.

A letter written by Bacon himself contains an allusion in which he seems to admit to being a secret poet. In correspondence to courtier Sir John Davies, soon after the succession of James I, Bacon urges Davies to influence the new King to favour him. As Davies was a well known patron of dramatists, Bacon implored him to help, knowing that he was 'good to concealed poets'. Bacon, it was surmised, is here referring to himself as one of the 'concealed poets'.

Another letter written to Bacon by his friend Sir Tobie Mathew in 1624 further suggests that Bacon was a popular writer under another name. Mathew writes:

> The most prodigious wit that I knew, of my nation and
> this side of the sea, is your lordship's name, though he be
> known by another.

Together, these letters seem to imply that Bacon was a secret
poet using a *nom de plume*, but neither offers any evidence that
his work was being fronted by William Shakespeare.

The Elizabethan satirists Joseph Hall and John Marston, however, are thought by Baconians to have recognised Bacon as the
true author of *Venus and Adonis* and *The Rape of Lucrece* as
early as 1597. As they satirise the author with the name Labeo, a
Roman lawyer, it is thought that both men are referring to
Francis Bacon. Although he fails to give his grounds for suspicion, Hall certainly makes it clear that he does not think William
Shakespeare wrote the poems when he says 'Write they that can,
through they that cannot do' (*Hall's Satires Book II*). On the
same subject in another work he reproaches Labeo, 'Who list
complain of wronged faith or fame, when he may shift it on to another's name' (*Hall's Satires Book IV*). As Hall calls the false
author of the poems 'the Cynic', and the poems had been openly
published under Shakespeare's name, 'the Cynic' must presumably be Shakespeare. But is Labeo, although perhaps a lawyer,
really Bacon?

Hall's colleague Marston, in *Pigmalion's Image* of 1598, also
calls the true author of *Venus and Adonis* and *The Rape of
Lucrece* Labeo, referring to him as *medioca firma*. As these were
two Latin words from Bacon's family motto, it can be convinc-
ingly argued that both Hall and Marston believed that Bacon was
the true author.

Although Hall and Marston's allusions are intriguing, they do
not prove that Bacon wrote the poems, merely that Hall and
Marston *thought* he did. Indeed, Hall and Marston's assertion
contradicts one of the Baconian's own arguments, that Bacon
chose William Shakespeare because Shakespeare was already
known as the author of *Venus and Adonis* and *The Rape of
Lucrece*. However, it certainly indicates one important point:
while Shakespeare was alive there were already suspicions that
he was not capable of composing the works attributed to him.
This again demonstrates the mystery shrouding Shakespeare's
educational background.

But were Hall and Marston right? Did Bacon ever admit authorship of the Shakespeare plays himself? Some Baconians believe that he did, but in code. They hold that Francis Bacon, though he dared not acknowledge authorship of works in his lifetime, was determined that future generations should know the truth, and accordingly left behind a number of clues which would one day be discovered.

In the late nineteenth century, the American lawyer Ignatius Donnelly conceived the idea that Bacon had left concealed messages in the plays themselves, and in 1888 published *The Great Cryptogram*. The most important was a deciphered message using letters alongside words beginning with letters from Bacon's name. The message supposedly concealed in *Henry IV: Part I* read:

Shakst spur never writ a word of them

The problem with Donnelly is that his codes show no consistency, the system changing from page to page, whereas a true cipher should conform to one solution only. American cryptographer Robert Cockrain has used exactly the same set of ciphers employed by Donnelly to obtain the identical message from the Book of Genesis. Moreover, back in 1888 (the very year Donnelly's book was published), the Reverend J. Nicholson, in *No Cipher in Shakespeare*, employed the same system on the very text used by Donnelly to arrive at the message:

Master William Shakespeare writ the plays

Although there were other attempts to uncover ciphers in Shakespeare's works, none have successfully convinced any reputable cipher expert. The problem was the lack of a key, the preconstructed chart explaining the precise solution to the code. However, one Baconian cryptographer, who concentrated on Shakespeare's tomb inscription, did discover a code key – one devised by Bacon himself.

In 1887 an American, Hugh Black, was convinced that Bacon had used a code which he personally invented to leave a message in the strange curse on Shakespeare's tomb. (According to

Black, the tomb inscription had been commissioned by Bacon himself.) Shakespeare's gravestone in the chancel of Holy Trinity Church is a few feet from the bust, lying between his wife Anne and his daughter Susanna. The present slab is a replacement and the wording, although the same, is not written in the peculiar style of the original.

The present slab was installed about 1830 when the original had crumbled, but from editor George Stevens in 1785 we know that the wording was 'an uncouth mixture of small and capital letters'. According to an illustration based on Stevens's rendition, and published in Edmund Malone's edition of Shakespeare's plays in 1821, the epigraph was laid out as follows:

Good Frend for Iesus SAKE forbeare

To diGG T-E Duft Enclo-Afed HERe

Blese be T-E Man $\frac{T}{Y}$ fpares T-Es Stones

And curst be He $\frac{T}{Y}$ moves my Bones

This strange lettering prompted Black to believe that a cipher might be involved. In an article in the *North American Review* of October 1887, Black referred his reader to a code that Bacon himself explains in his *De Augmentis Scientiarum* of 1623, a series of A and B letters grouped in fives, each corresponding to a letter in the alphabet:

A = aaaaa B = aaaab C = aaaba D = aaabb E = aabab

F = aabaa G = aabba H = aabbb I = abaaa K = abaab

L = ababa M = ababb N = abbaa O = abbab P = abbba

Q = abbbb R = baaaa S = baaab T = baaba V = baabb

W = babaa X = babab Y = babba Z = babbb

(N.B. The letter U was written as V, and J as I.)

The cipher can be installed in a message, with each of the letters in the message corresponding to an A or B of the code. By using lower case letters for all those that refer to a letter A, and capital letters for all those that refer to the letter B, the coded message can be included in anything with five times as many letters.

If the true message was 'go', for instance, any false message can be written with ten letters. For example, 'Must stay in'.

In code the word 'go' is G – aabba, and O – abbab. These letters are coupled together – 'aabbaabbab' – and then written down in order below the message:

```
M u s t   s t a y   i n
a a b b   a a b b   a b
```

All the letters over a B are then printed in capitals:

```
m u S T   s t A Y   i n
a a b b   a a b b   a b
```

So the message received would be:

muST stAY in

All the receiver need do is to write down the message without word spaces, place the As under lower case letters, the Bs under capitals, divide the resultant code into a series of five letters, and consult the key:

```
muST stAY in = m u S T s t A Y i n
               a a b b a a b b a a = aabba  abbaa
                                       G      O
```

Using Bacon's code, Black translated the tomb inscription thus:

GoodF	rendf	orIes	usSAK	Eforb
baaab	aaaaa	aabaa	aabbb	baaaa
S	A	E	H	R

eareT	odiGG	T EDu	ftEnc	loAfe	dHERe
aaaab	aaaaa	babba	aabaa	aabaa	abbba
B	A	Y	E	E	P

Blese	beT E	Man~T~ys	pares	T EsS	tones
baaaa	aabab	baaba	aaaaa	babab	aaaaa
R	F	T	A	X	A

Andcu	rstbe	He$_Y^T$mo	vesmy	Bones
baaaa	aaaaa	babaa	aaaaa	baaaa
R	A	W	A	R

Black then rearranged the resultant letters – SAEHR-BAYEEPRFTAXARAWAR – and formed the word SHAXPERE and FRA BA WRT EAR AY, which he took to mean Francis (FRA) Bacon (BA) wrote (WRT) Shakespeare's (EAR) plays (AY).

Although Baconians applauded this discovery, it failed to impress the Stratfordians who took issue on a number of points. They argued that Black altered the rules to make the anagram fit. He took the $_Y^T$ as a single capital, the GG of diGG as lower case, the hyphen of the T—H as a lower case, and ignored the hyphen in the Enclo-Afed. More importantly, it was emphasised that Bacon's code in his *De Augmentis Scientiarum* used italicised letters – *not* capitals – to indicate the Bs in his cipher.

In conclusion, it would seem more plausible, if he actually did want the world to eventually know that he wrote the plays, that Bacon would have made sure that the message was less ambiguous, by following his own rules exactly and leaving a straightforward message, not an incomplete and contestable anagram. Indeed, why not simply leave a posthumous confession with a lawyer?

Leaving aside the dubious cryptograms, how strong is the case for Francis Bacon? From the letter of Sir Tobie Mathew, and Bacon's own correspondence with Sir John Davies, there is reason to suspect that Bacon wrote poetry under an assumed name. But apart from Hall and Marston's apparent belief that Bacon wrote two of Shakespeare's poems, there is no other evidence that Bacon wrote under Shakespeare's name. The legal argument therefore remains the backbone of the Baconian case.

In 1859 Lord Chief Justice Campbell was asked if he thought the legal references in the plays meant that Shakespeare had at one time been a lawyer. In reply, Campbell stated that the legal knowledge was evident, but no more than should be expected from someone who had spent time 'in the office of a county attorney in good business'. The Shakespeare of Stratford could certainly have acquired such knowledge. One of the few facts known about the Stratford Shakespeare is his involvement in numerous legal matters. In fact, a considerable knowledge of legal terminology and court proceedings could have been gained by almost anyone; at a time when entertainment was sparse, the law courts drew large crowds of spectators.

The Baconian argument collapses with the discovery that so many other Elizabethan playwrights also exhibit equal familiarity with the law. In 1913 J.M. Robertson's *The Baconian Heresy* was published. Robertson spent five years in a lawyer's office, in his spare time, comparing Shakespeare with other contemporary playwrights, searching for legal references. He was able to demonstrate that the playwrights Robert Greene, Thomas Nashe and Philip Massinger often used precisely the same legal phraseology as Shakespeare, and that Ben Jonson used much more. As these playwrights had no formal legal training, the argument that the author (whoever it was) of the Shakespeare plays *must* be a trained lawyer was invalidated.

A strong case *against* the plays being written by an important lawyer was made by barrister W.C. Devecmon in 1889 (*Re Shakespeare's Legal Acquirements*), when he criticised the trial scene from the *Merchant of Venice* as good theatre but legal nonsense. He contrasted this with John Webster's realistic handling of trial scenes in three of his plays. Moreover, Devecmon stressed that Webster employed 'more legal expressions, some of them highly technical, and all correctly used, than any single one of Shakespeare's works'. It is difficult to imagine Francis Bacon, the most eminent lawyer of the age, being upstaged by the untrained Webster, a humble poet who was not even recognised in his day.

With the chief Baconian arguments in question, we are left with the frontman scenario itself: Bacon using the poet/actor William Shakespeare after the Essex rebellion of 1601. This reasoning relies on the notion that the Shakespeare plays which appeared before this date had been published anonymously. This assertion would appear to be wrong; three years earlier, in 1598, Francis Meres had already listed Shakespeare among 'the most excellent' English playwrights, naming twelve of his plays. It therefore seems that Shakespeare's name was already associated with the plays in 1598, three years before the Essex rebellion of

1601. Accordingly, Shakespeare must have written a third of his own plays before Bacon supposedly wrote them, making the Baconian theory absurd. Admittedly, some Baconians have countered this argument by suggesting that Bacon had previously used Shakespeare on other grounds. However, the most credible scenario evaporates, leaving the Baconian case firmly on the rocks. Moreover, there is considerable evidence *against* Bacon being the author of the plays.

Bacon lived an active life, most of it in public, yet none of it was in any way associated with the theatre. In his work *De Augmentis Scientarium*, published in the same year as the First Folio, Bacon actually attacks contemporary drama. Furthermore, in 1614 The King's Men appealed to James I to allow them to establish a theatre in a new location objected to by local tradesmen. When James referred the matter to the Commissioners for Suits, of whom Bacon was one, Bacon firmly opposed the move. As The King's Men were Shakespeare's company and the chief performers of his plays, surely Bacon, if he was the real author, would not have objected.

In conclusion, it seems unlikely that the answer to the Shakespeare enigma will be solved with Francis Bacon. The Baconians continue, although their attention has shifted from Shakespeare. With their arguments discredited, but still clinging to the notion that Bacon must have written *somebody's* plays, modern Baconians have ascribed Bacon's authorship to the works of other Elizabethan playwrights: Christopher Marlowe, Robert Greene, Thomas Nashe and George Peele. Whatever the truth regarding Bacon as a dramatist, other alternative Shakespeare authors have more recently ignited far greater controversy.

Summary

Because Shakespeare seems to have lacked the necessary experience to have written the plays accredited to him, others have been proposed as the true author. The first alternative author theory concerned the Elizabethan lawyer and politician Francis Bacon, although since the nineteenth century the Baconian case has been discredited.

1. The Baconian Theory: Bacon never intended to become a politician, but was persuaded to do so by his parents. His true

vocation as a poet-dramatist he was forced to conceal. For Bacon to have associated himself with the common theatre would have prejudiced his standing at Court. He was thus impelled to separate his name from his works, and employed the actor William Shakespeare to publish the plays in *his* name.

2. The Baconian Case: Bacon was quite capable of writing the works attributed to Shakespeare. Whereas Shakespeare left no evidence of education or political expertise, both considered by Baconians essential for authorship of the plays, Bacon was a leading politician, an historian and a philosopher. Most importantly, he was an accomplished writer, while Shakespeare evidently had no such background.

3. The Author as a Lawyer: As complex legal matters and terminology are included in the Shakespeare plays, the Baconians believed that the author possessed a profound knowledge of the law; accordingly, only a practising lawyer, such as Bacon, could have been the true dramatist. However, many other sixteenth-century dramatists exhibit equal familiarity with the law. In 1913 J.M. Robertson demonstrated that Elizabethan playwrights Robert Greene, Thomas Nashe and Philip Massinger often used precisely the same legal phraseology as Shakespeare, and that Ben Jonson used far more. As these playwrights had no formal legal training, the argument that the author of the Shakespeare plays *must* be a trained lawyer was invalidated.

4. Bacon as a Poet-Dramatist: In a letter written to courtier Sir John Davies around 1603, Bacon refers to himself as a 'concealed poet'. Another letter, written to Bacon by his friend Sir Tobie Mathew in 1624, further suggests that Bacon was a popular writer under another name. Mathew writes, 'The most prodigious wit that I know . . . is your lordship's name, though he be known by another'. Together, these letters seem to imply that Bacon was a secret poet using a *nom de plume*. However, both fall far short of proving Bacon was writing under the name William Shakespeare.

5. Bacon as Shakespeare: The Elizabethan satirists Joseph Hall and John Marston are believed by Baconians to have recognised

Bacon as the true author of *Venus and Adonis* and *The Rape of Lucrece* as early as 1597. As they satirise the author with the name Labeo, a Roman lawyer, and use a quote from Bacon's family motto, it is thought that both men are referring to Francis Bacon. Since Hall calls the false author of the poems 'the Cynic', and the poems had been openly published under Shakespeare's name, 'the Cynic' must presumably be Shakespeare. Although Hall and Marston's allusions are intriguing, they do not prove that Bacon wrote the poems, only that Hall and Marston thought he did.

6. The Secret Admissions: In the late nineteenth century, American lawyer Ignatius Donnelly believed that Bacon had left concealed messages in the Shakespeare plays, admitting authorship. The most important was a message deciphered by using letters beside words beginning with letters from Bacon's name. The message supposedly concealed in *Henry IV: Part I* read 'Shakst spur never writ a word of them'. However, in 1888, after reading Donnelly's claim, the Reverend J. Nicholson employed the same system on the very text used by Donnelly to arrive at the message 'Master William Shakespeare writ the plays'.

7. The Case Against Bacon: There is considerable evidence against Francis Bacon being the author of the Shakespeare plays. Bacon lived an active life, most of it in public, yet none of it was in any way associated with the theatre. In his work *De Augmentis Scientarium*, published in the same year as Shakespeare's First Folio, Bacon even attacks contemporary drama. Furthermore, in 1614 The King's Men appealed to James I to allow them to establish a theatre in a new location objected to by local tradesmen. When James referred the matter to the Commissioners for Suits, of whom Bacon was one, Bacon firmly opposed the move. As The King's Men were Shakespeare's company and the chief performers of his plays, surely Bacon, if he was the real author, would not have objected.

Chapter 6

Derby and Oxford

In the nineteenth century the Shakespeare controversy was a straightforward fight between the Baconians and the Stratfordians, but since the First World War new alternatives have been proposed. Although many candidates were ruled out in the early stages, two secured a considerable following: the earls of Derby and Oxford.

In 1919 the French professor Abel Lefranc first suggested that the true author of the Shakespeare plays was William Stanley, the Sixth Earl of Derby. The case, which initially received wide support, is similar to the Baconian argument in that, as a nobleman, Derby may have been impelled to separate his name from the plays, choosing the Stratford actor as a front. However, although the Derbyites offer a more direct link between Derby and William Shakespeare than their Baconian predecessors (Derby's elder brother, Ferdinando Stanley was Lord Strange, Shakespeare's patron), unlike Bacon, Derby had no demonstrable need for a frontman. He may have wished to keep his authorship secret, but why the deep cover? Why not simply use a pseudonym, or publish anonymously? Unlike the Baconians, most Derbyites failed to address this problem in any respect.

From the outset, the Derbyite case relied chiefly on comparisons between Derby's personal experiences and episodes in the plays, most of which have since been proved invalid. Others, such as Robert Cecil, Lord Leicester and Sir Francis Drake, have been shown to have had far more in common with the play-scenes than the Earl of Derby, but none of these have been seriously proposed as the Shakespeare author. Such comparisons mean nothing in themselves, since any imaginative dramatist

William Stanley, Earl of Derby. Does Stanley's handwriting
match Shakespeare's?

could incorporate the experiences of another person into his plays. Moreover, the Derbyites cannot produce *any* evidence likening Derby's work with Shakespeare's. Apart from a few business letters written during the later years of his life, none of Derby's writings have survived. Unlike Bacon, Derby leaves nothing for comparisons of thought, style or structure.

Only one piece of evidence associates Derby with drama at all, two letters written on 30 June 1599 by a Jesuit spy named George Fenner, both saying the Earl of Derby is busy penning comedies for the common players'. Although the Derbyites cite the Fenner letters as incontrovertible proof that Derby was a playwright, the Stratfordians argue that the message was a code alluding to Derby's subversive activities, claiming that because Derby's family were Catholics, whom the Jesuits wished to convert to their cause, 'penning comedies' for 'common players' meant 'well inclined' towards 'our cause'. In fairness to the Derbyites, there is no real evidence that this was a code, making it quite possible that Derby had tried his hand as a dramatist. All the same, in no respect does this constitute evidence that he wrote Shakespeare's plays.

The last effective Derbyite offensive occurred in 1952, when A.W. Titherley published *Shakespeare's Identity*. Initially, this new case for Derby seemed persuasive, since Derby's handwriting appeared to match Shakespeare's.

In the British Library, in manuscript Harley 7368, is the play *Sir Thomas More*, attributed to the Elizabethan playwright Anthony Munday. The surviving manuscript is believed to date from around 1590, being mainly in the handwriting of one author, probably Munday. However, six other hands had amended the work. One of these writers, the editor of three pages of the so-called Insurrection Scene, has been proposed as William Shakespeare. The idea was first suggested by Richard Simpson in 1871, although it was amplified by Sir E. Maunde Thompson, the British Museum's Principal Librarian, in 1916. Maunde Thompson's series of essays, *Shakespeare's Handwriting*, proposed that the six known examples of Shakespeare's signature are in the same handwriting as the editor of the Insurrection Scene; in particular, Shakespeare's peculiar letter S appears in both. The Maunde Thompson theory, endorsed by experts from Scotland

Yard, is now generally accepted by Shakespearean scholars. If correct, this is the only example of Shakespeare's handwriting (other than his signature) yet discovered.

Most Stratfordians accept that Shakespeare helped to edit *Sir Thomas More* during his early career, but Titherley held that the editing was the work of Lord Derby. However, if Titherley's comparison of handwritings is valid, it is also self-defeating. The sole argument for the Insurrection Scene editor being Shakespeare is that it is in the handwriting of the *Stratford* Shakespeare: the signatures to which the Insurrection Scene editor's handwriting was compared were of William Shakespeare 'of Stratford-upon-Avon'. In claiming that the true editor was Derby, Titherley is destroying his own case. If Derby edited the Insurrection Scene, then Shakespeare did not; consequently there is no longer anything to connect Derby with a Shakespeare manuscript.

The only counter-argument for the Derbyites would be that Derby signed Shakespeare's will, the Mountjoy deposition and the property deeds. This would mean that Lord Derby not only wrote under Shakespeare's name, but actually assumed Shakespeare's identity, living as a Stratford grain dealer, working as a humble actor, and leaving his second best bed to his 'wife' Anne Hathaway. Since this is patently absurd, the most Titherley could hope to prove was that as a playwright Lord Derby helped to edit *Sir Thomas More*, a play with which Shakespeare was unconnected. Regardless, Titherley's handwriting comparison did not receive the support of reputable handwriting experts and the Derbyite case has since evaporated.

Unless some of Derby's own works surface, if indeed there are any, then the Derby proposal seems dead and buried. For the Oxfordians, however, the case is far from closed. The theory that Edward de Vere, the Seventeenth Earl of Oxford, was the author of the Shakespeare plays has become the major Shakespearean controversy of the twentieth century.

It began in 1920, when Gateshead schoolmaster John Looney initiated the Oxfordian case. Although Oxford was originally proposed as the sole author, the theory was eventually modified; Oxford was the leader of a group of brilliant courtiers who produced the plays as a joint venture. This notion was popularised by Gilbert Slater in 1931 with the appearance of *Seven Shakespeares*. The case, in essence, is that Oxford became leader of an official propaganda department, established to produce plays in support of Queen Elizabeth's government. Like the Bacon and Derby scenarios, as a nobleman Oxford must employ the actor Shakespeare as the frontman.

The case for Oxford as a playwright is much more compelling than the arguments for Bacon or Derby. Meres, in his *Palladis Tamia* of 1598, not only states that Oxford wrote comedies, but that they were among the very best. Since Meres is academically accepted as a reliable critic of the period, it can be taken on good authority that Oxford *was* a dramatist. Unfortunately Meres does not name any of Oxford's works, and none have survived (at least under his own name). Oxford also wrote poems, and some of these *do* exist. So, unlike the Baconians and Derbyites, who lack conclusive evidence that their candidates were poet-dramatists, the Oxfordians set out on firm ground.

However, Meres is something of a double-edged sword for the Oxfordians, for he also mentions Shakespeare in his work, including a list of Shakespeare plays. As Meres not only names Shakespeare, but accredits him with these plays, it is safe to assume that Meres himself did not believe that Shakespeare and Oxford were the same author. The Oxfordian position, however, is that the earl had written under both his own and Shakespeare's name.

Since Oxford's poems survive, the Oxfordians sought comparisons on the style and content with Shakespeare's poems and sonnets. But there seemed little similarity between the two; like the Baconians and Derbyites, the Oxfordians were left with isolated verses. A typical example is the alleged similarity between a few lines of Oxford's *A Vision of a Fair Maid* and Shakespeare's *Venus and Adonis*. Where Oxford writes:

> . . . on her side she knocks . . .
> [and a few lines later]
> From sighs and shedding amber tears
> Into sweet song she broke
> When thus the echo answered her
> To every word she spoke.

Edward de Vere, Earl of Oxford. Did his Court syndicate write the Shakespeare plays?

Shakespeare writes:

> . . . she beats her heart . . .
> [and a few lines later]
> And twenty echoes twenty times cry so
> She marking them, begins a wailing note
> And sings extemporally a woeful ditty.

The Oxfordians highlight the similarities; a woman pounding her chest in anguish, crying aloud, before breaking into echoing song. As the Oxford poem was unpublished (although it was composed at the time Shakespeare's *Venus and Adonis* appeared), it was claimed that the second could only have been written by the author of the first, since no one but the author could have seen it. The Stratfordians, however, argue that although comparable, the theme is commonplace. Moreover, with literally thousands of Shakespeare lines from which to choose, chance alone would throw up such comparisons. It could also be argued that both writers had copied an idea from a common source, matter already published by someone else.

Regarding the plays themselves, the Oxfordians follow the Baconians and Derbyites, the mainstream of evidence concerning references in the plays, believed to refer to incidents in the candidate's life. Unfortunately, much of this evidence consists of little more than identifying certain characters in the plays with Oxford's relatives, usually because the name sounds similar. For instance, in *Hamlet* Horatio is said to be Sir Horace de Vere, Oxford's cousin, while Francisco is Sir Francis de Vere. Nonetheless, the evidence that Oxford was a secret poet, with something specific to hide, is ultimately more convincing than any argument from the Bacon and Derby camps.

A passage from *Arte of English Poesie*, by George Puttenham in 1598, actually refers to Lord Oxford as the leader of a group of secret, courtly poets:

> A crew of courtly makers, noblemen, and gentlemen, who have written excellently well as it would appear if their doings could be found out and made public with the rest, of which number is first that noble gentleman, the Earl of Oxford.

Oxford's courtly group might explain a mysterious warrant first issued by the Privy Council in 1586. In that year the Council endorsed a special grant of £1,000 to be paid annually to Lord Oxford. This annuity, for some undisclosed purpose, is thought to have been used to enable Oxford to promote poetry and drama of a patriotic nature. Since it continued to be paid annually throughout the reigns of Elizabeth and James, and neither monarchs were in the habit of handing out money for no return, Oxford must certainly have been involved in some important activity to earn it.

Although it is true that the Shakespeare plays evince a great love of England, a hatred of disorder and the need for strong government, few of them are truly patriotic in the usual sense. Furthermore, Queen Elizabeth was furious about the Essex affair and the performance of *Richard II*, believing herself ridiculed in the play. If the Oxfordians are right, and the Queen was knowingly sponsoring Oxford to write the Shakespeare plays, why was Oxford not called to account? His name was never connected with the matter and, more importantly, the annuity was continued. It therefore seems highly unlikely that the Shakespeare plays were written by Oxford's courtly poets mentioned by Puttenham.

There is a further argument against this syndicate being responsible for the Shakespeare plays. Like the Baconians and Derbyites, the Oxfordians incorporate the frontman scenario. Shakespeare was chosen to front the plays as it was inadvisable for Oxford to be associated with them. Once again, this seems a self-defeating argument; if Oxford was working for the Queen and the Privy Council, there is no need for a frontman – Shakespeare no longer has a feasible role. Accordingly, even if Oxford *was* writing official propaganda plays, they are unlikely to have included the Shakespeare plays.

The surviving Oxfordian argument, therefore, is that Oxford wrote the Shakespeare plays on his own initiative. As no direct evidence for this survives, the Oxfordians were impelled to search for secret, coded confessions. In this respect, the Oxfordian case fares little better than the Baconian ciphers. In *Romeo and Juliet*, for instance, Romeo says:

71

> For I am proverb'd with a grandsire phrase; I am a candle-holder, and look on.

The Oxfordian claim is that here Oxford is obliquely admitting to having written the play. A candle-holder was called a trestle, an old way of spelling trestle was 'trussell', and Oxford's grandmother was Elizabeth Trussell. Furthermore, Oxford's own coat of arms actually shows a candle flame. Accordingly, the author is saying:

> Here is a play on my grandparent's name, meaning candle-holder; I am one of the Trussells, look at my coat of arms.

Like the Baconian ciphers, such isolated puns, scattered throughout hundreds of pages of text, stretch the imagination considerably. Again, the Stratfordians argue that such phrases occur by chance alone.

However, there is an interesting motif in Oxford's coat of arms which the Oxfordians assert is no coincidence. The crest depicts Athena, the goddess of literature, and a lion shaking a spear. This, they claim, is evidence that Oxford was not only a literary figure, but that he used the pseudonym Shake-spear. Although of interest, the spear-shaking lion cannot have been Oxford's method of confessing to being the Shakespeare author, since the Oxford crest already existed before Shakespeare was born. Moreover, the lion appears to be static and there is no suggestion that it is actually *shaking* the spear in question.

In conclusion, the Oxfordian claim lacks concrete evidence. Moreover, a strong case can be made to bar Oxford entirely from the alternative author club. In the dedication to the first published Shakespeare work, *Venus and Adonis*, the author seems to be anything but an earl. It is dedicated 'To the Right Honourable Henry Wriothesley, Earl of Southampton and Baron of Titchfield', and reads:

> Right Honourable, I know not how I shall offend in dedicating my unpolished lines to your Lordship, nor how the world will censure me for choosing so strong a prop to

support so weak a burden; only, if your honour seem but pleased, I account myself highly praised, and vow to take advantage of all idle hours, till I have honoured you with some graver labour. But if the first heir of my invention prove deformed, I shall be sorry it had so noble a god-father, and never after ear so barren a land, for fear it yield me still so bad a harvest. I leave it to your honourable survey, and your Honour to your heart's content; which I wish may always answer your own wish and the world's hopeful expectation.

One point is certain about the author, whoever he was; he is of inferior rank to the Earl of Southampton. Not only was Lord Oxford of higher standing than Southampton (his earldom was a good deal more ancient), but at the time *Venus and Adonis* was published Southampton was in his teens and Oxford was forty-four. It is difficult to imagine an older, senior earl writing to Southampton in such terms as 'I know not how I shall offend', and referring to Southampton as 'so noble a god-father'. More-over, apart from it quite obviously being a dedication from an inferior to a superior, the words 'the first heir of my invention' shows that this is the poet's first published work. Even if the name William Shakespeare was a pseudonym, Oxford seemingly could not have been the author, for he had *already* written a number of poems.

Furthermore, we find exactly the same submissive phraseology in the dedication to Southampton in the second published Shake-speare work, *The Rape of Lucrece* on 9 May 1594:

The love I dedicate to your Lordship is without end; whereof this pamphlet, without beginning, is but a super-fluous moiety. The warrant I have of your honourable disposition, not the worth of my untutored lines, makes it assured of acceptance. What I have done is yours; what I have to do is yours; being part in all I have, devoted yours. Were my worth greater, my duty would show greater; meantime, as it is, it is bound to your Lordship, to whom I wish long life, still lengthened with all happiness.

All three alternative author theories so far examined have something in common, they present a convincing case for Shakespeare's seeming inability to write the plays, but their proposals for the 'true author' lack substance. Also, they point out a single – glaring – stumbling block that the Baconians, Derbyites and Oxfordians seem completely to ignore. Why choose a frontman who is seemingly incapable of writing the plays? If nothing else, William Shakespeare of Stratford-upon-Avon seems to have kept his writing activities as quiet as possible. The purpose of a frontman is to act the part of the playwright, accept responsibility for the plays and promote the fact. This, as we have already seen, is something that William Shakespeare certainly did *not* do.

There is, however, one alternative author theory which does not rely on the theme of a nobleman hiding his secret. It presents a far more intriguing and substantial case than its predecessors, providing many Shakespeare connections where the Baconians, Derbyites and Oxfordians have failed. The author advocated was an accomplished playwright, patronised by a Shakespeare patron, and was associated with many of Shakespeare's colleagues – the Elizabethan dramatist Christopher Marlowe.

Summary

Since the First World War two new alternative authors have been proposed for the Shakespeare plays: the earls of Derby and Oxford. However, like the Baconians, both cases have failed to produce anything other than contestable circumstantial evidence.

1. In 1919 the French professor Abel Lefranc first suggested that the true author of the Shakespeare plays was William Stanley, the Sixth Earl of Derby. The case was similar to the Baconian argument in that, as a nobleman, Derby was impelled to separate his name from the plays, choosing the Stratford actor as a front.

2. The only piece of known evidence to associate Derby with drama are two letters written on 30 June 1599 by a Jesuit spy named George Fenner. The first saying, 'The Earl of Derby is busy only in penning comedies for the common players', and the second, 'Our Earl of Derby is busy in penning comedies for the common players'. Although it is possible that Derby tried his

hand as a dramatist, this is far from being evidence that he wrote Shakespeare's plays.

3. The Derbyite case relied chiefly upon comparisons between Derby's personal experiences and episodes in the plays, most of which have since been proved invalid. Other Elizabethans, such as Robert Cecil, Lord Leicester and Sir Francis Drake, have been shown to have had far more in common with the play-scenes than the Earl of Derby, and none of these have seriously been proposed as the Shakespeare author.

4. The theory that Edward de Vere, the Seventeenth Earl of Oxford, was the author of the Shakespeare plays has become the major Shakespearean controversy of the twentieth century. It began in 1920, when Gateshead schoolmaster John Looney initiated the Oxfordian case. Although Oxford was originally proposed as the sole author, the theory was eventually modified, presenting Oxford as the leader of a syndicate who produced the plays as a joint venture. Like the Bacon and Derby scenarios, as a nobleman Oxford must employ the actor Shakespeare as the frontman.

5. A passage from *Arte of English Poesie*, by George Puttenham in 1598, refers to Lord Oxford as the leader of a group of secret, courtly poets who wrote for Queen Elizabeth. However, there is a powerful argument against this syndicate being responsible for the Shakespeare plays. If Oxford was working for the Queen there is no need for a frontman, and Shakespeare no longer has a feasible role. If Oxford was writing official propaganda plays, they are unlikely to have included the Shakespeare works.

6. Francis Meres, in his *Palladis Tamia* of 1598, not only states that Oxford wrote comedies, but that they were among the best. As Meres is academically accepted as being a reliable critic of the period, we can take it on good authority that Oxford was a dramatist. However, Meres also mentions Shakespeare in his work, including a list of Shakespeare plays. As Meres not only names Shakespeare but accredits him with these plays, it seems safe to assume that Meres himself did not believe that Shakespeare and Oxford were the same author.

7. Since Oxford's poems survive, the Oxfordians sought comparisons in their style and content with Shakespeare's poems and sonnets. However, like the Baconians and Derbyites, the Oxfordians were left with isolated verses. The surviving Oxfordian case concerned references in the plays, believed to refer to incidents in Oxford's life. Unfortunately, much of this evidence consists of little more than identifying certain characters in the plays with Oxford's relatives, usually because of similar-sounding names.

8. A powerful argument eliminates Oxford as the author of the Shakespeare plays. In the dedication to Lord Southampton in the first published Shakespeare work, *Venus and Adonis*, the author refers to his patron as 'so noble a god-father'. It is difficult to imagine Oxford, a senior earl, referring to Southampton in such terms. Not only was Lord Oxford of higher standing than Southampton, but at the time *Venus and Adonis* was published Southampton was in his teens and Oxford was forty-four.

Chapter 7

Christopher Marlowe

In 1955 Canadian journalist Calvin Hoffman reached the same conclusion as his Baconian, Derbyite and Oxfordian predecessors, in believing that William Shakespeare had been incapable of writing the plays ascribed to him. In *The Man Who Was Shakespeare* Hoffman proposed a new, alternative author, Christopher Marlowe. Unlike the previous theories, Hoffman's differed in two important respects. On the positive side, Marlowe *was* an accepted and brilliant playwright, arguably capable of writing the Shakespeare plays. On the negative side, Marlowe was officially dead at the time most of the plays were written. By 1593 Christopher Marlowe was the most successful playwright of his day, but at precisely the time that Shakespeare's works first appeared, Marlowe died. As Hoffman's case necessitated Marlowe still being alive after 1593, he proposed an intriguing theory – Marlowe's death had been staged. Certainly Marlowe had died in suspicious circumstances.

During the early months of 1593 a number of anonymous anti-government writings appeared throughout London, and on 22 April the Privy Council, both the cabinet and most powerful tribunal of the day, rounded up a number of possible authors for questioning. One of these was the playwright Thomas Kyd. Kyd's papers were examined, but although they failed to discover evidence of the Flemish Libels, the Council found something equally incriminating, atheistic writings questioning the authority of the Protestant Church. Under examination, Kyd denied that the papers were his, claiming they had been written by Christopher Marlowe while they were working together two years before.

On 18 May Marlowe was summoned for questioning, but Kyd's slender testimony was insufficient to have him detained. Marlowe had powerful friends and the Privy Council required further evidence. Marlowe was a close friend of Thomas Walsingham, whose cousin Francis had been the Secretary of State responsible for establishing England's Secret Service, an undercover network of spies and informers to detect supposed Catholic plots against the Protestant government of Queen Elizabeth. Francis Walsingham had died in 1590, but Thomas retained an influential position in the Secret Service.

By the end of May, the Privy Council found other witnesses prepared to testify against Marlowe. With his arrest imminent, at 10 o'clock on the morning of 30 May, Marlowe met with three acquaintances at a tavern in Deptford, south-east London: Nicholas Skeres, Robert Poley and Ingram Frizer. At around 6 in the evening the four men retired to a private room. According to the testimony of the other three, Marlowe began to argue over who was to settle the bill. The quarrel apparently became so heated that Marlowe attacked Frizer with a dagger, and in the ensuing struggle the weapon was driven into Marlowe's skull, killing him instantly. Frizer was detained, but later acquitted on grounds of self defence.

According to Hoffman, Marlowe was involved in a homosexual relationship with Walsingham, who had chosen to save his lover from torture, imprisonment and possible execution. Accordingly, Walsingham arranged to fake Marlowe's death. He hired the three drinking partners to claim Marlowe had been killed in self defence, a substitute body was found and the coroner was bribed to conceal the truth. The coroner passed a verdict of self defence, the body was quickly buried and Marlowe lived on in secret somewhere on the Continent. Thereafter, still inspired to write, Marlowe required someone to front his works.

Hoffman believed that William Shakespeare was at the time employed as an actor at the Shoreditch Theatre, where Marlowe was also working. As an actor, Shakespeare was chosen as the frontman and well paid for his cooperation. Hoffman claimed that this was why Shakespeare had been unknown as a writer in Stratford. He had journeyed to London as an actor, and when the offer was made to front Marlowe's plays he accepted, having much to gain and nothing to lose.

The Marlowe case was manifestly stronger in one respect than the previous alternative author theories in that Marlowe was already the leading playwright of his day. Hoffman's theory also accounted for Shakespeare's sudden wealth (it came from Walsingham in payment for his services), and it explained Shakespeare's low public profile (he was seeking to avoid being questioned about plays he had not written).

In addition to the fact that Marlowe and Shakespeare seem to have worked together at the Shoreditch Theatre, there are other connections between the two men. Shakespeare's first published work, *Venus and Adonis*, was similar in content to Marlowe's last work, *Hero and Leander*, on which he was working when he apparently died. Even the traditional Shakespeare biographers agree that there must have been some connection between the two poems, the usual explanation being that Shakespeare had acquired a copy from Marlowe while working with him at the Shoreditch Theatre.

Few scholars doubt that Marlowe and Shakespeare worked together. Around 1593 Shakespeare seems to have been attached to Lord Strange's company at the Shoreditch Theatre, and Marlowe's plays were performed by Lord Strange's Men at the same time. However, as *Venus and Adonis* was registered on 18 April, over a month before Marlowe's death, the idea that Shakespeare had taken over from Marlowe to complete the work seems incongruous. Hoffman believed that the plan to stage Marlowe's death may already have been hatched, and Shakespeare was being prepared in advance.

Marlowe was thus an accomplished playwright, he almost certainly worked with Shakespeare and his career ended precisely where Shakespeare's began. Indeed, it could be argued that unless Marlowe had been removed from the scene, Shakespeare might never have achieved such fame, as Marlowe's death left Shakespeare without a rival. Additionally, the two men were exactly the same age, and the works ascribed to both are of comparable quality.

Although Hoffman's theory is intriguing, it relies on Marlowe being alive at the time the plays were written. Many historians agree that the circumstances surrounding Marlowe's death are suspicious – occurring as he was about to be arrested – although it is argued that Marlowe was genuinely murdered to prevent him from incriminating Walsingham. The circumstances surrounding Marlowe's death must therefore be examined in greater detail.

In 1593, with government permission, a number of Flemish Protestant refugees had settled in London. Their presence was resented by local tradesmen who regarded them as business rivals, and before long protests were made. Accordingly, a number of slogans and placards were anonymously posted in public places, designed to whip up anti-Flemish feelings. Some were also anti-government in tone, so the Privy Council ordered the arrest of those responsible.

Among those arrested was the playwright Thomas Kyd, and when his rooms were searched atheistic writings were discovered. Atheism, by implication, denied the divine right of the Queen to be head of the English Church and so was legally considered treason, a capital offence. Understandably, Kyd denied that the document was his, claiming instead that it had been written by Christopher Marlowe, with whom he had shared rooms two years earlier. On 18 May the Privy Council summoned Marlowe, then staying with Thomas Walsingham at Scadbury Manor near Chislehurst in Kent. The instructions for Marlowe's apprehension were handed to the Queen's messenger, Henry Maunder:

> Repair to the house of Mr Thomas Walsingham in Kent, or to any other place where he shall understand Christopher Marlowe to be remaining, and by virtue hereof to apprehend and bring him to the Court in his company.

Maunder returned with Marlowe, who appeared before the Council on 20 May. The Privy Council's Register records:

> This day Christopher Marlowe of London, Gentleman, being sent for by warrant from their Lordships, hath entered his appearance accordingly for his indemnity therein, and is commanded to give his daily attendance on their Lordships till he shall be licensed to the contrary.

From this entry we know that Marlowe appeared before the Council and was allowed to go free as long as he continued to report each day. It can be assumed therefore that Marlowe had denied authorship of the document and that he was freed on 'bail' while subject to further investigation.

Some days later Marlowe's problems deepened when the Privy Council received a report from its agent Richard Baines, containing far more serious allegations. The Privy Council considered it important enough to send a copy to the Queen. According to the report (in part entitled 'the most horrible blasphemies uttered by Christopher Marlowe') Marlowe had been heard saying that 'Christ was a bastard and his mother dishonest'. Blasphemy was serious enough, but Marlowe was also accused of far worse: mocking the Protestant Church. According to the Baines report he had said 'all Protestants are hypocritical asses', and more damaging still, 'if there be a God or any religion it is the papists'. The report listed one and a half pages of similar accusations.

If found guilty, Marlowe would almost certainly have been executed, after days of interrogation and torture. His treatment would probably have been brutal, as the report also stated that Marlowe met with others – in high positions – who shared his opinions. Walsingham may well have fallen under suspicion as one of these. Not only was he Marlowe's friend and patron, but the playwright was actually staying with him at the time. Even if Walsingham was innocent, under torture Marlowe might admit to anything. It is therefore quite possible that Walsingham, learning of the Baines report from a friend in the Privy Council, quickly arranged for Marlowe's murder, or, in Hoffman's theory, the staging of his death.

There is no record of when the Baines report was received, but it must have been late on 30 May; if earlier, Marlowe would have been detained when he attended the Privy Council that morning. Historians suspecting Marlowe's murder draw attention to this timely demise; the Council receive the Baines report, Marlowe's detention is ordered and then he dies. There are certainly grounds for suspicion.

It is quite possible that the three drinking partners at the Deptford tavern, the only witnesses to the killing, were working for Thomas Walsingham. Poley and Skeres had previously worked for the Secret Service and Frizer was directly employed by Walsingham. That very morning Poley had returned from the

Netherlands on a Secret Service mission. According to Chamber Treasurer Sir Thomas Heneage, in his record of payment to Poley on 12 June 1593, Poley had been carrying 'letters in post for her Majesty's special and secret affairs of great importance'. Moreover, Heneage says that Poley was actually in the Queen's service from 8 May to 8 June, during the precise period Marlowe died.

Skeres had also worked for the Secret Service. He is mentioned by Francis Walsingham's assistant Francis Milles as an undercover agent helping to thwart the Catholic Babington Plot in 1586, and in July 1589 he is again in the pay of Francis Walsingham.

Although there is no surviving evidence to connect Frizer with the Secret Services, he *was* employed by Thomas Walsingham around the time of the Marlowe killing. According to a complaint lodged at the Chancery Court in 1598 by a Drew Woodleff of Aylesbury, Frizer and Skeres had tricked Woodleff out of £34 five years previously. The complaint mentions a legal document dated 29 June 1593, in which Thomas Walsingham is described as Frizer's 'master'. This was just one day after Frizer was acquitted of Marlowe's killing, so we know for certain that he was working for Walsingham a month after he supposedly killed Marlowe in self defence.

The testimony of these three unsavoury characters is the only available evidence of the events that occurred in the Deptford tavern when Marlowe died. Dated 1 June 1593, the coroner's report states that Marlowe met with Ingram Frizer, Nicholas Skeres and Robert Poley:

> . . . on 30th day of May, at Deptford Strand, within the verge, about the tenth hour before noon of the same day, met together in the room in the house of a certain Eleanor Bull, a widow, and there passed the time together, and walked in the garden belonging to the said house until the sixth hour after noon of the same day and then returned from the said garden to the room aforesaid and there together and in company supped. And after supper the said Ingram and Christopher Marlowe were in speech, and uttered one to the other divers malicious words for the

reason that they could not be at one nor agree about the payment of the sum of pence, that is, *le recknynge* [the reckoning] there. And the said Christopher Marlowe then lying upon a bed in the room where they had supped, and moved with anger against the said Ingram Frizer then and there sitting in the room aforesaid with his back toward the bed where the said Christopher Marlowe was then lying, sitting near the bed with the front part of his body towards the table, and the aforesaid Nicholas Skeres and Robert Poley sitting on either side of the said Ingram in such a manner that the same Ingram Frizer in no wise could take flight.

It so befell that the said Christopher Marlowe, then and there, maliciously gave the aforesaid Ingram two wounds on the head; of the length of two inches, and of the depth of a quarter of an inch. Whereupon the said Ingram, in fear of being slain, and sitting in the manner aforesaid between the said Nicholas Skeres and Robert Poley so that he could not in any wise get away, in his own defence, and for the saving of his life, then and there struggled with the said Christopher Marlowe to get back from him his dagger aforesaid. In which affray the same Ingram could not get away from the said Christopher Marlowe, and so it befell in that affray that the said Ingram, in defence of his life, with the dagger aforesaid, of the value of 12d, gave the said Christopher, then and there, a mortal wound over his right eye of the depth of two inches and the width of one inch; of which mortal wound the aforesaid Christopher Marlowe then and there instantly died.

In this, the accepted verdict, Marlowe was killed by Frizer in self defence. They had quarrelled over the bill, Marlowe jumped up, snatched Frizer's dagger, and attacked him. In the ensuing struggle, the weapon was driven into Marlowe's head, killing him instantly. Regrettably, it is only the word of the three drinking partners that this is actually what occurred, and there is certainly a compelling case that the killing was premeditated. Walsingham had motive (his neck), means (his agents) and opportunity (no other witnesses) to murder Marlowe. But is Hoffman correct in supposing that the killing was only staged?

For a year Hoffman lived in hope that proof of his theory would be found in Thomas Walsingham's tomb in St Nicholas's church in Chislehurst. It is not clear exactly what Hoffman hoped to find, but when he eventually received permission for it to be opened in 1956 he was disappointed. It did not contain the body of Christopher Marlowe, nor anything to connect him with the Shakespeare plays. Lacking proof that Marlowe had lived on, Hoffman was left to search for evidence of a cover-up of Marlowe's murder.

In October 1593, five months after Marlowe's apparent death, the poet Gabriel Harvey wrote the poem *Gorgon*, in which he implied that Marlowe died of plague. Plague had indeed been sweeping London at the time of Marlowe's death, and in a period before mass communication it is understandable that Harvey got it wrong. Hoffman disagrees. As Gabriel Harvey had been Marlowe's close associate (they had been at Cambridge together) he would be better informed. Hoffman discovered that Harvey's younger brother Richard was rector of St Nicholas's church in Chislehurst, Thomas Walsingham's own parish church. Hoffman suggested that the rector had seen Marlowe alive after 30 May in Chislehurst and that a cover story was formulated, explaining that Marlowe had since died of the plague. Quite how such a story would satisfy anyone who later heard of Marlowe's tavern-brawl death Hoffman fails to explain.

It seems unlikely that there is anything untoward in the report that Marlowe died of plague. It was probably a simple case of idle gossip. Indeed, four years later another distorted account of Marlowe's death appeared, adequately demonstrating the dangers of hearsay in Elizabethan London. In 1597 another Cambridge scholar, Suffolk clergyman Thomas Beard, said that Marlowe was killed while attempting to assassinate an enemy in a London street. Beard considered it God's retribution for Marlowe's atheism, and in his tirade *Theatre of God's Judgements* he writes:

It so fell out that in London streets, as he proposed to stab one whom he ought a grudge unto with his dagger, the other party perceiving, so avoided the stroke that withal catching hold of his wrist, he stabbed his own dagger into his own head, in such sort that notwithstanding all the means of surgery that could be wrought, he shortly after died thereof.

It is clear from this account how the original story has been exaggerated, from a drunken Marlowe quarrelling over a bill to a homicidal Marlowe attacking in cold blood. The coroner's version of events seems to have circulated by 1600, however, as the Welsh writer William Vaughan (in *The Golden Grove*) stated that Marlowe had been killed in a tavern brawl at Deptford by 'one named Ingram'. Without evidence to the contrary, therefore, we can assume that Gabriel Harvey could well have been misinformed about Marlowe's death, without resorting to any conspiracy theory.

Returning to Marlowe's authorship of the Shakespeare plays, like the Baconians and Oxfordians, Hoffman cannot resist searching for an 'I wrote Shakespeare's plays' cipher. However, his main line of argument linking Marlowe with the Shakespeare plays is far more ingenious.

Hoffman cites the work of Dr Thomas Corwin Mendenhall from Ohio, who in the late nineteenth century devised a means to 'fingerprint' an author's individual style. The process relied on the average number of word letters, which Mendenhall maintained were unique to every writer. Around the turn of the century Mendenhall had been asked by a Baconian to apply his theory to the works of Shakespeare and Bacon. Mendenhall concluded that they were not the same author, but after examining other playwrights he believed that Shakespeare's 'fingerprint' was identical to Marlowe's.

Taken at face value, the Mendenhall test seems persuasive. He counted the number of letters in a vast number of words in the playwright's works, then calculated the average number of letters per word down to eight decimal places (although at the time it was calculated in fractions). For example, the sentence 'The home is where the heart is' has 24 letters and 7 words. Dividing the 24 by 7 gives 3.42825714, the average number of letters per word. To establish an author's 'fingerprint' Mendenhall used thousands of words (400,000 from Shakespeare, and presumably as many from Marlowe). Although the average number of letters per word is about 4 in general texts, it varies from about 3.5 in children's books to around 5 in technical manuals. However, the eight decimal places provides almost a hundred million to one chance against any two people having exactly the same number.

Unfortunately, this is not as scientific as it might appear. We can only assume that Hoffman never carried out the tedious task of checking Mendenhall's results. Now, thanks to the universal accessibility of modern computers, many have since proved the theory invalid. For a start, the complete works of Shakespeare have a value of 4.24235672 and Marlowe's are 4.21563427, suggesting an understandable amount of miscounting in Mendenhall's laborious task. Bacon fares slightly better with 4.22352489. However, one writer has been shown to match Shakespeare exactly up to three decimal places, the modern novelist Jackie Collins. If Hoffman's theory is correct, then Ms Collins is more likely to have written Shakespeare's plays than either Bacon or Marlowe! In fact, taken individually, every single one of Shakespeare's plays differs from the others in its 'fingerprint' from the first decimal place. For the Mendenhall theory to work, each of Shakespeare's plays must have been written by a separate author, something even the most avid anti-Stratfordian has never advocated.

Although modern, sophisticated techniques have been devised to 'fingerprint' writers, employing factors such as the frequency of phrases, and words that regularly follow each other, they are still not generally accepted as reliable. But even if they were, 'fingerprinting' an Elizabethan playwright would be impossible. We know from many surviving manuscripts (such as the *Sir Thomas More* manuscript) that although a work may have been devised by one author, plays were amended and edited by others. The eventual wording would nearly always have been a group effort.

In final analysis, Hoffman's case for Marlowe's fake death falls apart. In 1925 the original coroner's report was discovered in the archives of the London Records Office by Harvard scholar Dr Leslie Hotson. The report begins:

> Inquisition indented taken at Deptford Strand in the aforesaid County of Kent, within the verge, on the 1st day of

June, 1593, in the Presence of William Danby, Gent,
Coroner of the Household of our said Lady the Queen,
upon the view of the body of Christopher Marlowe, there
lying dead and slain upon the oath of . . . [There follows
the names of sixteen members of the jury.]

The presence of Danby works against Hoffman. From the report
we know he was 'Coroner of the Household of our said Lady the
Queen'. He was therefore a high-class, royal official. If Walsingham had planned a fake death and used a substitute body, surely
he would have staged the event outside 'the verge' – the jurisdiction of the Queen's own coroner – not within it. A local
coroner would presumably be much easier to bribe or blackmail,
and would certainly attract far less attention. Moreover, we can
see from the report that no fewer than sixteen jurors viewed the
body. With so many involved, Walsingham would be leaving a
great deal to chance, hoping that none had previously seen the
country's most famous playwright.

There is no record of how the Privy Council regarded Marlowe's death, but with the Queen informed it is certain they
would wish to verify the identity of the body. Many of the offi-
cials attached to the Privy Council knew Marlowe by sight,
Henry Maunder for one. As the parish register shows that Marlowe was buried at St Nicholas's Church in Deptford on 1 June,
the body could easily have been exhumed if necessary. In conclusion, if there really had been a substitute body, Walsingham
would have to trust the coroner, bribe the jury and risk exhuma-
tion. Surely he would have planned a safer form of 'death', one
that disfigured the corpse beyond recognition – a fire perhaps.

There seems little reason to doubt that Christopher Marlowe
did die in the brawl at the Deptford tavern and therefore he cannot be accredited with Shakespeare's plays. However, did the
events occur as Poley, Skeres and Frizer described? A murder
may well have been committed and may present a solution to the
mystery of Shakespeare's life.

Summary

In 1955 Canadian journalist Calvin Hoffman published his
conclusion that Shakespeare's plays had been the work of Elizabethan dramatist Christopher Marlowe. However, it seems

highly unlikely that Marlowe was still alive by the time most of the plays were written.

1. On the positive side, Marlowe *was* an accepted and brilliant playwright, arguably capable of writing the Shakespeare plays. On the negative side, Marlowe was officially dead at the time that all but the earliest plays were written. As Hoffman's case necessitated Marlowe still being alive after 1593, he proposed that Marlowe's death had been staged.

2. In April 1593 the Privy Council arrested playwright Thomas Kyd for suspicion of writing seditious literature. When Kyd's papers were examined, the Council found atheistic writings questioning the authority of the Protestant Church. Under examination, Kyd denied that the papers were his, claiming they had been written by Christopher Marlowe while they worked together two years before.

3. On 18 May Marlowe was summoned for questioning, but Kyd's slender testimony was insufficient to have him detained: Marlowe had powerful friends and the Privy Council required further evidence. Marlowe was a close companion of Thomas Walsingham, whose cousin Francis had been the Secretary of State responsible for establishing the Elizabethan Secret Service, a spy network to uncover supposed Catholic plots against the Protestant government. Francis Walsingham had died in 1590, but Thomas retained an influential position in the Secret Service.

4. By the end of May the Privy Council found other witnesses prepared to testify against Marlowe. With his arrest imminent, at 10 o'clock on the morning of 30 May, Marlowe met with three acquaintances at a tavern in Deptford: Nicholas Skeres, Robert Poley and Ingram Frizer. At around 6 in the evening the four men retired to a private room. According to the testimony of the other three, Marlowe began to argue over who was to settle the bill. The quarrel apparently became so heated that Marlowe attacked Frizer with a dagger, and in the ensuing struggle the weapon was driven into Marlowe's skull, killing him instantly. Frizer was detained, but later acquitted on grounds of self defence.

5. Hoffman's Case: Marlowe's friend Thomas Walsingham decided to save him from the gallows and arranged to fake his death. Walsingham hired the three drinking partners to claim Marlowe had been killed in self defence, a substitute body was found, and the coroner was bribed to conceal the truth. Marlowe lived on in secret, using the actor William Shakespeare (with whom he had worked at the Shoreditch Theatre) to front his plays.

6. It is quite possible that the three drinking partners at the Deptford tavern, the only witnesses to the killing, *were* working for Thomas Walsingham. Poley and Skeres had previously worked for the Secret Service, and Frizer was directly employed by Walsingham. However, although Walsingham may well have arranged Marlowe's death to prevent the playwright from incriminating him, it is most unlikely that the killing was a fraud.

7. There is no record of how the Privy Council regarded Marlowe's death, but with the Queen informed it is certain they would wish to verify the body's identity. As the parish register shows that Marlowe was immediately buried at St Nicholas's Church in Deptford, the body could easily have been exhumed if necessary. Had there been a substitute body, surely Walsingham would have planned a safer form of 'death', perhaps one which disfigured the corpse beyond recognition.

8. For a year Hoffman lived in hope that proof of his theory would be found in Thomas Walsingham's tomb in St Nicholas's church in Chislehurst, Kent. It is not clear exactly what he hoped to find, but when he eventually received permission for it to be opened in 1956 he was disappointed. It did not contain the body of Christopher Marlowe, nor anything to connect him with the Shakespeare plays.

Chapter 8

The Strange Connection

With the alternative author theories falling well short of their objectives, we return to Shakespeare himself. Lacking any substantial evidence to the contrary, we must assume that he *was* the true author of the plays published in his name. Consequently, we are again confronted by the peculiarity of his life style. From what can be deduced, he maintained a low public profile in London, kept his writing a secret in Stratford and lived very differently in each location. Why?

The lack of historical record in respect of his education raises the question of how Shakespeare acquired the necessary knowledge and experience to write the plays. There is no record of him attending any university or being privately tutored. He must presumably have been self taught, following a modest schooling in Stratford. So where are his books? He appears to have bought none himself and he left none in his will. There is also the question of the play themes, many literary authorities agreeing that Shakespeare must have spent time in the company of aristocrats, travelling widely abroad. How did this occur?

As Shakespeare's father was a middle-class Warwickshire trader, with no aristocratic, cultural or academic connections, and as no one else in the immediate family is known to have had any such associations, we can only surmise that the answers to all these questions lie in the so-called 'lost years', the period between his marriage and the publication of his first work. What do we know of Shakespeare's life during this time? Following his marriage in 1582, at the age of eighteen, there are only three records pertaining to his life prior to the publication of *Venus and Adonis*, by which time he had reached the age of twenty-nine:

Mr. WILLIAM
SHAKESPEARES

COMEDIES,
HISTORIES, &
TRAGEDIES.

Publifhed according to the True Originall Copies.

Martin Droeshout fculpfit London.

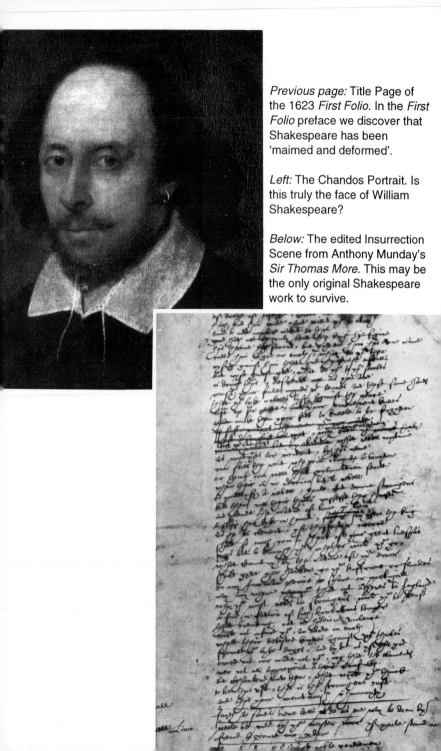

Previous page: Title Page of the 1623 *First Folio*. In the *First Folio* preface we discover that Shakespeare has been 'maimed and deformed'.

Left: The Chandos Portrait. Is this truly the face of William Shakespeare?

Below: The edited Insurrection Scene from Anthony Munday's *Sir Thomas More*. This may be the only original Shakespeare work to survive.

Poet and dramatist Sir Philip Sidney, whose influence may have launched Shakespeare's career.

Playwright and government agent Christopher Marlowe. Did Marlowe recruit Shakespeare for the Elizabethan Secret Service?

Richard Burbage (left) and Ben Jonson (below), Shakespeare's closest friends.

William Cecil, Queen Elizabeth's prime minister. Was Shakespeare involved in a conspiracy to remove him from office?

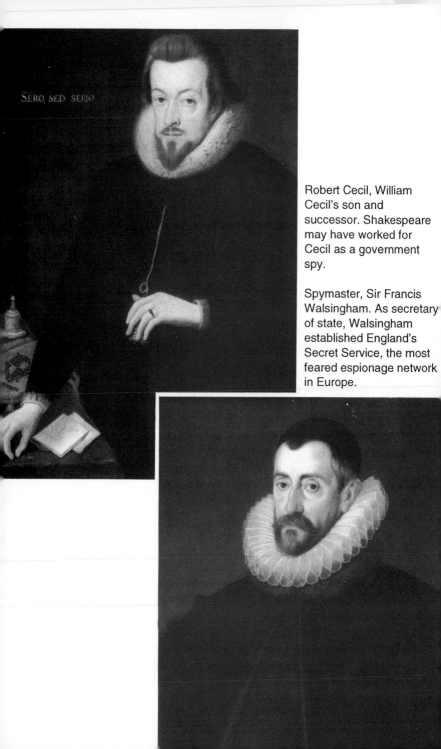

SERO, SED SERIO

Robert Cecil, William Cecil's son and successor. Shakespeare may have worked for Cecil as a government spy.

Spymaster, Sir Francis Walsingham. As secretary of state, Walsingham established England's Secret Service, the most feared espionage network in Europe.

Sir Walter Ralegh, enemy of the Cecils. Was Ralegh responsible for Shakespeare's death?

Ferdinando Stanley, Lord Strange, Shakespeare's patron. Was Shakespeare involved in his murder?

Queen Elizabeth I, survivor of the myriad conspiracies.

Shakespeare's tomb memorial at Holy Trinity Church, Stratford. Is this bust an eighteenth-century fake?

1583. 26 May: Baptism of Shakespeare's daughter Susanna.

1585. 2 February: Baptism of Shakespeare's twins Hamnet and Judith.

1589. William Shakespeare named in legal proceedings regarding an unpaid mortgage on his mother's property in Wilmcote.

From these brief allusions we can assume that he was still present in Stratford until at least the summer of 1584, in order to father the twins. The legal matter, however, tells us little; as the case concerned Mary Shakespeare's property, William himself may not have been present.

The one other *possible* reference to Shakespeare before the registration of *Venus and Adonis* on 18 April 1593 is Greene's *Groat's-worth of Wit* of 1592, warning other writers of the arrogant 'upstart crow'. If it is accepted that this does refer to Shakespeare, then it must be supposed that by this time he was already acting (if that is what Greene's reference to a 'shake-scene' implies) and that he was making a name for himself as a writer. Moreover, for Henry Chettle to have bothered to castigate Greene's criticism the following year (which seemingly appeared before *Venus and Adonis* was actually published) further implies that Shakespeare's work was fairly well known, at least in literary circles.

Indeed, Shakespeare must have been quite a prolific author by 1593. It is otherwise difficult to imagine the Earl of Southampton patronising his work. Yet in the dedication of *Venus and Adonis* Shakespeare himself admits that it is his *first* work. This, however, may simply mean that it was his first poem rather than a play. As Henry Chettle seems to include Shakespeare (if he is Greene's 'upstart crow') among other playwrights in 1593, then he may already have been a recognised dramatist. Certainly by the following year early Shakespeare plays were published, and 'several' seem to have been performed before the Queen. This suggests a number of years' theatrical experience, an inference further supported by the appearance of at least six published plays during the mid-1590s: (*Henry IV: Parts I & II, Richard III, Titus Andronicus, Romeo and Juliet* and *Richard II*).

Where was this experience acquired? It is known from surviving records that Shakespeare was a member of The Lord Chamberlain's Men when they came into existence in 1594, but what was he doing previously? The most probable answer is that he began his career at James Burbage's Theatre in Shoreditch. It was the first, and one of the only, purpose-built theatres in England at the time, and although the Rose (in Southwark) and Curtain (north of Shoreditch) were attracting crowds, Burbage's Theatre was by far the most popular. Indeed, its very name the Theatre (coming from the Roman *amphitheatre*) lent its name to all the playhouses that followed. Moreover, James Burbage's sons Cuthbert and Richard were closely associated with Shakespeare for the rest of his life.

In 1597 James Burbage died and his sons inherited the Theatre. Cuthbert seems to have continued with the administration, while Richard organised the productions. Although there appears to have been no 'director' in Elizabethan theatre, Richard seems to have been the nearest equivalent. Richard Burbage was also an accomplished actor and evidently became Shakespeare's close friend. He is not only mentioned in Shakespeare's will, he is also referred to by John Manningham in 1602, regarding the joke that Shakespeare intended to play on Richard and the young lady (see Chapter 2).

In 1598 the Burbages decided to rebuild their theatre near London Bridge on the more accessible south bank, and with timbers from the original building constructed the Globe which opened the following year. Although Cuthbert Burbage was the chief shareholder with 50 per cent, Shakespeare purchased a 10 per cent holding in February 1599. Along with the Burbage brothers, Shakespeare also became a shareholder in the Blackfriars Theatre, erected in 1608. On the drama front, in early 1594 Richard Burbage and William Shakespeare, along with William Kempe, were paid £20 for 'several' comedies acted before the Queen. Thereafter, Richard's name appears alongside Shakespeare's nearly every time the company is recorded.

Such a close working relationship between Shakespeare and the Burbages makes it a reasonable guess that Shakespeare's theatrical experience was originally gained at the Burbage's Theatre in Shoreditch, which had been open since 1576. But this tells only half the story. How did Shakespeare become involved in the theatre in the first place? Are the traditional biographers correct in their notion that Shakespeare arrived in London one day with a pack on his back, hoping to find a job? It seems highly improbable. This was the golden age of drama, with scores of dramatists and many more actors, most of them centred on London. The Burbage group were the *corps d'élite*. Not only did they own one of drama's few permanent homes, but they were the originals – the name of their playhouse had lent its name to the very concept of stage drama. Consequently, the Burbages would not have been in the habit of hiring anyone who turned up. They ran a successful commercial enterprise, providing the best (and virtually the only) dramatic entertainment in London. For William Shakespeare to have joined the company, in whatever capacity, he must already have had considerable expertise.

We can only deduce that Shakespeare must previously have been associated with another company of actors. It is possible, as some scholars have advocated, that he first became an actor by joining The Queen's Men when they visited Stratford on 13 June 1587. As we have seen, William Knell's widow eventually married John Heminge, who later became Shakespeare's associate. However, no collaborative evidence to support this conjecture has been discovered, despite the fact that the Stratfordians have spent years searching.

The most effective way to solve the riddle is to work backwards from the first publication of a Shakespeare play. Although published anonymously, *Titus Andronicus* in 1594 is probably the earliest surviving edition of any Shakespeare play. Its title page proclaimed that it 'was played by the Right Honourable the Earl of Derby'. Although the earls of Pembroke and Sussex are also named, Derby heads the list, suggesting that he was the original patron, while the latter two had successively purchased the script. From what little is known of Derby's players, it seems that they ran into financial difficulties in 1590, when they were forced to amalgamate with The Lord Admiral's Men. It was probably then that the rights were sold to Pembroke. Pembroke's Men themselves ran into trouble in December 1593, when they are recorded as being in debt. They probably resold the script at this time to The Sussex Men.

The same fate also seems to have befallen one or other of the *Henry VI* plays, and probably accounts for one of the Shakespeare mysteries, notably why, between 1594 and 1598, six of Shakespeare's plays were all printed minus the author's name. To raise finance, his company had evidently been impelled to sell them, along with all rights.

Returning to the *Titus Andronicus* manuscript, we can clearly see who the original patron was: the Earl of Derby. If we accept the First Folio as a definitive edition of Shakespeare's plays, then *Titus Andronicus*, which it contains, *was* a Shakespeare play. Accordingly, the Earl of Derby was Shakespeare's patron when it first appeared. Also, as it is most likely to have been sold around 1590, we can also conclude that it had been written by that date, meaning that Shakespeare was already an accomplished writer in the late 1580s.

So the Earl of Derby may have been Shakespeare's patron before he teamed up with the Burbages. The Earl of Derby in 1594, at the time the *Titus Andronicus* manuscript appeared, was Ferdinando Stanley, the Fifth Earl. He was the elder brother of William Stanley, later to become the Sixth Earl of Derby, the man to whom the Derbyites accredit authorship of the Shakespeare plays. On 25 September 1593 Ferdinando had succeeded to his father's title, but before that time he went by the title Lord Strange. (To avoid confusion, we shall continue to use the name Lord Strange when referring to Ferdinando Stanley.) Lord Strange had patronised a company of actors from 1589 to 1594. Known as Lord Strange's Men, they included in their number one of the most popular Elizabethan actors, Edward Alleyn.

Whether Shakespeare originally acted in Lord Strange's company, or merely wrote for them, is impossible to tell from the *Titus Andronicus* manuscript. However, a number of clues suggest that the relationship between Lord Strange and William Shakespeare was considerably closer than is suggested by collaboration in just one or two works.

Elizabethan theatres were hired out to various acting companies, and Lord Strange's Men staged performances at a number of London theatres. Burbage's Theatre had its own company, although it too hired its stage to others. Around 1593 it appears that a merger took place which was to create the finest and most successful company of the era: the amalgamation of Lord Strange's Men with the Burbage company. Although there is no surviving record of this transaction, there are two firm indicators that it occurred. First, Strange's company was performing almost exclusively at the Theatre at this time. Second, when Strange died on 16 April 1594, the Queen's cousin Lord Hunsdon immediately patronised the Burbage players, thereafter called The Lord Chamberlain's Men. As the takeover tallied precisely with Strange's death, Strange was almost certainly the previous patron. Accordingly, it seems that Shakespeare's company *were* Lord Strange's Men until 1594.

If Shakespeare was working with Lord Strange's Men from (at least) 1590 until 1594, then he would have crossed paths with Christopher Marlowe. On 26 February 1592 Marlowe's *The Jew of Malta* was first performed by Lord Strange's Men at the Theatre, and in January the following year the same company performed the premiere of Marlowe's *The Massacre at Paris*. Dramatist Thomas Middleton, in his *Black Book* of 1604, says that he watched a performance of Marlowe's *Doctor Faustus* at the Theatre in January 1593. It is almost certain that Marlowe would have been personally involved in the premieres of his own work, and for the same company to have performed at least two premieres suggests an affiliation between Marlowe and Strange's company. Moreover, for *Doctor Faustus* to have been performed at the Theatre in January 1593 is evidence that Marlowe was working there just prior to his death.

This is precisely the time that Marlowe was composing *Hero and Leander*, and since Shakespeare was almost certainly working at the Theatre at this time it would adequately explain how he acquired a copy, either with or without Marlowe's approval. Such a close association between the two playwrights would certainly have been beneficial to Shakespeare. He would have worked alongside the most successful playwright of the time. It also explains the enigma, observed by many literary historians, that Marlowe's hand is evident in two of Shakespeare's early works, *Henry VI* and *Titus Andronicus* – Marlowe and Shakespeare were obviously close colleagues.

Shakespeare's professional association with Strange and Marlowe during the early 1590s would explain a number of

Shakespeare mysteries. It solves the *Hero and Leander/Venus and Adonis* riddle, without resorting to the frontman theory; it partly explains how Shakespeare managed quickly to assume Marlowe's status – he had Strange's contacts and the benefit of Marlowe's expertise; and it provides a plausible theory for the Earl of Southampton as patron of Shakespeare's poems. Strange knew Southampton well; Southampton's mistress later married Strange's brother. However, although this scenario goes some way towards explaining Shakespeare's theatrical schooling and his rapid success – he had wealthy backers, the most professional company and the best teacher – we are still left in the dark concerning his academic background, his education and his initial acquaintance with Lord Strange.

A possible explanation for the Strange connection may be found in Ernst Honigmann's *Shakespeare: The Lost Years*, published in 1985. In Lancashire, Honigmann discovered a record of a young tutor first employed by Alexander Houghton of Lea Hall near Preston, and possibly later by a nearby Catholic landowner, Sir Thomas Hesketh. The tutor's name was William Shakeshafte. Although he failed to prove it, Honigmann believed that this was William Shakespeare. The name is remarkably similar and the man does appear during Shakespeare's missing years. As yet, nothing has been discovered about Shakeshafte's background to disprove he was William Shakespeare; so far, he simply appears and disappears during Shakespeare's missing decade. Until proof can be found either way, William Shakeshafte *could* be William Shakespeare.

Shakespeare's name does appear in various renderings during his lifetime: Shaksper, Shaxpere, Shagspere and so on. Not only was there an inconsistency of spelling in the sixteenth century, there were often different forms of the same person's name. Marlowe, for instance, appears as Morley in various documents. Even Shakespeare himself has his christian name entered as a Latinized Gulielmus in the Stratford church register. As standardisation of spelling was not achieved until after the publication of Samuel Johnson's *Dictionary* in 1755, during the Elizabethan era Shakespeare could conceivably have been written as Shakeshafte. If Shakeshafte is Shakespeare, it might explain how he was introduced to Lord Strange. Sir Thomas Hesketh was a close friend of the Fourth Earl of Derby, Lord Strange's father.

The Shakeshafte theory, although offering a possible link with Lord Strange, still fails to account for Shakespeare's education. If the Shakeshafte theory is right, then Shakespeare, as a tutor, is already well educated before he leaves Stratford. The truth about Shakespeare's missing years might not be revealed until we have examined the most perplexing conundrum of all, Shakespeare's bizarre double life.

The logical solution to this mystery would seem that Shakespeare had something to fear. Marlowe certainly did, and may have paid for it with his life. Could there be a connection? At first glance there seems no reason to think so. Shakespeare is not known to have been pursued by the authorities for anything more serious than tax dodging, and nothing he said or wrote in his plays is usually interpreted as being seditious or blasphemous. However, when we discover that Lord Strange also met with a suspicious death, in circumstances closely paralleling Marlowe's final days, we may be forced to reconsider.

Strange was a lapsed Catholic who had spent many years studying the occult under the famous Elizabethan magician John Dee. Magic itself was not an offence in England, only the supposed use of sorcery to commit a felony. In fact, John Dee was court astrologer to Queen Elizabeth herself. As long as a citizen continued to believe in God, and adhered to the contemporary principles of the Church of England, occultism may have been frowned upon but was not considered heresy. It was atheism and the denial of the divine right of the Queen to be head of the English Church that constituted the capital offence of blasphemy.

In the spring of 1594 Lord Strange fell under suspicion of atheism and his case came before the Privy Council. Some days later, perhaps in the hope of saving his own neck, Strange wrote to Secretary of State William Cecil, claiming he had evidence of a conspiracy against the government. However, before Strange could meet Cecil, he suffered a horrible death. The manner of Strange's death appears to indicate arsenic poisoning. From the account, it is easy to understand why many believed Strange had been bewitched.

He was seized and tormented by vomiting matter of a

dark rusty colour, which was so violent and corroding that it stained the silver and irons in the chimney of his room. When he died, though his body was wrapped in sear cloth and covered with lead it so corrupted and putrefied that for a long time after, none could endure to come near the place it was laid in till his burial.

Strange died on 16 April 1594 at Lathom House in Lancashire and was buried at the neighbouring church of Ormskirk. His terrible demise is shrouded by circumstances so reminiscent of Christopher Marlowe's death that a link may well exist. Both were under investigation by the Privy Council for alleged atheism, both could seemingly implicate others, and both died under suspicious circumstances before they were able to testify. Were Marlowe and Strange both killed for the same reason and by the same assailants? Moreover, Strange and Marlowe have something else in common. Both appear closely linked with the early career of William Shakespeare.

Summary

Shakespeare seems to have begun his career writing for Lord Strange's Men in the late 1580s, joining the Burbage Theatre in Shoreditch when the two companies amalgamated around 1590.

1. Following his marriage in 1582, there are only three certain records pertaining to Shakespeare before the publication of *Venus and Adonis* in 1593. From these brief allusions we can assume that he was still present in Stratford until at least the summer of 1584. His life throughout the following decade has long remained a mystery.

2. Although published anonymously, *Titus Andronicus* in 1594 is arguably the earliest surviving edition of any Shakespeare play. Its title page shows that it had originally been written for the theatrical patron Lord Strange, probably in the late 1580s. Strange may therefore have been Shakespeare's first patron.

3. If Shakespeare was with Lord Strange's Men around 1590, he would have known Christopher Marlowe who was working with

the same company. Such a close association between the two playwrights would certainly have been beneficial to Shakespeare, as he would have been working alongside the most successful playwright of the time. It also explains why Marlowe's hand is evident in two of Shakespeare's early works, *Henry VI* and *Titus Andronicus*.

4. A possible explanation for Shakespeare's association with Lord Strange may be found in Ernst Honigmann's *Shakespeare: The Lost Years*, published in 1985. In Preston, Lancashire, Honigmann discovered evidence of a young tutor named William Shakeshafte who may have been employed by the Catholic landowner Sir Thomas Hesketh. Although he failed to prove it, Honigmann believed that this was William Shakespeare. The name is remarkably similar, and the man does appear and disappear during Shakespeare's missing years. If Shakeshafte is Shakespeare, it might explain how he was introduced to Lord Strange; Sir Thomas Hesketh was a close friend of the Fourth Earl of Derby, Lord Strange's father.

5. Around 1593 it appears that Lord Strange's Men amalgamated with the Burbage Theatre in Shoreditch. Although there is no surviving record of this merger, there are two firm indicators that it occurred. First, Strange's company were performing almost exclusively at the Theatre by this time. Second, when Strange died on 16 April 1594, the Queen's cousin Lord Hunsdon immediately patronised the Burbage players, thereafter called The Lord Chamberlain's Men. As the takeover precisely tallied with Strange's death, Strange was almost certainly the previous patron. Shakespeare had certainly joined the Burbage players by the time of their association with Strange; from the early 1590s Shakespeare was closely associated with the Burbage family throughout his career.

6. In the spring of 1594 Lord Strange fell under suspicion of atheism and his case came before the Privy Council. Some days later, perhaps in the hope of saving his own neck, Strange wrote to Secretary of State William Cecil, claiming he had evidence of a conspiracy against the government. However, before Strange

could meet Cecil, he suffered a horrible death. The manner of his death, on 16 April, suggests he died from arsenic poisoning.

7. Strange's death is surrounded by circumstances so reminiscent of the Marlowe killing that there may well be a link. Both men had worked closely together, both were being investigated by the Privy Council for alleged atheism, both could seemingly implicate others, and both died under suspicious circumstances before they could testify.

Chapter 9

The School of Atheism

Shakespeare's plays appeared soon after Marlowe's death in May 1593, and before long they were among the most popular in London. Following Strange's death in April 1594, Lord Hunsdon became the patron of the Burbage players. As Lord Chamberlain, chief authority overseeing all royal entertainments, he ensured that the company appeared at court. This is shown in the accounts of the Chamber Treasurer, recording that in December 1594, 'Will Kempe, Will Shakespeare, and Richard Burbage, servants to the Lord Chamberlain' were paid £20 for 'several comedies' acted before the Queen. The prestige for the company was immense, with London society falling over itself to see The Lord Chamberlain's Men perform.

Within a year Shakespeare had lost his rival, secured a new and important patron and performed at court, all as a direct consequence of his two colleagues' sudden and suspicious deaths. But was Shakespeare somehow associated with the same, seemingly ruthless, characters as Marlowe and Strange? Such a link would certainly give Shakespeare reason to fear, perhaps explaining his low profile and life of apparent secrecy.

Who were the 'others in high places' mentioned in the Baines Report, and the 'conspirators' referred to by Lord Strange, the names that Marlowe and Strange took with them to their graves? Richard Baines's report on Marlowe to the Privy Council in May 1593 may provide the answer. Referring to Marlowe's alleged blasphemies Baines says:

He [Marlowe] affirmeth that Moses was but a juggler

[conjurer], and that one Hariot, being Sir Walter Ralegh's man, can do more than he.

Here Baines seems to implicate Sir Walter Ralegh, the explorer and Queen's favourite, in Marlowe's circle of acquaintances. Although he was not a member of the Privy Council, Ralegh had enjoyed considerable influence with the Queen. Consequently, when a copy of the Baines Report was sent to Her Majesty, Ralegh's name was removed. But even as the Marlowe case was being considered by the Privy Council, Ralegh was already under investigation. He had a dangerous enemy in the Council, William Cecil, the Secretary of State. Although Cecil was the prime minister of the day, the Queen's power was absolute. Anyone who had her ear could effectively undermine Cecil and the Privy Council. Ralegh had been doing so for years and Cecil wanted him stopped. He and others in the Council had long sought a way to be rid of Ralegh and were looking for anything that would discredit him.

Sir Walter Ralegh had long questioned the authority of the Church in the affairs of government. In an age of religious intolerance, he stood almost alone for freedom of worship and intellectual liberty. As a Member of Parliament, he had often risen in defence of those accused of heresy. His charm and personality, together with his seafaring seizures of Spanish gold, had enshrined Ralegh as the royal favourite, and for many years his outspoken opinions went unchecked. In 1592, however, his esteemed position was terminated when he married Elizabeth Throckmorton, one of the Queen's maids of honour, and the couple were imprisoned in the Tower of London. They were released a few months later, but although the Queen had cooled off, she now refused Ralegh at court, and he retired to his estate at Sherborne Abbey in Dorset.

On 10 March 1593 the poet George Chapman wrote to his friend, the scientist Walter Warner, concerning a group who met regularly at Ralegh's home at Sherborne. In the letter, Chapman referred to discussions on the subject of atheism, and a copy somehow fell into the hands of the Privy Council.

Although Ralegh was no longer the Queen's idol, no one knew how long her disfavour would last. Elizabeth had an unsettling habit of changing her mind about her friends; indeed, after Ralegh's next voyage, and his seizure of more Spanish gold, he received many honours and again found royal favour. It was while the Privy Council were seeking to uncover evidence to damage Ralegh that the Chapman letter came into their possession. While pursuing these allegations of atheism, hoping to discover something more substantial, the Council were furnished with the Baines report on Christopher Marlowe. As we have seen, one sentence in the report seemed to suggest that Ralegh and Thomas Hariot held the same subversive notions as Marlowe.

Hariot was the mathematician and astronomer who, along with Johannes Kepler, was among the first to demonstrate that the earth was not the centre of the universe, as taught by the established Church. Although in a Catholic country Hariot might have found himself in serious trouble, the less stringent Protestant regime in England more readily absorbed such ideas. However, Hariot had long been suspected of overstepping the mark, and moving from modernism to atheism. The Council therefore inferred from the report that both Hariot and Ralegh expressed views similar to Marlowe's. But the Council needed more.

As the Chapman letter, or at least the Council's report on it, had also included the names of Hariot and Marlowe as those attending Ralegh's atheistic meetings, the Privy Council no doubt believed that they had found a way to discredit Ralegh – through Christopher Marlowe. Perhaps they could persuade Marlowe to implicate Ralegh directly, or otherwise reveal those who could.

So it appears that Thomas Walsingham was not the only one who stood to lose if Marlowe was interrogated, but Ralegh as well. Yet there was another whom the Chapman letter also implicated: Lord Strange. It therefore appears that through his association with Ralegh, Lord Strange was familiar with those who stood to gain from Marlowe's death. Could the 'conspirators' mentioned by Strange in his letter to Cecil have been the Ralegh circle?

Next to nothing is known of Ralegh's group, although it seems to have included Thomas Hariot, Christopher Marlowe and Lord Strange. We have the Privy Council's report of the Chapman letter, which seems to have been intercepted on its way to Walter

Warner. Like Hariot, Warner was a scientist and mathematician patronised by Ralegh. He was also a close friend of George Chapman, explaining why Chapman should have written to him about the group. It can be concluded, therefore, that George Chapman and Walter Warner may also have been involved. We would know more if the letter itself had survived. Unfortunately, there is only one reference to its contents via the Council's second and third-hand reports. Different copies name different people and some omit the names altogether. So were Marlowe and Strange really associated with this group, if it existed at all?

Among the Harley collection of manuscripts in the British Library is a document which shows that the Privy Council had at least one other witness to swear to Marlowe's connection with Ralegh's atheists. Entitled *Remembrances of words and matters against Richard Cholmeley*, it is a report on the activities of a Secret Service agent named Richard Cholmeley, who had been employed by the Privy Council in the early 1590s to help in the 'apprehension of Papists and other dangerous men'. From the report, it seems that Cholmeley had also been instructed to spy on Marlowe in 1593, probably after the latter's release on 20 May. Cholmeley believed that:

> Marlowe is able to show more sound reasons for atheism than any divine [theologian] in England is able to give to prove divinity.

We also learn that:

> Marlowe told him [Cholmeley] that he hath read the atheist lecture to Sir Walter Ralegh and others.

Does this refer to the same group as that mentioned in the Chapman letter? Also, George Chapman provides further evidence that Lord Strange was a member of Ralegh's group. In 1594 Chapman published *The Shadow of Night*, and in its preface writes of two men he suggests are in Ralegh's entourage, 'ingenious Derby and deep-searching Northumberland'. Northumberland is Henry Percy, Earl of Northumberland, a known associate of Ralegh's and a patron of Hariot; Derby is almost certainly Lord Strange, as he had become the Fifth Earl of Derby early in 1594.

Thomas Kyd, under interrogation by the Privy Council just prior to Marlowe's apprehension, also linked Marlowe with Thomas Hariot and Walter Warner, saying that they met together for atheistic conversations. According to Kyd's testimony:

> For more assurance that I was not of that vile opinion, let it but please your Lordship to enquire of such as he conversed withal, that is (as I am given to understand) with Hariot, Warner, Roydon, and some stationers in [St] Paul's Churchyard.

Kyd denied any association with this group, claiming he only knew of it through Marlowe. Again it is evidence extracted, presumably under torture, by the Privy Council, so Kyd's testimony may be unreliable. However, there are at least three independent references to the Ralegh group, dating from around the same period.

The exiled Catholic priest Robert Persons, in his *Responsio ad Elizabethae Edictum* of 1592, talks of 'the popular school of atheism of Walter Ralegh . . . which he is said to maintain in his own house'. In the autumn of the same year a broadsheet entitled *An Advertisement written to a Secretary of my Lord Treasurer's of England* was printed in London which mounted an attack on Ralegh:

> At Sir Walter Ralegh's school of atheism, Moses, Our Saviour, and both the Old and New Testaments, are jested at.

Although Persons and the author of the *Advertisement* were probably basing their opinions on rumour and hearsay, one reference constitutes more substantial evidence. In 1592 the Italian poet Giordano Bruno refers to 'Ralegh's School of Atheism' from first-hand experience. Bruno's reference is of particular interest, since it implies that these meetings had been continuing for some years. Apparently the meetings, organised by Ralegh himself, had originally taken place at the home of Fulke Greville (later to become Baron Brooke of Warwick) in Whitehall, as early as 1585. Bruno writes of one such meeting in his *Ash-Wednesday Supper*, and also admitted to the Venice Inquisition in 1592 (when he was interrogated by the Catholic authorities regarding accusations of heresy) that he had been present on at least one occasion with his patron the French Ambassador, the Marquis de Castelnau.

It seems therefore that Ralegh's 'School of Atheism' really existed, and that Marlowe and Strange were probably involved. But what was the 'School of Atheism'?

Ralegh had become close friends with Thomas Hariot after he engaged him as his mathematical tutor in the early 1580s. Ralegh helped sponsor Hariot's scientific investigations, in which both shared a common interest. Both were materialists and realists – one, the explorer who had travelled half way round the world, the other, the mathematician who helped develop modern algebra. It seems unlikely, therefore, that either would have founded a society to ridicule the scriptures for the sheer hell of it. They may not have believed in God, but it seems unlikely that such men would run the risk of recklessly blaspheming, as Marlowe is purported to have done. In all likelihood, their intentions would have been far more practical.

The important scientific and navigational discoveries made during the sixteenth century successfully challenged the orthodox view of the universe. Due to these new discoveries, not only the power of the Church but also the State itself came into question. If the Church had been wrong about universal order, could it be trusted regarding its influence on government? There were those who came to question the Anglican Church as the State religion of England, and its teachings concerning the divine right of monarchs to rule by hereditary succession. Although dangerous, Ralegh may well have found such ideas appealing, particularly after he was banished to Sherborne. He was certainly a liberal, by Elizabethan standards, and had never been a religious man. Could Ralegh and Hariot have based the 'School of Atheism' on such ideas?

The two men may have believed that significant cultural and political changes were imminent, and decided to select a small group of like-minded intellectuals to share opinions, perhaps in preparation for an imagined new age. The atheism of which they stood accused may only have concerned an eccentric fringe element, like the flamboyant Marlowe, or the occultly-inclined Lord Strange. There is no evidence that Ralegh or Hariot ever uttered a word of blasphemy. In March 1594, just a few weeks before Strange's death, the Privy Council intensified their efforts in search of evidence to incriminate Ralegh. A commission was established at Cerne Abbas in Dorset, headed by Lord Thomas Howard, to enquire thoroughly into these allegations of blasphemy and atheism. But although the commission found local witnesses prepared to testify that Ralegh had an unorthodox attitude to religion, the evidence proved too vague to warrant prosecution and the matter was dropped.

If Ralegh's group were the 'conspirators' mentioned by Strange, then the conspiracy would almost certainly have been potentially more threatening to the government than a few words of heresy. Ralegh seems to have ridden the accusations of atheism for years, and the Queen knew of them. She was a shrewd woman who knew Ralegh well, something of which the Privy Council would have been acutely aware. There was no way they could have arrested Ralegh without the Queen's consent. If a case was to be brought against him it had to be watertight, not the ravings of eccentrics, or a handful of confessions extracted under torture. If Lord Strange really had been silenced by the Ralegh group, it was probably concerning information more damaging than blasphemy. Indeed his letter to Cecil actually mentioned a conspiracy against the government.

Following the Cerne Abbas enquiry, Ralegh wrote to the Queen, announcing his intention to undertake a voyage to Venezuela in search of gold. The Queen granted him an audience and offered to reinstate him at court provided he returned with sufficient spoils. The letter to the Queen was sent on 22 April, just six days after Strange's death. Was Ralegh's attempt to rekindle royal favour somehow connected? Unquestionably, Cecil would have considered Strange's death suspicious. As the Council had already linked Strange with Ralegh via the Chapman letter, suspicion would undoubtedly have fallen on Sir Walter. By invoking the Queen's avarice, Ralegh may well have saved his neck.

After the spring of 1594 the Sherborne meetings seem to have been abandoned and there is no record of further enquiries into Ralegh's atheistic activities. In all likelihood, the Queen instructed the Privy Council to cease their enquiries, and instructed Ralegh to concentrate on preparing for his expedition. When he eventually returned from Venezuela, and made Elizabeth richer than she had ever been before, Ralegh regained his old naval commands and was appointed governor of Jersey.

Unfortunately for Ralegh, his enemies eventually triumphed. With the death of Queen Elizabeth, and the accession of James I in 1603, the Privy Council lost no time in poisoning the King's mind against Ralegh. He was dismissed as governor of Jersey, evicted from his London home, implicated in a plot against the King, and imprisoned in the Tower of London for the next thirteen years.

Was William Shakespeare ever a member of Ralegh's group? Although there is, as yet, nothing to link Shakespeare directly with Ralegh himself, the circumstantial evidence is persuasive. Of the handful of names associated with Ralegh's 'School of Atheism', two appear to have been closely connected to Shakespeare: Marlowe and Strange. Shakespeare certainly seems to have known of Ralegh's group and, furthermore, Marlowe's involvement. In the play *Love's Labour's Lost* he seems to be referring to Ralegh's group when his Berowne character is made to parody Marlowe's *Hero and Leander*:

> For valour, is not love a Hercules
> Still climbing trees in the Hesperides?

Marlowe had written:

> Leander now like Theban Hercules
> Enter'd the orchard of the Hesperides.

In *Love's Labour's Lost* Berowne also exclaims:

> O paradox! Black is the badge of hell,
> The hue of dungeons and the School of Night.

Here it is generally thought that Shakespeare is referring to

Ralegh's dark complexion, his atheism, his recent imprisonment, and his group. If this is Ralegh, as many literary scholars believe, then Shakespeare is associating Marlowe with both Ralegh and the atheistic group. Indeed, the name 'School of Night' has been used to identify this group ever since. For the sake of convenience, the name 'School of Night' will be used when referring to the Ralegh group, though it is unlikely that Ralegh himself ever called it that.

The mystery of Shakespeare's influential friends might be explained if he was in the School of Night. Ralegh seems to have surrounded himself with poet-dramatists; like Marlowe, they could serve an essential function.

At a time before mass media, theatre was virtually the only means of reaching a wide audience. As a playwright, therefore, Marlowe would have been an important element in disseminating the group's ideas. Indeed, Marlowe's *Edward II* preached the underlying message of monarchistic fallibility, while *Doctor Faustus* contained many dialogues regarding the nature of the universe. For example, Marlowe included Hariot's discoveries concerning the orbit of the Earth and planets around the Sun when Faustus uses his magic to learn the truth about the heavens. Packaged as fiction, theatrical drama was the ideal medium for any subversive message.

Shakespeare's mysterious life style is partly understandable if he had been one of Ralegh's playwrights. If he was, then the 1590s would have been harrowing years, ever fearing a midnight knock at the door. Would Ralegh fail to seize his Venezuelan gold? Would the Queen have a change of heart? Would his own associates decide to silence him? Such concerns would certainly explain Shakespeare's low profile in London. It would explain why, although he was openly associated with the theatre company, his name was seldom associated with the performances of his plays when they were first staged. It would also explain why he seems to have kept himself to himself.

Even as time passed, Shakespeare would still have reason to play safe. In 1601 the Earl of Southampton was suspected of being involved in the Earl of Essex's rebellion against the Queen and was imprisoned in the Tower. In 1603 Ralegh was himself arrested. Thereafter, the new regime of James I was less tolerant than Elizabeth's and violent persecution followed the abortive Gunpowder Plot of 1605. If Shakespeare had in some way been involved in Ralegh's activities, he may have spent the rest of his life living with uncertainty.

This theory leaves many unanswered questions. It may account for Shakespeare's apparent low profile, but it fails to explain, for example, why no one in Stratford appears to have had an inkling of his profession until years after his death. However, it does provide us with a starting point to investigate the enigma of his education and the lost years. An association with the 'School of Night', no matter how informal, may provide some important clues.

Summary

Evidence suggests that through his colleagues Marlowe and Strange, Shakespeare became involved with a group of seditious atheists, led by the explorer and politician Sir Walter Ralegh. Government investigations into this group might explain Shakespeare's low profile in London.

1. Evidence for the Ralegh Group's Existence: In 1592 the exiled Catholic priest Robert Persons, in his *Responsio ad Elizabethae Edictum*, wrote of 'the popular school of atheism of Walter Ralegh'. In the autumn of the same year a broadsheet entitled *An Advertisement written to a Secretary of my Lord Treasurer's of England* was printed in London which also mounted an attack on Ralegh's 'school of atheism'. In 1592 the Italian poet Giordano Bruno referred to 'Ralegh's School of Atheism' from first-hand experience. Apparently the meetings, organised by Ralegh himself, had originally taken place as early as 1585.

2. Involvement of Marlowe and Strange: On 10 March 1593 a letter from the poet George Chapman was intercepted by the Privy Council. It concerned the group that met regularly at Ralegh's home at Sherborne in Dorset. In the letter Chapman referred to discussions on the subject of atheism, implicating Christopher Marlowe and Lord Strange. While pursuing these allegations of atheism (a capital offence in Elizabethan times), the Council were furnished with the Baines Report on Christopher Marlowe.

The report also suggested that Marlowe was acquainted with this group.

3. Further Evidence for Marlowe's Involvement: There were others who swore to Marlowe's connection with Ralegh's atheists. From a report on the activities of Secret Service agent Richard Cholmeley, we learn that Cholmeley had also been instructed by the Privy Council to spy on Marlowe around May 1593. In his report Cholmeley claimed that Marlowe was an active member of Ralegh's atheist group. Also, the playwright Thomas Kyd, under interrogation by the Privy Council in the spring of 1593, linked Marlowe with the Ralegh group.

4. The End of the Ralegh Group: Around April 1594 the Sherborne meetings seem to have been abandoned and no record exists of further enquiries into Ralegh's atheistic activities. In all likelihood, the Queen ordered the Privy Council to cease its investigation, instructing Ralegh to concentrate on preparing his forthcoming expedition to South America.

5. Shakespeare's Involvement: Although there is nothing conclusively to link Shakespeare with Ralegh himself, the circumstantial evidence associating him with the Ralegh group is persuasive. Of the handful of names associated with Ralegh's 'School of Atheism', two appear to have been closely connected to Shakespeare: Marlowe and Strange. Shakespeare certainly appears to have known of Ralegh's group. In *Love's Labour's Lost* he seems to refer to it as the School of Night, a name applied to the group ever since.

6. Shakespeare as Marlowe's Replacement: Ralegh seems to have surrounded himself with poet-dramatists who served an essential function. At a time before mass media, theatre was virtually the only means of reaching a wide audience. When Marlowe, probably Ralegh's most important playwright, died in 1593, Shakespeare may have been called to replace him as an important element in disseminating the group's ideas.

7. Shakespeare's Low Profile: Shakespeare's mysterious life

style is partly understandable if he had been one of Ralegh's playwrights. If he was, then the 1590s would have been harrowing years, ever fearing arrest by the Privy Council. Such concerns would certainly explain Shakespeare's low profile in London. It would explain why, although he was openly involved with the theatre company, his name was seldom associated with the performances of his plays when they were first staged.

Chapter 10

Cue Shakespeare

We have so far traced Shakespeare's theatrical activities to around 1590, when he appears to have worked alongside Marlowe in Lord Strange's company at the Shoreditch Theatre. But how did he first become acquainted with Marlowe and Strange? Although it is possible that he was already working for Burbage when Lord Strange's Men merged with the Shoreditch Theatre players, this fails to explain how Shakespeare was affiliated to so prestigious a troupe in the first place. As we have seen, it is more likely through Marlowe and/or Strange that he first came to work with the Burbage company.

Even though he appears to have had Marlowe's help, Shakespeare's earliest plays were already superior to the work of most other contemporary dramatists. He must therefore have been involved in theatrical circles for some considerable time. By 1590 he already possessed the necessary experience to have written *Titus Andronicus*, which, as we have demonstrated, must have been in existence by that time. Was this early work made possible through contacts in the Ralegh group? What do we know of this group?

Ralegh's circle was suspected of harbouring sinister intentions, prompting the Privy Council's enquiries and the subsequent disclosure of some of the School of Night members. On closer inspection, these members, and the chain of events that tied them together, may reveal an early connection to William Shakespeare.

Early in 1593 the Chapman letter named Ralegh, Hariot and Strange. Chapman further implicated Strange in 1594, while Hariot is mentioned by Richard Baines in his Marlowe report.

So, together with Ralegh, Hariot and Strange seem to be leading members of the group. What is known of their lives prior to Shakespeare's appearance around 1590?

Walter Ralegh was born into a prominent Devonshire family in 1552. In 1572, after leaving Oriel College, Oxford, he travelled to France to fight with the Protestant army in its religious war against the Catholics. After five years he returned to England, taking up residence at the Middle Temple where he wrote poetry, eventually published in George Gascoigne's *The Steel Glass*. Ralegh's favourite poetic theme was the impermanence of material things; consequently, he was a metaphysical rather than a romantic poet.

After two years in obscurity, Ralegh accompanied his half-brother Sir Humphrey Gilbert on a voyage in search of the Northwest Passage to the Orient. The trip soon degenerated into a privateering venture, and on their return in 1579 the two men faced the displeasure of the Privy Council, who considered them little better than pirates. Ralegh's subsequent conduct did nothing to placate the Council, and he engaged in several verbal attacks on their hypocrisy. He was imprisoned, and on release six months later departed for Ireland. Here he again fought the Catholics as commander of an infantry company.

Ralegh's two years of campaigning in Ireland demonstrates a violent side to his nature; after bombing a garrison into surrender, he oversaw the massacre of those inside. Ralegh's ruthlessness impressed the authorities and he was appointed as the military commander of Munster. By the end of 1581 he returned to England in glory and was invited to Court.

Handsome and confident, Ralegh rose quickly in prominence. His opinion on Ireland was sought by the Queen, and he was appointed her official adviser on the subject. Ralegh soon became the Queen's favourite and by 1584 she had rewarded him with a house in London, two estates in Oxford and a knighthood. The following year he became warden of the mines in Devon and Cornwall, sat for Devonshire in Parliament, and in 1586 succeeded Christopher Hatton as the captain of the Queen's guard. The same year, after founding the American colony of Virginia, he returned home with his most famous gifts to Europe, potatoes and tobacco. In 1588 Ralegh played a minor role in the defeat of the Spanish Armada as a member of Elizabeth's War Council, although he did not participate in the naval battle itself.

After the defeat of the Spanish Armada, Ralegh's fortunes began to wane. When he returned to Court he clashed with Elizabeth's new favourite, the Earl of Essex, with whom he almost fought a duel. Afterwards, he left for Ireland, where he spent time on his estates, befriending the poet Edmund Spenser, whom he patronised and later presented at Court. The two men became close associates, and in 1590 Spenser published *The Fairy Queen*, with lengthy dedications to Walter Ralegh.

In 1590 Ralegh himself had returned to Court, and the following year led a fleet against the Spanish. In his absence the Queen discovered his relationship with Elizabeth Throckmorton, her maid of honour. Furious, she had them both imprisoned. However, after the fleet returned with vast quantities of gold, seized by Ralegh's sailors, she permitted Ralegh to go free, but he and his new wife were banished from Court. For the next four years Ralegh was to spend much of his time at Sherborne Abbey in Dorset. It was during this Court exile that his political enemies conspired against him; in particular, William Cecil.

From what we know of Ralegh's activities, there is no reason to suppose that William Shakespeare, a glover's son from Stratford, would have known him before this time. However, it is around 1590 that we have our earliest evidence of Shakespeare in London (the *Titus Andronicus* manuscript), which is precisely when Ralegh was banished from Court. Ralegh had already patronised one poet, Spenser, and it seems that he also patronised Shakespeare's friend Ben Jonson.

Turning to Thomas Hariot, it is also unlikely that Shakespeare could have known Hariot before 1590. Hariot was born in Oxford in 1560, where he later entered St Mary Hall. After his graduation with a BA in 1580, he was immediately employed by Ralegh as a tutor in mathematics. The two men become firm friends and business associates, and five years later Ralegh sent Hariot to his colony of Virginia as a surveyor. He returned the following year and wrote *A Brief and True Report on the New-Found Land of Virginia*, one of the earliest examples of a large-scale statistical survey in existence. Around this time Ralegh introduced him to Henry Percy, Earl of Northumberland, who greatly admired Hariot's scientific work, offering him a lifetime patronage of £100 a year. Hariot had no interest in theatre, as far as is known, and his activities were confined to logistic and scientific work prior to 1590. It therefore seems unlikely that Shakespeare would have known him (unless via the Ralegh group) before this time.

There also seems no way in which Shakespeare could have become associated directly with Lord Strange in the early 1580s, unless Shakespeare was the William Shakeshafte discussed previously.

Ferdinando Stanley – the son of Henry, Fourth Earl of Derby – was born in London in 1559. In 1573, at the age of fourteen, he attended the Queen at Windsor; from 1585 he acted as Deputy Lieutenant of Lancashire; in 1588 he became Mayor of Liverpool, and in the same year he was granted the title Lord Strange and entered Parliament. He completed his education late in life, receiving an MA from St John's College, Oxford, in 1589. Thereafter, he became fascinated with literature, composing a number of poems later published in John Bodenham's *Garden of Muses* in 1600. He eventually settled for being a patron of the arts, founding his acting company and befriending Ralegh's poet-friend Edmund Spenser, whose cousin Alice he married. Spenser had great admiration for Strange, typified in his poem *Colin Clout's Come Home Again*:

> He, whilst he lived, was the noblest swain
> That ever piped upon an oaten quill:
> Both did he other, which could pipe, maintain
> And eke could pipe himself with passing skill.

Strange's literary interests began at Oxford, before which time he was chiefly involved in politics. It appears most unlikely, therefore, that Strange would have befriended Shakespeare much before 1590.

It seems clear how Ralegh, Hariot and Strange came together. They had all graduated from Oxford and shared much in common. Hariot was directly employed by Ralegh, and Strange shared a friend in Edmund Spenser. But, as yet, there seems no portal through which Shakespeare might enter the scene. Is it perhaps more probable that it was via Marlowe that Shakespeare was introduced to Ralegh's circle?

Born in Canterbury, Christopher Marlowe's early life is uncannily similar to Shakespeare's. He was born in 1564, the same year. His father, also named John, was a middle-class shoemaker (Shakespeare's father made gloves) and he received a modest education at a local grammar school. But the similarities end there. There is no mystery about Marlowe's higher education. At the age of sixteen he received a scholarship from the Archbishop of Canterbury and entered Corpus Christi, Cambridge. Three years later, he obtained his BA and commenced an MA in 1587.

With his Cambridge contacts and consequent circle of wealthy friends, Marlowe slipped easily into the world of drama, moving to London to begin his theatrical career. His *Tamburlaine the Great* (in two parts) first appeared around 1587, and was arguably the finest tragedy yet produced for the English stage. *Doctor Faustus, The Jew of Malta* and *Edward II*, followed over the next three years, and *The Massacre of Paris* around 1591. His final work, *The Tragedy of Dido*, was left unfinished when he died.

We know for certain that Marlowe was working with Lord Strange in the early months of 1592. In January *Doctor Faustus* was performed at the Theatre and in February *The Jew of Malta* was performed by Lord Strange's Men. His early plays were performed primarily by the Lord Admiral's Men, so his earliest association with Strange may have come when the two companies amalgamated around 1590. However, a number of indications in Marlowe's life suggest that he may already have been associated with Ralegh's group well before this time. This appears to have arisen from his involvement with a much more sinister organisation, the Elizabethan Secret Service.

On 18 September 1589 Marlowe was arrested for fighting a duel in Finsbury. He and fellow poet Thomas Watson were accused of killing an innkeeper's son, William Bradley. Both men were imprisoned for a time at Newgate, but were acquitted on 3 December. Marlowe was found not guilty, while Watson was pardoned on grounds of self defence. From these proceedings we know that Marlowe and Watson were not only colleagues but close friends. Via Watson, Marlowe seems to have been introduced to Secret Service agents Thomas Walsingham and, more intriguingly, Robert Poley, one of the three drinking partners at Deptford.

Watson's poem *Meliboeus*, a eulogy on the late Secret Service chief Sir Francis Walsingham, is addressed and dedicated to Thomas Walsingham (Francis's cousin). Written in 1590, it records that in 1581 Watson first became associated with the Walsinghams in Paris. This means that Watson certainly knew Thomas Walsingham well before Marlowe, while Marlowe was still in his first year at Cambridge.

Robert Poley first appears at Clare College, Cambridge, in 1564, where he is recorded as recently marrying 'one Watson's daughter'; so it seems that Poley may well have been Thomas Watson's son-in-law. Poley next surfaces in 1583, when he is recorded as living at a house belonging to Francis Walsingham at Barn Elms and described as working for Sir Philip Sidney, Francis Walsingham's son-in-law. Poley's associations with the Walsingham family had brought him into contact with Thomas Walsingham by 1586, as he then worked alongside him in helping to uncover the Babington Plot to murder the Queen.

We already know that Poley and Thomas Walsingham had been working for Francis Walsingham's Secret Service, but it appears that Watson was also in their employ. In 1581, while in France meeting with Thomas Walsingham, Watson is recorded as carrying despatches for the Secretary of State. It therefore appears that his meeting with Thomas was originally on a Secret Service matter.

Through Watson, Poley and Thomas Walsingham, Marlowe was also drawn into the Secret Service as a courier. In 1587 he travelled widely throughout Europe, being mentioned in despatches to the Secretary of State from Utrecht in Holland on 2 October that year. He is again referred to as a messenger between the government and the British Ambassador in Paris in 1592. In all but name Marlowe was working as a spy for the Secret Service. As a courier, he would be expected not only to carry messages, but to report on the situation in the countries he visited.

We have established Marlowe's initial link with Walsingham, but how did he become involved with Ralegh's atheist group? The contact here may originally have been made via Sir Philip

Sidney. Since the latter was Poley's employer in 1583, Marlowe is very likely to have known him quite early on and Sidney was the lifelong friend of Fulke Greville, in whose house Ralegh's meetings were once held. Greville had been at school with Sidney in Shrewsbury and a close friendship continued thereafter. Like Sidney, Greville was a fine poet and playwright, although his works were not published until after his death. Greville's association with the Ralegh group is mentioned by Giordano Bruno, the Italian poet who spent two years in England between 1583 and 1585, staying at the French embassy with his patron. He had himself attended a meeting of the group at Greville's house in Whitehall. Bruno was also a close friend of Sidney and he mentions him in association with such meetings.

We have seen, too, how part of the group might have come together. Hariot already worked for Ralegh, Ralegh befriended Spenser, and Spenser befriended Strange, his cousin's husband. Ralegh held meetings at Greville's house, and Marlowe was introduced by Greville's friend Sidney, Poley's employer. But there still seems no way in for Shakespeare. We must therefore move on to other possible group members.

George Chapman, the poet who wrote the original letter about Ralegh's circle, seems to have been well informed, so was he personally involved? Chapman falls immediately into place. Not only was he an associate of Marlowe – he published *Hero and Leander* after Marlowe's death, with a long sequel praising his dead friend – but he was patronised by Thomas Walsingham's wife, Lady Audrey Walsingham. The man Chapman wrote the letter to, Walter Warner, also fits neatly into the picture. As the scientist who helped initiate theories on blood circulation, he was a lifelong friend of Thomas Hariot. As we have seen, Warner was implicated by Kyd in his Privy Council testimony as being involved in the group along with Marlowe, Roydon and 'some stationers in St Paul's Churchyard'. Before returning to this enigmatic statement about the 'stationers' we must examine Roydon.

Roydon appears to have been Matthew Roydon, a one-time law student at Thavies Inn, London. He was also a poet, although little of his work has survived. Roydon knew many of those involved. In 1582 Thomas Watson included Roydon's poems, together with personal praise, in his *Ekatompathia*. In 1586 Roydon wrote for Sir Philip Sidney, and in 1594 George Chapman not only refers to Roydon as 'my good Mat' but implies that he is closely associated with Lord Strange. In January 1582 Roydon signed a bond to repay £40 to a London goldsmith, and the bond is co-signed by Nicholas Skeres, another of Marlowe's shady drinking partners on his last, ill-fated day. Moreover, Marlowe appears to have been planning to escape with Roydon's help, had he not been killed at Deptford on 30 May 1593. According to Kyd in his testimony shortly after Marlowe's death, Marlowe intended to flee to Scotland to be with Roydon:

> He would persuade with men of quality to go unto the King of Scots, whither I hear Roydon is gone.

From the various letters and testimonials, the circle seems to involve Ralegh, Hariot, Strange, Marlowe, Warner, Chapman, Roydon, Greville, Bruno, Sidney and Henry Percy. Others associated with Thomas Walsingham lurk on the fringes: Watson, Poley and Skeres. Kyd also seems to have been well informed. But again, where does William Shakespeare sit in the equation? We know that he was almost certainly involved with Marlowe and Strange, but does his mysterious arrival on the London theatre scene actually involve the School of Night? The answer may lie in the enigmatic statement made by Thomas Kyd.

During interrogation by the Privy Council concerning Marlowe's activities, Kyd denied he was involved with Marlowe's circle of friends, who were supposedly making atheistic statements:

> For more assurance that I was not of that vile opinion, let it but please your Lordship to enquire of such as he conversed withal, that is (as I am given to understand) with Hariot, Warner, Roydon, and some stationers in [St] Paul's Churchyard.

We have already seen how Hariot, Warner and Roydon all link closely together, almost certainly via the Ralegh group, so who are the mysterious 'stationers'? The answer might be found on

The Frontispiece of the 1594 *Venus and Adonis*. Did Shakespeare work for the printer Richard Field?

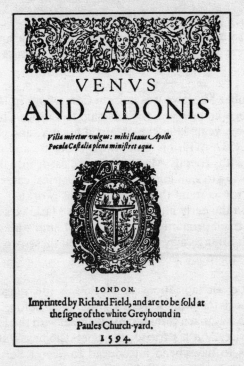

the cover of Shakespeare's first published work, *Venus and Adonis*. The publisher's note reads:

> Venus and Adonis. Imprinted by Richard Field, and to be sold at the sign of the White Greyhound in St Paul's Churchyard 1594.

Although there were other stationers operating from St Paul's Churchyard at the time (it was the centre for the London book trade), there can be little doubt that Richard Field's company were the 'stationers' Kyd refers to in association with Marlowe, Hariot, Warner and Roydon. Earlier in his testimony Kyd mentions that they met beneath 'the sign of the White Greyhound'. The Greyhound pub is precisely where Field's books were sold, as stated on the cover of *Venus and Adonis*. With Field, we have a direct link between the Ralegh circle and William Shakespeare.

Summary

Shakespeare may have become involved with Marlowe and the Ralegh circle via a Stratford colleague, his publisher Richard Field.

1. Christopher Marlowe was born in Canterbury in 1564. At the age of sixteen he received a scholarship to Corpus Christi, Cambridge. Three years later, he obtained his BA, and commenced an MA in 1587. With his Cambridge contacts, and consequent circle of wealthy friends, Marlowe slipped easily into the world of drama, moving to London to begin his theatrical career. The first we know for certain that Marlowe was working with Lord Strange is in the early months of 1592. As Marlowe's early plays were performed primarily by the Lord Admiral's Men, his association with Strange may have begun when these two companies amalgamated around 1590.

2. A number of indications in Marlowe's life suggest he was already associated with Ralegh's group well before 1590. This appears to have arisen from his involvement with the Elizabethan Secret Service. Via his friend, the poet Thomas Watson, Marlowe seems to have been introduced to Secret Service agents Thomas Walsingham and Robert Poley.

3. Robert Poley first appears at Clare College, Cambridge, in 1564, where he is recorded as recently marrying 'one Watson's daughter', so it seems that Poley was Thomas Watson's son-in-law. Poley next surfaces in 1583, when he is recorded as living at a house belonging to Francis Walsingham at Barn Elms and is described as working for the dramatist Sir Philip Sidney, Francis Walsingham's son-in-law. Poley's associations with the Walsingham family had brought him into contact with Thomas Walsingham by 1586, as he then worked alongside him in helping to uncover the Babington Plot to murder the Queen.

4. Through Watson, Poley and Thomas Walsingham, Marlowe

was also drawn into the Secret Service as a courier. In 1587 he travelled widely throughout Europe, being mentioned in despatches to the Secretary of State from Utrecht in Holland on 2 October that year. He is again referred to as a messenger between the government and the British Ambassador in Paris in 1592. In all but name Marlowe was working as a spy for the Secret Service. As a courier, he would be expected not only to carry messages, but to report on the situation in the countries he visited.

5. Marlowe's original contact with the Ralegh circle may initially have been made via Philip Sidney. Since the latter was Poley's employer in 1583, Marlowe is very likely to have known him quite early on; and Sidney was the lifelong friend of Fulke Greville, in whose house Ralegh's meetings were once held. The Italian poet Giordano Bruno was also a close friend of Sidney, and he mentions him in association with such meetings.

6. Shakespeare may have become involved with Marlowe and the School of Night via his publisher Richard Field. During interrogation by the Privy Council concerning Marlowe's activities, Thomas Kyd named a number of School of Night members, including 'some stationers in [St] Paul's Churchyard'. Although there were other stationers operating from St Paul's Churchyard at the time (it was the centre for the London book trade) there can be little doubt that Richard Field's company were the 'stationers' Kyd refers to. Earlier in his testimony Kyd mentions that they met beneath 'the sign of the White Greyhound'. The Greyhound pub is precisely where Field's books were sold, as stated on the cover of Shakespeare's *Venus and Adonis*. With Field, we have a direct link between the Ralegh circle and William Shakespeare.

Chapter 11

To London

Sufficient records have survived from Richard Field's publishing concern for us to discover a good deal about his life. He had served his apprenticeship with Thomas Vautrollier, a French Huguenot from Rouen, and when Vautrollier died in 1587 Field married his widow Jacqueline, inheriting their business in Blackfriars. The main sales outlet for his publications was through fellow stationer John Harrison, whose premises were in St Paul's Churchyard, beside the White Greyhound pub. In fact, when Shakespeare's *The Rape of Lucrece* was published by Richard Field, the printer's note actually states that it had been printed *exclusively* for sale by John Harrison. Romantic poetry was not in Field's usual line, as the Stationers' Register shows that most of his books were theological, technical or classical works. Why, therefore, had he suddenly decided to publish the work of an unknown poet like Shakespeare?

The answer is clear: they had known each other for many years – in Stratford-upon-Avon. The surviving property deeds and business transactions of the Blackfriars enterprise clearly show that Field had entered into apprenticeship, having come to London from Stratford-upon-Avon. In Stratford there are also records of Richard Field. He was born in 1561, the son of Henry Field, a tanner who lived in Bridge Street, very close to the Shakespeare home in Henley Street. William Shakespeare is certain to have known Richard Field. Not only were they approximately the same age, but their fathers were in the same line of work, in leather goods. Moreover, when Henry Field died in 1592, Shakespeare's father helped value his estate.

In London, in 1596, it seems that Shakespeare retained close ties with Field. Field's name appears on a document proposing the building of the Burbage Theatre in Blackfriars. Furthermore, Shakespeare may well have found lodgings with Christopher Mountjoy in 1604 through their mutual acquaintance Field. Mountjoy lived in Cripplegate, on the corner of Silver Street and Monk Street, while Richard Field lived in nearby Wood Street. Like Field's wife Jacqueline, Mountjoy was of the Huguenot religion, and living so closely together their respective wives probably attended the same church.

That the association between Shakespeare and Field was closer than simply a printer/author relationship is further demonstrated by the registration papers for *Venus and Adonis* on 18 April 1593. The notice filed with the Stationers' Register shows that Field was not only the printer and publisher, but that he was the *owner* of the work 'entitled *Venus and Adonis*'.

If it was via Field that Shakespeare came to meet Marlowe, Strange or the Ralegh group, we have a credible scenario. Richard Field was Sir Philip Sidney's publisher; indeed by 1598 Field had published Sidney's collected works. We have already demonstrated Sidney's association with the Ralegh group – Bruno includes him in a meeting at Greville's house. We have also seen how those named in Thomas Kyd's list of Marlowe's associates were almost certainly involved with the Ralegh group. If the 'stationers' are Field and/or Harrison then they were also involved. It would certainly have made good sense for the School of Night to have included a publisher, so influential in moulding public opinion. Moreover, there seems little doubt that Field/ Harrison were associated with the Ralegh group, as Kyd includes the 'stationers' along with Marlowe, Hariot, Roydon and Warner. Two scientists and two poet-dramatists would seem to have little else in common other than the School of Night.

This appears to be the most credible explanation of how Shakespeare became involved in the London theatre. Richard Field could well have introduced William Shakespeare to those people uniquely beneficial to his career as a poet-dramatist.

Before investigating how Shakespeare might have come to join forces with Field in London, another member of the Ralegh group requires examination. Someone who may hold the key to the mystery of Shakespeare's subject knowledge, and even his lack of books: the Earl of Northumberland.

We have already examined George Chapman's inclusion of Lord Strange in the School of Night, but he also named Northumberland. In 1594 Chapman published *The Shadow of Night*, in its preface writing of two men he suggests are in Ralegh's entourage, 'ingenious Derby, and deep-searching Northumberland'.

Henry Percy, Ninth Earl of Northumberland, was an Elizabethan nobleman-scholar born in 1564. He was educated in Paris around 1582 and succeeded to the earldom in 1685 at the age of twenty-one. Much of his life was spent at his stately home at Petworth in Sussex, where he engrossed himself in the study of history, science, mathematics and philosophy. Percy writes freely about his friendship with Walter Ralegh, speaking of their many shared interests. They rode together, played endless games of cards (which Ralegh usually won) and shared an enjoyment of tobacco. Unfortunately, Percy fails to describe the content of their more important conversations.

Percy seems to have been *a*, if not *the*, key figure in Ralegh's group. He was on intimate terms with Thomas Watson, who dedicated two works to him, *Helenae Raptus* and *Waters and Foundations*, around 1586. Walter Warner was also a close friend, and he was patronised by Percy. Even when Percy was eventually imprisoned in the Tower of London by James I in 1606, following suspicions that he had been involved in the Gunpowder Plot the previous year, Warner visited him regularly for the duration of his captivity. Thomas Hariot, however, seems to have been his chief protégé. Percy provided him with a handsome £100 a year to continue his research for the rest of his life. Furthermore, Percy granted him exclusive use of his Sion House, near Isleworth, generously equipped with a sophisticated laboratory. Together with Warner, Hariot also paid regular visits to Percy during the period of his imprisonment.

It is Percy's house, Petworth in Sussex, that may provide an answer to Shakespeare's education. As Shakespeare was the author of some of the greatest works in the history of literature, he was unquestionably a genius; he would, we can safely assume, have been quick to learn. Such a man, provided he knew how to read and write, could presumably educate himself. We have seen that Marlowe, of comparable ability and with an almost identical

126

background, was able to secure a scholarship to Cambridge. If Shakespeare had become attached to the Ralegh group, and hence to Henry Percy, then he would have had access to one of the finest libraries in England.

At Petworth House, Percy had amassed a huge library to satiate his enquiring mind. Inventories of the period show that it contained well over 2,000 books – a vast number at the time – and was considered to be one of the best of its kind anywhere in Britain. We can imagine something of its size from the posthumous records of his estate, which note fifty-two chests full of books, with enough additional volumes to fill a further twelve cases. The library was used by many of Percy's acquaintances, one of whom describes the book-lined chamber, complete with Ralegh's famous Molyneux globe of the world, and many mathematical instruments provided by Hariot.

The library housed some of the most respected tomes of the day: books of history, politics, mathematics, philosophy and the new geography. It also contained many of the classics from ancient Greece and Rome. Consequently, it included almost all the subject matter required to produce the works of William Shakespeare. Many of Percy's other poet friends made use of the library while composing their works. Watson, for instance, used it when characterising Helen and others in his *Helenae Raptus* of 1586.

Recalling one of Shakespeare's mysterious disappearances, we discover a tantalising reference which may allude to his use of the Petworth library, or at least a visit to Henry Percy's home. In October 1599, when Shakespeare is sought by the tax collectors of London's St Helen's parish, he is traced to Sussex. The authorities appear to have been correct that he was in Sussex, as the tax was eventually collected by the Bishop of Winchester, who had fiscal jurisdiction over all ecclesiastical matters in the county. Since it was a year later, in October 1600, that the bishop eventually received the money, it appears that Shakespeare had been in the county throughout this time, or that he was a frequent visitor.

It has long remained a mystery to Shakespeare's biographers why he should have resided in Sussex. Shakespeare seems to have been well established in London during this time; an inventory in May 1599, concerning property belonging to Thomas

Brend (the son of the Globe leaseholder), lists Shakespeare as occupying a new house in St Saviour's parish. Moreover, the Globe had only just been opened and Shakespeare had a 10 per cent holding. This would have been one of the company's busiest periods in London, rendering his prolonged trip to Sussex of considerable importance to warrant the time spent there. Work on a fresh set of plays for the new theatre is a plausible explanation.

It could be argued that Shakespeare had simply fled the debt collectors. But, as we have seen, such an explanation seems incongruous. He not only had a shareholding in the theatre, he also had considerable assets in Stratford. Whatever the reason for his non-payment of the tax, it was not through lack of capital. But even if this was the reason for his absence from London, why choose Sussex? The Percy library at Petworth House may provide the answer.

Shakespeare's possible association with the Ralegh group answers a number of unsolved questions about his life. It provides a link between his life in Stratford and his life in London; it explains his entry into the world of theatre; it offers a route for his educational knowledge, and it also explains how he fared so well so quickly. Moreover, it also goes a long way towards explaining his low profile.

So how did Shakespeare come to be in London in the first place? The answer to this may lie with his father's misfortunes.

William Shakespeare's father, John, made a good living as a glover in the 1550s, and by 1556 had purchased two houses in Henley Street. Over the next two years his prosperity earned him recognition in Stratford, and by 1568 he had risen from chamberlain, to burgess, to alderman (a town councillor). In that year he was appointed bailiff and by 1571 was the chief alderman in the town. The Shakespeares were obviously well respected during this period, but sadly in the same year John Shakespeare's luck was to run out. The town records of 1571 show that he proceeded against Richard Quiney for £50, which he required to settle his own debts. By 1573 the situation had become so grave that a warrant was issued for John's arrest for the non-payment of £30. By 1577 he had fallen on such hard times that he was forced to mortgage a property inherited by his wife Mary. Ultimately, he failed to keep up the repayments and the property was seized.

In 1579 he was finally unable to pay the town levies – the rates – and in 1580 appears to have taken to the bottle, being arrested for disorderly conduct and fined £20. By 1582 he had even ceased attending church, when the parish record shows that he would not attend 'for fear of process for debt'. In other words, he was afraid that his creditors would catch up with him during matins. It is around this time that William married, so his life with Anne Hathaway was doubtless troubled from the outset. John Shakespeare hit rock bottom in 1587 when he failed to attend municipal meetings and was suspended from the council.

But just as the Shakespeare family were about to find themselves on the street, along came William to the rescue. By 1589 William Shakespeare had somehow amassed enough capital to attempt the repossession of his mother's house. From the records, we know that in this year he took legal action in an effort to regain his mother's property in Wilmcote.

What conclusions can reasonably be drawn from this information? It seems that by 1589 William was making money on his own account, but *not* in his father's business, which was bankrupt. Yet there is absolutely no record of William Shakespeare's commercial activities in Stratford during the 1580s. The Stratford civic records of this period have survived fairly intact. It can clearly be seen how John Shakespeare, the Quineys, the Fields and others made their livings, and later there are many records pertaining to the business interests of Shakespeare himself. Shakespeare must therefore have made his money elsewhere. As this is seemingly too early for him to have earned enough as a playwright, we must look further afield.

Given that his father's business had already crashed by the time he married in 1582, and within three years he had three children to support, it seems reasonable to assume that Shakespeare sought a living outside Stratford, sometime in the early to mid 1580s. The key question is did he go straight into theatre, or was there some prior employment?

If Shakespeare was the William Shakeshafte discovered by Honigmann, he may have been a tutor in Lancashire. The first reference to Shakeshafte is in 1581, when Alexander Hoghton of Lea Hall, near Preston, included the name in his will. Hoghton made provision for Shakeshafte, asking that his brother Thomas

Hoghton 'be friendly unto' William Shakeshafte, and requesting that he either find him work or help him obtain another position. Honigmann suggests that Shakeshafte then worked briefly for the neighbouring landowner Richard Hesketh. If this is William Shakespeare then he is only seventeen at the time, which seems young for a tutor.

Nonetheless, there were possible connections between Shakespeare and the Hoghtons of Lancashire. One of the schoolmasters at King's School in Stratford, where Shakespeare may have been educated, was John Cottom, between the years 1579 and 1581. Cottom's father was a tenant of the Hoghtons and John returned to the estate in 1581. This is known because he left the school after his brother had been arrested as a Jesuit priest, and in the same year Cottom was fined in Lancashire for recusancy (the term used for Catholics who failed to attend the Church of England services on a Sunday).

Even if Shakespeare *is* Shakeshafte, he was back in Stratford by 1582 to father his first child and to marry some three months later. This brings us back to square one. If Shakespeare had worked for the Heskeths for some time prior to this, he could have met Lord Strange in Lancashire. As we shall see, Richard Hesketh was closely associated with Strange, whose Lancashire home was at Lathom House in neighbouring Ormskirk. However, even if Shakespeare had met Lord Strange around 1582, it was a good seven years before Strange became interested in poetry, drama or theatre.

The only demonstrable connection Shakespeare has with London is Richard Field. Field was already doing well as a publisher/printer by 1585 and by 1587 he had inherited the business. It is possible that Shakespeare either asked, or was invited, to join Field's publishing concern in Bishopsgate. The apprenticeship records are incomplete, so we do not know the names of most of Field's employees. Shakespeare could, therefore, have started life in London as an apprentice printer working with Richard Field. Indeed, this offers a tenable theory for Shakespeare's theatrical grounding. Unlike Marlowe, who had entered through the academic door, Shakespeare may have slipped in through the tradesman's entrance.

Working in a publishing house would certainly have given

Shakespeare a more practical approach to drama than many of his contemporaries. Unlike most of his compeers, Shakespeare displays a practical, commercial approach to his work. It can even be argued that this was his formula for success. He not only wrote plays, but maintained a direct input at each successive stage of their development (acting, performing, promoting). Moreover, his shareholding in the Globe and Blackfriars theatres made him far more prosperous than had he been a playwright alone. Coupled with his perceptive and sound investments in a completely separate venture in Stratford (a grain dealer), this evidences a level-headed entrepreneur. To have acquired such acumen suggests a commercial background. Working in Field's publishing house would have provided an excellent grounding for Shakespeare's unique style.

In Field's company, Shakespeare would not only have gained the necessary business experience, he would also have been enveloped in the world of literature at the sharp end, in printing, publishing and in sales. Furthermore, surrounded by many different kinds of publication, he could learn as he went along. Editing work for printing, he could gradually gain a wide experience of style, content and grammar, not afforded the academic poets. He would also have learned the most important lesson of all – what sold. Shakespeare became the world's most successful dramatist not only because he was the best writer, but because he knew what people wanted. A background among the booksellers and publishers of Blackfriars and St Paul's would have given excellent grounding.

In conclusion, the hypothesis that Shakespeare worked with Field would explain his move to London, his business acumen, his access to the theatre and his unique style, and – perhaps most importantly of all – it explains his missing years. Although in the final analysis it cannot be *proved* that Shakespeare worked with Richard Field, the argument is ultimately more compelling than the traditional, unsupported notions of theatre valets, strolling players, or the lad with a pack on his back.

The missing years of Shakespeare's life may therefore be as follows. By the time Shakespeare is married with children, his father's business has failed. Shakespeare must make his own living. He joins Field in London, working as an apprentice printer. After some years he is working as a publisher, helping to edit, print and perhaps even sell the company's books. He tries his own hand at writing and the quality of his work is appreciated by Sir Philip Sidney. Eventually, he is introduced to the poets in Ralegh's circle, meets Marlowe, and writes for Lord Strange's Men. Strange's company ultimately becomes attached to the Burbage Theatre in Shoreditch and Shakespeare is up and running.

Given this scenario, to what extent was Shakespeare tied to the School of Night? At least three men we have closely associated with Shakespeare – Marlowe, Strange and Field – seem to have been involved in the group. What exactly was the School of Night? What did it stand for? What was Shakespeare's role?

Summary

An association between Shakespeare and the Ralegh group answers a number of hitherto unsolved questions. It provides a link between his life in Stratford and his life in London. It explains his entry into the world of theatre and offers a tenable scenario of his educational background.

1. The only demonstrable connection Shakespeare has with London before his theatrical career is Richard Field, his publisher in the early 1590s. Sufficient records have survived from Richard Field's publishing concern for us to discover much about his life. He had served his apprenticeship with Thomas Vautrollier, a French Huguenot from Rouen, and when Vautrollier died in 1587 Field married his widow Jacqueline, inheriting their business in Blackfriars. The surviving property deeds and business transactions of the Blackfriars enterprise clearly show Field had entered into apprenticeship, having come to London from Stratford-upon-Avon.

2. In Stratford we also find record of Richard Field. Born in 1561, he was the son of Henry Field, a tanner living in Bridge Street, very close to the Shakespeare home in Henley Street. William Shakespeare is certain to have known Richard Field. Not only were they approximately the same age, but their fathers were in the same line of work, leather goods. Moreover, when

Henry Field died in 1592, Shakespeare's father helped value his estate.

3. Field was already doing well as a publisher/printer by 1585, and by 1587 had inherited the business. It is possible that Shakespeare either asked, or was invited, to join Field's publishing concern in Bishopsgate. The apprenticeship records are incomplete, so we do not know the names of most of Field's employees. Shakespeare could, therefore, have started life in London as an apprentice printer working with Richard Field.

4. Working with Field as a publisher would account for all the attributes Shakespeare later exhibited. In Field's company, Shakespeare would not only have gained the necessary business experience, he would also have been enveloped in the world of literature at the sharp end – printing, publishing and sales. Furthermore, surrounded by many different kinds of publication, he could learn as he went along. Editing work for publication, he would gradually gain a wide experience of style, content and grammar, not afforded the academic poets. He would also have learned the most important lesson of all – what sold. Shakespeare became the world's most successful dramatist not only because he was the best writer, but because he knew what people wanted. A background amongst the booksellers and publishers of Blackfriars and St Paul's would have given excellent grounding.

5. Petworth House in Sussex, the home of Ralegh's friend Henry Percy, may provide the solution to Shakespeare's education. At Petworth Percy had amassed a huge library to satiate his enquiring mind. Inventories of the period show that it contained well over 2,000 books – a vast number at the time – and was considered to be one of the best of its kind anywhere in Britain. The library housed some of the most learned tomes of the day; books on history, politics, mathematics, philosophy and the new geography. It also contained many of the classics from ancient Greece and Rome. Consequently, it included almost everything required to underpin the works of William Shakespeare. Many of Percy's other poet friends used the library while composing their works.

6. In October 1599, when Shakespeare is sought by the tax collectors of London's St Helen's parish, he is traced to Sussex. The authorities appear to have been correct concerning his whereabouts, as the tax was eventually collected by the Bishop of Winchester, who had fiscal jurisdiction over all ecclesiastical matters in the county of Sussex. As it was a year later, October 1600, that the bishop eventually received the money, it appears that Shakespeare had been in the county throughout this time, or was a frequent visitor. As the Globe Theatre had recently opened, and new plays were in demand, Shakespeare may have spent the year at Petworth writing these new works.

Chapter 12

Intrigue

We have developed a credible scenario incorporating Shakespeare's education, his missing years and his early association with the theatre, which also goes some way to explaining his low profile. However, it does not solve the strangest mystery of all – why nobody in Stratford appears to have been remotely aware of his career as a poet-dramatist. Even in later life, and for years after his death, when Shakespeare had become something of a literary legend, no one in the Warwickshire town seems to have been in the slightest bit interested. It has been argued that the people of Stratford, having no interest in the theatre, had no reason to mention their most famous son. But this fails to account for the tomb memorial, installed either on Shakespeare's or his family's request, showing him as a dealer in bagged commodities. It does not explain the complete lack of family pride, or even acknowledgment, and it conveniently ignores the absence of literary references left by Shakespeare himself. Even his executor – Thomas Russell, the stepfather of the poet Leonard Digges, who so praises Shakespeare in the First Folio, seven years after his death – fails to include reference to Shakespeare as a poet-dramatist in any of his writings.

It may be that William Shakespeare wanted it that way. Otherwise, even if – for some inexplicable reason – everyone else ignored his success, he would surely have acknowledged himself. But why embark on a deliberate policy of concealment? The answer may lie in a desire to protect his family. Aspects of his work as a poet-dramatist might put them in jeopardy if they discovered too much. Since the School of Night provides a link with a world of potential danger, the solution may lie here.

Thus far we have established the following:

In 1593 George Chapman wrote to Walter Warner concerning the Ralegh group, naming Marlowe, Hariot and Strange. The following year he further implicates Strange and also Percy. In 1594 Hariot and Ralegh are again implicated by Baines in his Marlowe report. Both Chapman and Baines refer to blasphemous talk, resulting in the term 'Walter Ralegh's school of atheism' being used to identify the group. This same 'school of atheism' is mentioned by the Italian poet Giordano Bruno as meeting at the home of Fulke Greville in 1585, where Philip Sidney is present. Greville is a friend of Philip Sidney, and both he and Hariot were close associates of Bruno. Finally, Thomas Kyd's testimony further implicates Marlowe along with Walter Warner (a lifelong friend of Hariot and Percy), Matthew Roydon (a known associate of Marlowe, Chapman and Sidney), and perhaps Richard Field.

Our group of suspected atheists now comprises Ralegh, Percy, Hariot, Marlowe, Sidney, Bruno, Greville, Strange, Chapman, Warner, Roydon and possibly Field. In addition, there is a second, seemingly more sinister, circle associated with the Walsinghams.

Between 1587 and 1592, Marlowe worked for Francis Walsingham's Secret Service as a courier. During this period, Marlowe is a close associate of Thomas Watson and Watson had been working for the Secret Service with Thomas Walsingham since 1581. Marlowe's drinking partner Robert Poley married Watson's daughter around 1564, worked for Francis Walsingham and lived in his house in 1583, and worked alongside Thomas Walsingham as a spy uncovering the Babington Plot in 1586. Nicholas Skeres is also involved as a Secret Service agent and an associate of Marlowe, Watson, Poley and Thomas Walsingham.

Francis Walsingham's Secret Service group therefore includes Thomas Walsingham, Christopher Marlowe, Robert Poley, Nicholas Skeres and Thomas Watson. Other than Marlowe, is this circle in any way linked with the Ralegh group? At least three others in the School of Night may also have Secret Service connections.

The first is Philip Sidney. In 1583 Poley is recorded as working for him in some undefined capacity – 'Sir Philip Sidney's man' –

while he is actually living in a house belonging to Francis Walsingham. Moreover, Philip Sidney is Francis Walsingham's son-in-law (married to his daughter Frances). The second is Matthew Roydon. Not only is Roydon a friend of Thomas Watson, he is also known to one of the three men present at Marlowe's death, a man with whom he co-signed the goldsmith's bond in 1582: Nicholas Skeres. The third man is George Chapman, who may be involved with both groups as he is patronised by Thomas Walsingham's wife, Lady Audrey.

Although there is, so far, no direct evidence linking the Walsinghams to the Ralegh group, at least four of the Walsingham associates – Marlowe, Sidney, Roydon and Chapman – are involved with Ralegh. Of these, Marlowe is unquestionably a Walsingham agent, as are Sidney and Roydon.

There are thus two groups: one accused of subversive atheism, the other consisting of government agents. Logic appears to dictate a conflict of interest, the purpose of the latter apparently being to undermine the activities of the former. But on examination the reality seems to be just the opposite. The Privy Council were working to bring about Ralegh's downfall, so why is Marlowe – a Secret Service man, at the very heart of the Ralegh group – first arrested by the Council before apparently being killed by Walsingham's agents? Why arrest and/or seemingly kill your key informant? Furthermore, the three other Walsingham associates and/or agents are never called to inform against Ralegh. It therefore seems likely that Walsingham's Secret Service is not being used by the Privy Council at all. But if the Privy Council are aiming to bring down Ralegh's group, why not enlist Secret Service help? The answer, it appears, is that Walter Ralegh and Thomas Walsingham were on the same side. To understand how the Ralegh and Walsingham groups may have come to cooperate, we must examine the background to the Secret Service, which takes us back to the Reformation.

* * *

In the early years of the sixteenth century the State religion of Western Europe was Roman Catholicism. Although separate countries had their own rulers, the power of the Catholic Church was woven into the fabric and government of each nation. In the second decade of the sixteenth century the picture began to change, with an avalanche of unprecedented events initiated by the Augustinian priest Martin Luther. As Professor of theology at Wittenberg University, Luther's conception that the Catholic Church had strayed from Bible teachings received considerable support in Germany. The final straw for Luther came in 1517, when he protested bitterly against the Pope's policy of selling indulgences; remissions of temporal punishments due after absolution – in plain English, signed documents forgiving sins. In the concept of indulgences the kind of life a person lived had no bearing on spirituality. Provided you had enough money, you could buy your way into heaven.

In 1517 Luther publicly posted a list of criticisms of the Pope to a church door in Wittenberg. When he refused to recant, he was summoned to appear before the Holy Roman Emperor, Charles V.

The Holy Roman Empire was the empire of the Austrian Hapsburgs, covering Austria, Germany, Hungary, the Netherlands, Bohemia and northern Italy. Although it had once been a powerful empire, the hundreds of small states of which it comprised were now virtually autonomous. Except in Austria and Hungary, the Emperor was little more than a figurehead. Luther's own prince, the Elector of Saxony, was therefore able to offer him protection, and the Emperor was powerless to intervene. In 1521, however, the Pope responded by excommunicating Luther.

With nothing to lose, Luther continued to preach an alternative form of Christianity. His followers progressed even further, rejecting the very essence of Catholicism, the belief that during Mass the wine and bread quite literally became the blood and body of Christ. In Wittenberg services were now held without the Mass. The followers of this new Christianity – denying the infallibility and authority of the Pope, rejecting the Mass and confession as essential for salvation, and believing in the ordination of married priests – came to be called Protestants (protestors against Rome). Luther himself gave up monastic life and married a former nun, Catherine von Bora, in 1525.

Throughout Christendom people had lost patience with the Catholic Church. Secular rulers resented its authority and wealth. Once someone made the first move, many followed suit. In most cases it was opportunism, an excuse for dukes and princes to seize Church land and possessions. In 1527 Protestantism became the State religion in Denmark and Sweden, and within a few years some 50 per cent of German duchies had converted. This marked the beginning of the fragmentation of Europe into two armed camps, Catholic and Protestant, and was the cause of untold bloodshed for centuries to come. It was the beginning of the Reformation, the Protestant intent to reform the Christian Church.

In England, between 1529 and 1536, Henry VIII had his own quarrels with the Pope, particularly when the pontiff refused to annul his marriage to the Spanish Catherine of Aragon. Accordingly, Henry passed a number of progressively anti-Catholic acts, severing completely from Rome when excommunicated in 1533. The following year, Henry had himself appointed head of the English Church by the Act of Supremacy. By 1535 papal authority was rejected by most English bishops. Some, who refused to comply, were beheaded. The final stage in the English Reformation came between 1536 and 1540, when Henry ordered the dissolution of the monasteries and monastic assets were seized by the Crown.

By the time of Henry's death in 1547, Europe was markedly divided into Protestant and Catholic factions. Much of Germany and Scandinavia were Protestant, as was England, while France, Spain and Italy remained Catholic. The remainder of the Holy Roman Empire became the battleground for the two factions. Elsewhere, John Calvin had established Protestantism in Switzerland in 1541; in 1546 John Knox led a Calvinist revolt in Scotland; and at the same time the Mennonites were refuting Catholic authority in the Netherlands.

The Catholics fought back and counter-Reformation massacres occurred, such as the slaughter of the Protestant Huguenots by the French King Francis I in 1535. Around the same time Ignatius Loyola founded the Jesuit Society in Paris. Officially recognised by the Pope in 1540, the Jesuit priests risked their lives entering Protestant countries to perform Mass for those who still followed the old religion. Moreover, the Jesuits often acted as spies and agents for the Catholic monarchs, travelling in disguise across Europe under assumed names. Finally, in 1542, the Pope reinstated the Inquisition, leading to the execution of an untold number of Protestants on the charge of heresy. There were atrocities on both sides, committed with equal vigour by Catholics and Protestants alike.

In England, when Henry VIII died, his young son Edward VI became king; but as he was only a child, his uncle Edward Seymour became the temporary ruler, the protector of the realm. In 1549 Seymour was replaced by John Dudley, Earl of Warwick. As a Protestant, Dudley endeavoured to ensure that England, deeply divided on this issue of religion, should not revert to Catholicism. The young king was ill, however, and not expected to live much longer. Dudley therefore tried to persuade Edward's sister Mary Tudor, as next in line to the throne, to convert from Catholicism to Protestantism. When Mary refused, Dudley encouraged the King to break with tradition and name his daughter-in-law Lady Jane Grey as heir. Edward died in 1553, but Jane only remained Queen for nine days, before forces loyal to Mary removed her from office. Mary became Queen and Jane was executed.

Queen Mary immediately ordered the arrest of all bishops not recognised by Rome. The following year the English Church was reconciled to the Catholic Church and the anti-heresy laws were revived. Mary's policy of ruthless persecution and burning those who refused to revert to Catholicism earned her the name Bloody Mary.

When Mary died without child in 1558, her younger sister Elizabeth came to the throne, opening her reign by re-establishing the Protestant Church. Not being particularly religious herself, she was initially tolerant towards the Catholics. But her patience did not last.

Elizabeth's cousin, Mary Queen of Scots, a Catholic, was next in line to the English Throne. In Scotland, in 1567, a Protestant revolt against Mary forced her to abdicate in favour of her baby son James. In May the following year she escaped captivity and raised an army, but was defeated at the battle of Langside. She fled to England, hoping to find asylum with her cousin. Elizabeth, however, knowing that many Catholics expected Mary to replace her, had her cousin confined to house arrest for the next nineteen years. But although many Protestants wanted Mary dead, Elizabeth refused to endorse her execution until she had proof implicating Mary herself in conspiracy.

Here, Francis Walsingham entered the scene. In the 1570s Walsingham rose to become one of Elizabeth's chief Secretaries of State and a member of the Privy Council. A puritanical Protestant, he planned to ensure that Britain never again reverted to Catholicism, to this end establishing the Secret Service as his principal instrument; an espionage network of spies and informers to uncover Catholic plots at home and abroad. In 1586 Walsingham's Secret Service uncovered the Babington Plot to murder Elizabeth and place Mary on the throne. 'Orchestrated' is probably a more apt term than 'uncovered', as it seems that Walsingham manipulated Anthony Babington to discredit the Catholics.

In May 1586 Anthony Babington, a Catholic lawyer, met with the Jesuit priest John Ballard at the Plough in London's Temple Bar. Here, it seems, the plot was hatched. Ballard had recently returned from France with news of an imminent Catholic invasion. Some 60,000 French, Spanish and Italian troops were preparing to cross the Channel. There was one proviso, a simultaneous uprising in England. Ballard believed that there was only one way to ensure such a rebellion; Elizabeth must die, and Mary must replace her as Queen. Babington was given the task of organising the rebellion, while another Catholic lawyer, John Savage, was chosen as the assassin.

From the outset Walsingham knew of the plot and could have immediately arrested the conspirators. One of those present at the conclave was Barnard Maude, a Walsingham agent working undercover as Ballard's aide. But Walsingham chose to wait, instructing Maude to keep watch and report developments.

The first development was Babington's change of heart. Having no stomach for regicide, he decided to flee the country. His initial attempts to obtain a passport failed, but succeeded in alerting Walsingham to his intentions. Maude, it seems, was instructed to befriend Babington and also express doubt about the planned rebellion. The plan worked and Babington was referred to a man employed in the home of Walsingham's daughter, whom he was told could acquire him a passport – Robert Poley.

Soon, Babington was taken by Poley to Walsingham's office, believing he was to be granted a passport. Unfortunately for him, he received an audience with Walsingham himself.

There is no surviving transcript, if ever there was one, concerning what took place at that meeting, although we can make an informed guess. Walsingham confronts Babington with his predicament – either he helps, or he finds himself on the rack. By the month of June Babington is once again with the conspirators, accompanied by Poley, now posing as a Catholic reactionary. Babington must therefore have been made an offer he could not refuse. Although Babington is disenchanted, Walsingham forces him to return as an informer, with Poley assigned to keep watch. The other conspirators seem none the wiser and the plot continues as planned.

Presumably on Ballard's instructions, on 6 July Babington wrote to Mary Queen of Scots, outlining the aims of the conspiracy and seeking her consent. Eleven days later Walsingham's plan paid off. Mary replied. Although the Queen of Scots did not agree to the assassination, she acknowledged the conspiracy, requesting further information. Walsingham now had exactly what he wanted, evidence to implicate Mary, the one condition the Queen had demanded before considering her execution. Regardless, he let the plot run its course for another month in the hope of entrapping more rebels.

On the morning of 4 August Walsingham's agents, including Thomas Walsingham, surrounded the house of another agent, Anthony Hall (a skinner), where Poley had arranged a meeting of the conspirators. Inside, along with the plotters, were Poley and another Secret Service colleague named only as Skeres. This was almost certainly Nicholas Skeres, later involved with Marlowe's death. Sometime earlier, Babington at last realised he was being framed, having discovered Poley compiling a secret message in an upstairs room. Somehow he managed to escape. When Walsingham's agents moved in to arrest John Ballard and the others at midday, Babington was nowhere to be found.

Fleeing north to Harrow, Babington lived off the land for eight days before finding sanctuary in the home of a Catholic friend, Jeremy Bellamy. But his freedom was short-lived. On 14 August the Bellamy house was stormed and Babington was arrested.

Despite protesting his innocence, Babington was tortured into confession along with his fellows. Moreover, he was portrayed as the instigator of the plot, his name having been associated with it ever since. The interrogation was severe, even by Elizabethan standards. Ballard had to be carried into court and Bellamy died in the dungeons. On 13 September fourteen conspirators were tried for high treason and all were condemned to death.

The method of execution was horrific, so much so that Queen Elizabeth ordered it to cease when only seven had died. On 20 September, at St Giles's Field near Holborn, Ballard, Babington and five of the plotters were drawn through the streets on sledges. They were hanged from the gallows, but cut down before death. While still alive, and fully conscious, their genitals were cut off, their guts sliced open, and their intestines drawn out in a long, bloody trail. Finally, they were released from their suffering by being hacked into four writhing pieces. This barbaric form of execution, minus the castration, eventually became the accepted death penalty for Catholic conspirators by the time that James I came to the throne a few years later. To be hanged, drawn and quartered, as it came to be called, was the eventual fate of Guy Fawkes and the Gunpowder Plotters in 1605.

Walsingham's plan had paid off. The Catholics were thoroughly discredited and Elizabeth agreed to a trial for Mary. The Queen of Scots was found guilty and beheaded at Fotheringhay Castle near Peterborough on 8 February the following year.

In Walsingham's Secret Service Poley, Skeres and Thomas Walsingham were key players. The evidence demonstrates their ruthless efficiency. So why were they not used to undermine Ralegh a few years later? It seems that after his death in 1590, Francis Walsingham's Secret Service had become something of a rogue outfit, led by Thomas Walsingham. The Queen's Chief Minister and Lord High Treasurer, William Cecil, became understandably concerned about its power and, realising its potential, attempted to draw it into his own sphere of control.

It was at this time, in the early 1590s, with Thomas Walsingham trying to maintain his influence over the Secret Service, that he and Ralegh found themselves with a common adversary: William Cecil. Cecil not only intended to take over the Secret Service, he also wanted to destroy his old enemy Walter Ralegh.

Both Walsingham and Ralegh posed a threat to Cecil. Ralegh might regain his influence with the Queen, while Walsingham had control over the most sophisticated espionage network in Europe.

The Privy Council's inquiries into Ralegh's activities, and the death of Christopher Marlowe, now come into perspective. The Privy Council was the most powerful body in England, beside the monarchy, and Cecil all but controlled it. He used its influence to pursue Ralegh and discover the Marlowe allegations. Eventually, armed with the Baines report, he was ready to detain Marlowe. Both Ralegh and Walsingham had reason to fear Marlowe's interrogation. Marlowe knew too much about the Secret Service and could name names. We have seen how the Secret Service operated, and the ruthlessness of its agents. Walsingham, Skeres and Poley helped frame the hapless Babington. Aware of his innocence, they watched him arrested, tortured and butchered to death. There can be little doubt that such men would have no compunction silencing someone in Marlowe's predicament.

Still seeking evidence against Ralegh, after Marlowe's death Cecil turned on Lord Strange, whose association with the occult was possibly seen as a potential weak link in the Ralegh entourage. But again Cecil had to tread carefully. Since the Queen's own astrologer, John Dee, was Strange's mentor, the latter could not simply be accused of blasphemy, for fear the Queen herself might be implicated. In the spring of 1594 Strange was summoned before the Privy Council. No record survives of his questioning, but it may have concerned his beliefs. It seems to have achieved little, however, as he was allowed to go free.

Nine days later Strange wrote to Cecil, requesting a meeting to discuss his knowledge of a conspiracy. Before the meeting could be arranged, Strange fell violently ill and never recovered. Cecil was hoping that Marlowe could prove Ralegh an atheist, but the Strange allegations were far more serious, a conspiracy to bring down the government. Oddly, Strange does not mention the Queen in his letter. Could the conspiracy have therefore been aimed at Cecil himself. Whatever the truth, both the Ralegh and Walsingham circles had every reason to want him eliminated.

Having progressed from accusations of atheism into the realms of conspiracy, we are moving into ever darker waters. Knowing the ruthlessness of those who appear to be involved, it is understandable that anyone linked to the Ralegh or Walsingham circles would have reason to fear for their family's well-being. This brings us full circle to William Shakespeare and evidence that he, too, was employed by the Secret Service.

Summary

The evidence indicates that William Shakespeare kept his work in London a secret in Stratford-upon-Avon. The most likely solution is that he wished to protect his family. Shakespeare's association with members of the Ralegh group, and a possible plan to overthrow the prime minister William Cecil, could account for the playwright's actions.

1. A credible sequence of events incorporates Shakespeare's education, his missing years and his early association with the theatre, which also goes some way to explaining his low profile. However, it does not solve the strangest mystery of all – why no one in Stratford appears to have been remotely aware of his career as a poet-dramatist.

2. The only feasible explanation for this mystery is that Shakespeare himself wanted it that way. Otherwise, even if everyone else in Stratford ignored his success, Shakespeare would surely have acknowledged himself. But why embark on a deliberate policy of concealment? The answer may lie in a desire to protect his family. Aspects of his work as a poet-dramatist might place them in jeopardy if they discovered too much. The solution to this mystery may lie with Shakespeare's involvement with the School of Night, and an alliance between Walter Ralegh and the Walsingham Secret Service.

3. In the 1570s Francis Walsingham rose to become one of Queen Elizabeth's chief Secretaries of State and a member of the Privy Council. A puritanical Protestant, he planned to ensure that Britain never reverted to Catholicism, to this end establishing the Secret Service as his principal instrument; an espionage network of spies and informers to uncover Catholic plots at home and abroad.

4. It seems that after Francis Walsingham's death in 1590 the Secret Service had become something of a rogue outfit, led by Francis's cousin Thomas Walsingham. The Queen's Chief Minister and Lord High Treasurer, William Cecil, became understandably concerned about its power and, realising its potential, attempted to draw it into his sphere of control. It is at this time, in the early 1590s, with Thomas Walsingham trying to maintain his influence over the Secret Service, that he and Ralegh find themselves with a common adversary: William Cecil. Cecil not only intended to take over the Secret Service, he also wanted to destroy his old enemy Walter Ralegh.

5. A group of suspected atheists comprises Ralegh, Percy, Hariot, Marlowe, Sidney, Bruno, Greville, Strange, Chapman, Warner, Roydon and possibly Field. A second, seemingly more sinister, circle also seems associated with the Walsinghams. At least four of the Walsingham associates – Marlowe, Sidney, Roydon and Chapman – are involved with Ralegh. Of these, Marlowe is unquestionably a Walsingham agent and Sidney and Roydon almost certainly are.

6. In March 1594 Lord Strange wrote to Cecil, claiming he had evidence of a conspiracy against his government. A plot involving Cecil's enemies Ralegh and Walsingham seems the most likely identity of this mysterious conspiracy. However, before the meeting could be arranged, Strange fell violently ill and never recovered, the terrible symptoms suggesting arsenic poisoning. Although murder could not be proven with the inadequate medical facilities of the day, both the Ralegh and Walsingham circles are chief suspects. As Shakespeare was closely involved with Strange and Marlowe, both of whom had died under similar circumstances, he may well have had reason to fear for his own life.

Chapter 13

The Superspies

By the time of the Babington Plot, Queen Elizabeth's relatively lenient attitude to Roman Catholicism had evaporated. The celebration of Mass was now a serious offence, and Catholics remaining true to their faith were compelled to worship in secret. Risking life imprisonment to continue saying Mass, the priests were based chiefly in Rheims, northern France, where the English Seminary became a centre for Catholic resistance.

Rheims became an espionage capital of Europe and Walsingham's spies were everywhere. Amongst his agents was Richard Baines, the informer against Marlowe in 1593. Between 1578 and 1582 Baines had become Walsingham's superspy, having infiltrated the Rheims seminary. He was even ordained as a priest, saying Mass and, more importantly, hearing confession. In consequence, he was able to discover everything that was going on in Rheims, becoming one of the most important figures in the Secret Service. In 1583 he returned to England under the guise of a Catholic propagandist, disclosing to Walsingham everything he knew. Baines fell under suspicion when he returned to France, however, and he was lucky to return home alive.

Baines was not the only top agent to have his cover blown. Others soon followed. After the Babington Plot, Robert Poley was suspected by the Catholics. The Jesuit Robert Southwell wrote of Walsingham's agents:

> The matter of Babington was wholly of their plotting and forging, of purpose to make Catholics odious and to cut off the Queen of Scots.

Southwell was also aware that Poley had been the key figure:

> It is known that Poley, being Francis Walsingham's man, and thoroughly seasoned to his master's tooth, was the chief instrument to contrive and prosecute the matter.

The Catholics were now wise to Walsingham's methods. It was no longer going to be so easy to work, in the words of Southwell, in the way Poley had:

> He heard Mass, confessed, and in all things feigned to be a Catholic.

Walsingham was compelled to find new blood, choosing the best possible recruits – poets and dramatists, whose lifestyles were ideally suited to his purpose. They had the perfect cover, travelling widely and receiving welcome everywhere, and since many were also actors, role playing was often second nature. They possessed all the necessary qualifications for spying. Not only were they educated, but many knew foreign languages. Furthermore, as the usual social barriers were often dropped for poets, they were equally at home in back street pubs or in the palaces of the mighty. They were thus in the privileged position of having their eyes and ears everywhere. Moreover, they were often impecunious, and money was something that Walsingham could provide. The standard payment for a play was around £2 for months of work. Agents like Poley and Baines were being paid £15 or £20 for trips lasting just a few days.

By the late 1580s the poet-dramatists had replaced the fake Catholics as the tentacles of the Walsingham network. It was in this way that Marlowe became involved as a courier and Watson as a spy, both doubtless recruited by Poley. Three other playwrights were almost certainly Walsingham agents in some capacity: Sidney, Roydon and Chapman. But there was one poet-dramatist who was so deeply involved in the Secret Service that he took over from superspy Baines: the playwright Anthony Munday.

Anthony Munday was involved in the Secret Service from the outset, and revelled in it. In 1580 he was in Rheims with Baines, scheming to capture the leader of the English Jesuits, Edmund Campion. Munday successfully induced Campion to return to England, duping him into a sham conspiracy. Believing he was to meet with fellow Catholics, Campion arrived in England only to find himself arrested. When Campion was hanged in 1581, Munday attended the execution, gleefully writing up the event in his diary. Later, Munday openly boasted of his exploits in Rheims, publishing them in *The English Romain Life*.

Like Shakespeare and Marlowe, Munday came from humble beginnings; he was the son of a London draper. Munday may have had more in common with Shakespeare, as he served an apprenticeship as a printer-publisher. He eventually moved into the world of theatre, but continued with his espionage activities. He was also working with the Poley set, in particular Anthony Hall, the skinner whose house Poley had made use of during the Babington affair. After at least a dozen priests were hanged because of him, Munday was too infamous to continue as a spy. However, he seems to have loved the work so much that in 1588 he worked publicly for the Archbishop of Canterbury, arresting extremists of all religious persuasions. He was even granted the title of Archbishop's Pursuivant, a position akin to that later held by Mathew Hopkins, Oliver Cromwell's famous Witchfinder General. Incredibly, while Munday was entertaining theatregoers with plays such as *The Downfall of Robert the Earl of Huntingdon*, which gave us the modern Robin Hood story, he was simultaneously persecuting Catholics.

Munday wrote for The Lord Admiral's Men, which seems to be why Shakespeare came to work with him on *Sir Thomas More*, when The Lord Admiral's Men and Lord Strange's Men amalgamated in the early 1590s.

With Marlowe and Munday, we have *two* close colleagues of William Shakespeare who worked for the Secret Service, one of them its superspy. Additionally, there are a number of other likely associates who also seemed to have been involved with the Walsingham network: Sidney, Roydon and Chapman. These connections imply a link between Shakespeare and the Secret Service; indeed, further investigations reveal that his company's patron, Lord Strange, was also implicated.

Lord Strange's involvement occurred in a period of double-dealing following Francis Walsingham's death. Between 1590 and 1594, Secret Service agents began increasingly to defect to the Cecil camp. By 1594, all but a few of the most loyal had deserted Thomas Walsingham. Baines was already working for Cecil in 1593, compiling his report on Marlowe. Even Poley had gone over by the following year, and was working for Cecil in the Netherlands, Scotland and France. Strange also seems to have been recruited by William Cecil, although his role reveals a new dimension to the whole affair.

In the summer of 1593, a fresh Catholic initiative was launched. Known as the Hesketh Plot, it was doomed from the outset. On 27 September the Catholic landowner Richard Hesketh arrived at the home of Lord Strange, who had just become the Earl of Derby, inviting him to join a planned Catholic uprising. A Lancastrian, Hesketh had known Strange for many years. Since Strange's father was Catholic, it was assumed that his son would be sympathetic to the cause. Strange led Hesketh to believe that he would give the rebellion serious consideration. Instead he informed William Cecil. On 10 October Hesketh was arrested and after two months of interrogation he was hanged, drawn and quartered. The fact that Strange had immediately told Cecil of the planned uprising does not in itself constitute evidence that he had been working as an agent for Cecil, but it certainly arouses suspicion. In the first instance, why should the conspirators have trusted Strange?

The answer lies in the city of Prague, the cold-war Berlin of its day. Prague was the capital of Bohemia, in what is now the Czech Republic. A small country, surrounded by forested mountains, it was also wealthy; in the Middle Ages its silver mines had been the richest in Europe. In 1526 Prague had been absorbed into the Austrian-dominated Holy Roman Empire, and by the 1590s, as the Empire fell apart, it found itself wedged between the Protestant German states and Catholic Austro-Hungary. Consequently, the Holy Roman Emperor Rudolf II temporarily held court in Prague, hoping to utilise its strategic setting as a base from which to unite his crumbling Empire. Prague thus became a focal point for Catholic resistance throughout Europe, and many English Catholics made it their home.

Yet unlike Rheims, which was purely Catholic, a peculiar

situation existed in Prague. The Emperor Rudolf had an unusual interest for a Catholic in that he was fascinated by the occult. Accordingly, many accused of witchcraft and black magic also found asylum in Prague, even those escaping from Catholic countries. It is here that Lord Strange enters the scene. Strange was himself intrigued by the occult, studying with Queen Elizabeth's astrologer John Dee, whom he met through a mutual acquaintance, fellow Lancastrian Edward Kelly.

Kelly was one of the most colourful and bizarre characters of the Elizabethan era, an occultist who openly practised alchemy and necromancy, the purported raising of the dead. Understandably, it was not long before he was in trouble with the authorities. In 1580 he was found guilty of counterfeiting, placed in the pillory, and had his ears chopped off. Shortly after, he was discovered removing corpses from Walton Dale churchyard, just outside Preston, presumably in the hope of resurrecting them. This was a much more serious offence and Kelly was hauled before the local squire Thomas Langton. Fortunately, Langton was a friend of Lord Strange, whose father, as Earl of Derby, was Lord Lieutenant of the County. Strange intervened to free Kelly and the two men became occult colleagues. Strange was infatuated by Kelly's unholy activities, and soon the pair were experimenting with alchemy.

In 1582 Kelly joined forces with John Dee, and together with Strange they met frequently at Dee's house at Mortlake. Eventually, Kelly and Dee left England, travelling around Europe performing what can only be described as a spiritualist show. Billed as an 'angelic conference', Dee would recite magical incantations, while the entranced Kelly offered advice to a playing clientele. Dee and Kelly were constantly on the move, just one step ahead of the Church and civic authorities. In cities across the Continent, warrants were issued for their arrest on charges of witchcraft and deception.

By 1590 Dee had grown weary of this life style, returning to England to discover his home had been ransacked by Puritans. Like Baron Frankenstein in the Boris Karloff film, Dee was driven into hiding by a torch-wielding mob. Events turned out much better for Kelly, however, who made his way to Prague, his arrival setting in motion one of the strangest affairs in Reformation history. The Holy Roman Emperor was in the city and, hearing of Kelly's spiritualist antics, summoned the conjurer to court. To Kelly's relief, the 'angelic conference' demanded by the Emperor appeared to work. Rudolf was so impressed with Kelly's 'spirit messages' that he appointed him as an official advisor. Kelly had been granted estates and offered a government post in Bohemia.

Thereafter, Prague became the occult capital of Europe, with Kelly as its chief magus. He also wielded considerable authority. In England William Cecil, hearing of Kelly's elevated position in a city rife with Catholic intrigue, made a proposition. If Kelly provided intelligence regarding the English Catholics in Prague, he would be well rewarded. Kelly agreed, and in May 1591 Cecil wrote expressing his appreciation. The messenger involved in the exchange of letters is referred to as 'Mr Roydon', almost certainly the poet Matthew Roydon.

Roydon is another familiar name. His appearance not only confirms the suspicion that he was working for the Secret Service, it also shows that he had moved to the Cecil camp. In Roydon, Cecil had a man in both the Walsingham and Ralegh circles. Roydon may therefore provide the answer to an historical mystery regarding the Baines report. Where had Baines received his information regarding Marlowe? Historians have long suspected that Baines had merely compiled a report from intelligence submitted by an informant closer to Marlowe. Matthew Roydon could well have been that man. But if, like Baines, Roydon had switched sides, he was not the only one. Around this time, Strange also seems to have been recruited by Cecil.

Richard Hesketh had arrived in Prague in 1589, and over the next couple of years formulated his plan to lead a Catholic revolt in England. Many of those who became embroiled in the conspiracy were, like Hesketh, Lancashire exiles. With Kelly in Cecil's pocket, the Secretary of State would certainly have been aware of the planned uprising well in advance, a notion supported by the fact that Kelly was also a Lancastrian and Hesketh already knew Kelly's friend Dee in London. It is therefore reasonable to assume that Hesketh knew Kelly well before his arrival in Prague.

Lord Strange was probably recruited by Cecil once the conspiracy had come to his attention, sometime around 1591. Strange was uniquely valuable. Not only was he a close friend of Kelly, and already knew Hesketh, but his father had been a loyal Catholic and a natural focus for any Catholic insurgence in the North. The approach to Strange, therefore, was probably suggested by Kelly, as the bait to entice Hesketh and his associates back to England.

Most of Cecil's clandestine activities during the period he was attempting to gain control of the Secret Service are unknown. Many of his interviews at the Privy Council went unrecorded, and the little information available has survived in the documents of his own family. However, the Cecil papers that still exist at Hatfield House, Hertfordshire, and contemporary accounts recorded in William Camden's *Annales* (*c*1625), cast sufficient light on the events to permit some informed guesswork.

We know from these sources that Strange was summoned to the Privy Council on 10 March 1594, evidently to answer allegations of blasphemy. No record was apparently kept of his interrogation, but after a few hours he was allowed to go free. At the very least, Cecil must have intervened to have had him released, as we now know that Strange had been the willing bait in the Hesketh Plot. Strange was thus an exceptionally valuable asset and doubtless Cecil intended using him again. Strange's summons is therefore likely to have been a cover for a private meeting with Cecil.

The content of their discussion will probably never be known. However, in the last week of March, just two weeks after his visit to the Privy Council, Strange wrote to Cecil informing him of a further conspiracy against the government and requesting a meeting. It is not known exactly when the letter was sent, but Cecil's secretary records its arrival on 29 March. By this time Strange had left London and returned to his country home at Lathom House. Soon after his arrival, around 1 April, he became violently sick, and by 16 April he was dead.

It appears that Cecil was neither aware of Strange's condition nor his whereabouts, as a new summons was issued for him to appear before the Privy Council on 9 April. Since the summons was again to answer allegations of blasphemy, this appears to indicate a cover for the appointment requested by Strange himself. On Cecil's instructions, a man who has just volunteered information of a conspiracy against the government is called in to answer questions relating to a comparatively minor matter of blasphemy. This seems incongruous. It appears that Cecil intended Strange to act for him in a similar capacity to his role in the Hesketh affair.

What was this conspiracy? As we have seen, it almost certainly involved Ralegh and/or Walsingham. Ralegh heads the list, for it coincides precisely with the Cerne Abbas enquiry in Dorset. Moreover, Ralegh's activities after Strange's death are suspicious. Within the week he had requested an audience with the Queen, promising her vast quantities of Spanish gold if she granted him leave to return to sea.

Whatever conspiracy was being planned, and whoever was involved, it never materialised. If it included the Ralegh/Walsingham groups and a proposed coup to remove Cecil, resulting in Strange's murder, then it would seem to have been abandoned. After this time no more is heard of Ralegh's School of Night, while Walsingham, perhaps too young and inexperienced (at age twenty-six) to tackle a man like Cecil, surrendered his stake in the Secret Service. The power struggle had been won by William Cecil, who became the most influential man in England.

Returning to William Shakespeare, setting aside the host of possible associates involved in the Secret Service, we now know that Shakespeare's three most important colleagues in the early 1590s were all deeply involved – Marlowe, Munday and Strange. Not only were they Shakespeare's mentors and his patron, but they were almost certainly those who launched his career. Shakespeare was surrounded on all sides by espionage. Is it conceivable that he passed his life untouched by this world of intrigue? All the circumstances seem to hint towards Shakespeare's involvement.

Cecil's ace cards in his cold war with Ralegh and Walsingham were Marlowe (inadvertently) and Strange (willingly). When Marlowe dies, Cecil loses his key witness. When Strange dies, he loses his key informant.

Shakespeare's career as a playwright is launched when the Cecil/Ralegh/Walsingham struggle is at its height, in the early 1590s. When Marlowe dies, Shakespeare's work is immediately patronised by the Queen's favourite, Southampton. When

Strange dies, Shakespeare's company is immediately patronised by the Queen's Chamberlain, Lord Hunsdon. These are the primary elements that ensure Shakespeare's success.

Were Southampton and Hunsdon's patronage influenced by the only person other than the Queen who could bring pressure to bear: William Cecil? Like Roydon and others, had Shakespeare become Cecil's man?

It is with Lord Strange and the Hesketh Plot that we discover persuasive evidence directly linking William Shakespeare to the Secret Service.

Summary

In the late 1580s Secretary of State Francis Walsingham recruited a number of poet-dramatists to act as spies and informants. By 1593 many of Shakespeare's closest colleagues were working as agents in the Elizabethan Secret Service. Was Shakespeare himself involved?

1. By the late 1580s Francis Walsingham began to recruit poets and dramatists to work as Secret Service agents. They possessed all the necessary qualifications for spying. Not only were they educated, but many knew foreign languages. Marlowe became involved as a courier and Watson as a spy. Other playwrights who were almost certainly Walsingham agents included Sidney, Roydon and Chapman. One poet-dramatist was so deeply involved in the Secret Service that he became its superspy, the playwright Anthony Munday.

2. Anthony Munday was involved in the Secret Service from the outset and revelled in his role. He had been in Rheims in northern France in 1580, scheming to capture the leader of the English Jesuits, Edmund Campion. Munday successfully induced Campion to return to England, duping him into a sham conspiracy. Believing he was to meet with fellow Catholics, Campion arrived in England, only to find himself arrested. When Campion was hanged in 1581, Munday attended the execution, gleefully writing up the event in his diary. Later, Munday openly boasted of his exploits in Rheims, and published them in *The English Romain Life*. Ultimately, at least a dozen priests were hanged as a consequence of Munday's spying activities.

3. Munday eventually wrote for The Lord Admiral's Men, doubtless how Shakespeare came to work with him on *Sir Thomas More* when The Lord Admiral's Men and Lord Strange's Men amalgamated in the early 1590s. With Marlowe and Munday, we have *two* close colleagues of William Shakespeare who worked for the Secret Service. Additionally, a number of other likely associates also seemed to have been involved with the Walsingham network: Sidney, Roydon and Chapman. Further investigation reveals that Shakespeare's patron Lord Strange also worked for the Secret Service.

4. Lord Strange's involvement occurred in a period of double-dealing following Francis Walsingham's death. Between 1590 and 1594, Secret Service agents were defecting to the Cecil camp. By 1594, all but a handful of the most loyal had deserted Thomas Walsingham.

5. On 27 September 1593 the Catholic landowner Richard Hesketh arrived at the home of Lord Strange, who had just become Earl of Derby, inviting him to join a planned Catholic uprising. A Lancastrian, Hesketh had known Strange for many years. As Strange's father was Catholic it was assumed that his son would also be sympathetic to the cause. Strange led Hesketh to believe that he would give the rebellion serious consideration. Instead he informed William Cecil. It seems very possible that Strange was working in the same capacity, as a Cecil informant, when he appears to have betrayed Ralegh and/or Walsingham in March 1594.

6. After Strange's death in 1594 no more is heard of the School of Night, while Walsingham, too young and inexperienced to tackle a man like Cecil, surrendered his stake in the Secret Service. The power struggle had been won by William Cecil, who became the most influential man in England.

7. Besides the host of possible associates who were embroiled in the Secret Service, we now know that Shakespeare's three most important colleagues in the early 1590s were all deeply involved – Marlowe, Munday and Strange. Not only were they his mentors

and his patron, they were almost certainly the individuals who launched his career. Shakespeare is surrounded on all sides by espionage. Is it conceivable that this world simply passed him by? The circumstances certainly hint towards Shakespeare's involvement.

8. Shakespeare's career is launched when the Cecil/Ralegh/Walsingham struggle is at its height, in the early 1590s. When Marlowe died Shakespeare's work was immediately patronised by the Queen's favourite, Southampton. When Strange died his company was as promptly patronised by the Queen's Chamberlain, Lord Hunsdon. These are the primary elements that ensured Shakespeare's success. Were Southampton and Hunsdon's patronage influenced by the only individual other than the Queen able to bring pressure to bear: William Cecil?

Chapter 14

William Hall

On 28 August 1593, just before Hesketh made his ill-fated return to England, a letter was despatched from William Cecil to Edward Kelly in Prague. The contents of the letter are unknown, although the payment for the messenger was recorded by the Chamber Treasurer at the time. It was seemingly a message somehow connected with the Hesketh Plot.

Kelly undoubtedly knew Hesketh, having worked with his ex-colleague John Dee. He also knew Lord Strange, the man who had once saved his life. It was probably Kelly, therefore, who suggested using Strange as the bait. It would certainly be difficult to persuade Hesketh to return to England to meet anyone he did not already know and trust. As a neighbour, Hesketh already knew Lord Strange and had admired his father, who had risked his wealth and standing to remain true to the Catholic faith. Accordingly, the letter may well have contained the instructions which Kelly, having feigned sympathy with the plot, was to relate to Hesketh; details of the meeting with Strange on 27 September. The opportunist Kelly would doubtless have had no hesitation in selling out someone like Hesketh.

Cecil's clerk's record of this letter, which still survives in the Cecil collection at Hatfield, names the courier as William Hall. Since Anthony Hall was the Secret Service agent who allowed his house to be used in the Babington affair, it has been suggested that the William in question was his brother, although no record of such a brother survives. Under various spellings, the name occurs in association with the Secret Service a number of times, and each time there is a connection to William Shakespeare. Is it possible that William Hall was a cover name used by William Shakespeare as a Secret Service agent?

The ecclesiastical archives of Canterbury Cathedral show that on 17 June 1592 a 'Will Hall' was paid £10 for services to the Archbishop's Pursuivant, Anthony Munday. And on 19 March 1596 the Chamber Treasurer paid £15 to 'Hall and Wayte' for 'messages' conveyed from the Netherlands to the Secretary of State. If this is the same Hall, there are two associations with possible colleagues of Shakespeare. First, it is known that Shakespeare was working with Munday around 1592 – the *Sir Thomas More* play dates from around that time, and Munday's troupe, The Lord Admiral's Men, had already amalgamated with Lord Strange's Men. Second, Shakespeare *was* associated with a man named Wayte in 1596; indeed, this is exactly the year in which the Rolls of the Queen's Bench record that a William Wayte craved sureties of the peace against William Shakespeare 'for fear of death and so forth'.

Shakespeare working as a courier might explain the knowledge of foreign culture exhibited in many of his plays. Indeed, on one occasion when the agent Hall surfaces, he has just returned from Denmark. On 2 October 1601 a 'Willm Halle' is mentioned by the Secretary of State's clerk as having returned with intelligence from Denmark. This presents another possible link to Shakespeare. *Hamlet* was written around 1601 (it was registered in 1602) at the same time that Hall returned from Denmark. Did Shakespeare acquire first-hand experience of the Danish Court, which inspired him to write the play, because he had recently travelled there incognito?

If Shakespeare was using an alias to cover Secret Service activities, he would not have been the only dramatist to do so. As a Secret Service agent, Anthony Munday, for example, used the name George Grimes. As a popular playwright Munday was a well-known figure, so was obviously not attempting to conceal his identity. Rather the name Grimes was used as a false account, a name for the records of payment. A similar cover may have been used by Shakespeare. Indeed, the very purpose of the poet-dramatist agents was for them to be themselves. If Hall was Shakespeare, therefore, the name was only his code name within the network – for *Hall* read *Shakespeare*. A further case for Hall being Shakespeare is the choice of name. Munday, for instance, seems to have used the name Grimes since his godfather was called Matthew Grimes. Shakespeare's family in Stratford seems to have been closely attached to the local family called Hall. Indeed, Shakespeare's daughter eventually married a member of this family, physician John Hall. Moreover, the Christian name is the same – William.

We have seen how the poet-dramatist Matthew Roydon was used by the Secret Service in Prague in May 1591 to relay messages between Cecil and Kelly. Had Roydon now been replaced by fellow poet-dramatist William Shakespeare? (If Shakespeare was the William Shakeshafte in Lancashire, then he would already be known to Richard Hesketh, since Shakeshafte had apparently worked for him. If Hesketh knew him, then his presence would be all the more credible, making it less likely that he would be suspected as a Cecil agent.)

Shakespeare would have been at home in late sixteenth-century Prague, the city having become something of an alternative culture capital. Indeed, the word 'bohemian', describing someone with an unconventional life style, was originally applied to the eccentrics who congregated in the state of Bohemia. Amongst other artists, many poets made an academic pilgrimage to Prague, and many were fascinated by the occult. Strange, for instance, studied magic with John Dee; Bruno was burned at the stake for witchcraft; Sidney, Roydon and Greville were accused of sorcery; Marlowe wrote about Devil worship; Chapman's *Shadow of Night* is often referred to as his occult rhapsody; and Shakespeare's works are riddled with references to the supernatural.

Doubtless there are many who would find it difficult to equate Shakespeare the Bard with Shakespeare the spy, believing the author of the Shakespeare plays to be a kindly, virtuous individual, who would never lend himself to such skulduggery. The historical evidence of Shakespeare's life reveals that this is a mythologised image unsupported by the facts. Nothing in Shakespeare's background precludes him from espionage. Like Marlowe and Watson, Shakespeare was not beyond resorting to physical violence. It is a matter of historical record that in 1596 Shakespeare threatened the life of William Wayte. The range of human emotions and behaviour displayed in Shakespeare's works stands as a testament to the life experiences and depth of character of the man. It is too cosy an ideal to believe that only a mild-mannered saint could create such literary classics. Anthony Munday's plays exhibit considerable warmth and tenderness, but in his 'other' life his zealous persecutions bordered on the pathological. Over a century before Shakespeare was writing, Sir Thomas Malory penned the cornerstone work of chivalry, courtly romance and knightly idyll, *Le Morte D'Arthur*. Malory, of Newbold Revel just south of Warwick, is historically recorded as a robber and rapist; indeed the work itself is believed to have been compiled in prison.

Although there is a circumstantial case for Shakespeare as spy William Hall, is there any evidence that proves that Shakespeare himself ever used this name? The evidence may be on the cover of the 1609 edition of the Shakespeare *Sonnets*.

The *Sonnets* appear to have been written as early as 1598, since they are referred to by Francis Meres in that year. Unfortunately Meres only mentions them in passing, referring to 'his sugared sonnets among his private friends'. A year later William Jaggard published two sonnets (numbers 138 and 144) in his *Passionate Pilgrim*. In 1609 the entire collection, as we now know it, was published by the London printer Thomas Thorpe.

Thorpe was a minor figure in the London book trade, having neither a press nor sales outlet of his own. His books were printed by publisher George Eld, and sold via a John Wright of Christ Church gate. Why, then, after his successful association with Richard Field, did Shakespeare opt to downgrade to Thorpe? The answer, it seems, is that Shakespeare had no intention of publishing the *Sonnets*, and that Thorpe had pirated them. Since the idea of copyright did not exist in the early seventeenth century, there was very little Shakespeare could have done, at least not in law. This certainly seems to have been the case as, unlike *Venus and Adonis* and *Lucrece*, there is no dedication by the author himself. The dedication is by the publisher, Thomas Thorpe. The cover reads simply:

Shake-speares Sonnets. Never before Imprinted
At London. By G. Eld for T.T. and are to be

sold by John Wright, dwelling at Christ Church
gate, 1609.

This is prefixed by Thorpe's curious dedication:

> To the only begetter of these ensuing sonnets, Mr W.H.,
> all happiness and that eternity promised by our ever-
> living poet, wisheth the well-wishing adventurer in setting
> forth.

What does this mean? Thorpe appears to be dedicating the *Sonnets* to the author, a Mr W.H. But we know from the prefatory
note that they are 'Shake-speares sonnets' and two of them, bearing Shakespeare's name, had already appeared in 1599. Why then
is the author referred to as Mr W.H.? Thorpe seems to be referring to Shakespeare as Mr W.H. Could W.H. be William
Hall?

This perplexing dedication is the subject of controversy, the
argument concerning the meaning of the word begetter. The
begetter is clearly Mr W.H. 'To the only begetter of these ensuing sonnets, Mr W.H.' But what exactly is a begetter? A
begetter is someone who begets something, as a father begets a
son. Presumably, therefore, the begetter of the *Sonnets* is its
creator, the author. However, as Thorpe tells us that the author
is Shakespeare, and as the begetter is Mr W.H., begetter has
been taken to mean something different. It has been suggested
that in Elizabethan times the word might also mean 'the getter',
one who 'gets' something. If this was the intended usage it would
mean that the begetter of the *Sonnets* was the acquirer, the person who obtained them for the publisher. By this reasoning, Mr
W.H. was merely the procurer of the *Sonnets*.

Historians maintaining this alternative have attempted to identify Mr W.H. Although there have been a number of candidates,
three are the most popular. The first, initiated by the eighteenth-
century scholar Edmund Malone, suggested that the procurer of
the *Sonnets* was a man named Will Hues. Malone arrived at this
conclusion because in Sonnet 20 the word 'Hue' is erroneously
printed with a capital H, while the word 'will' is used as a pun.
Not only has an appropriate Will Hues never been found, but the

argument itself is weak. An examination of the original printing shows that many other words are printed in exactly the same fashion.

Another popular candidate is William Herbert, the Earl of Pembroke. There *were* connections between Shakespeare and Pembroke, but he is unlikely to be W.H. The prefix 'Mr' is an inappropriate form of address to an earl, particularly in a dedication. Moreover, Thorpe actually published another manuscript which included a personal dedication to Pembroke, in which he addresses the earl 'To the Honourable, William, Earl of Pembroke'. It therefore seems improbable that Thorpe would have used 'Mr W.H.' in referring to William Herbert.

The most widely accepted theory is that W.H. was Henry Wriothesley, the Earl of Southampton. Southampton was Shakespeare's patron, to whom he had already dedicated his first published works. But there are two clear objections. First, as with Pembroke, using the title 'Mr' seems an odd way to address an earl. Second, and the most obvious problem, is that the initials are the wrong way around. Subscribers to the Southampton theory offer a variety of explanations, principally that Southampton was a man who 'put his family first', hence the initial for the Christian name comes after the initial for the family name. The best argument for Southampton being W.H., however, is that he is the subject of the *Sonnets*. For this theory to hold water, the word begetter must refer to the inspirer, and not to the creator. In other words, Southampton begot (inspired) the *Sonnets* in the writer's imagination.

We must therefore examine the *Sonnets* in an effort to discover if Southampton really was the subject of the poems.

The *Sonnets* have fired heated debate, as they constitute the only hint at a Shakespeare autobiography to survive. Thus far we have avoided, wherever possible, readings of the plays themselves, focusing instead on the historical evidence. As works that are ostensibly fiction, the plays themselves have often led biographers to erroneous assumptions about the playwright. However, as the *Sonnets* are written in the first person, presumably the author himself, they do present a special case. But do they really reveal anything about the poet's life?

The *Sonnets* consist of two distinct sections. The first series addressed to a young man of great beauty and high station (1–125), the second addressed to a dark and troublesome woman. The scenario is summarised by the author himself in Sonnet 144:

> Two loves I have of comfort and despair,
> Which like two spirits do suggest me still;
> The better angel is a man right fair,
> The worser spirit is a woman, colour'd ill.
>
> To win me soon to hell, my female evil
> Tempteth my better angel from my side,
> And would corrupt my saint to be my devil,
> Wooing his purity with her foul pride.
>
> And whether that my angel be turn'd fiend,
> Suspect I may, yet not directly tell;
> But being both from me, both to each friend,
> I guess one angel in another's hell:
>   Yet this shall I ne'er know, but live in doubt,
>   Till my bad angel fire my good one out.

So we have a young man, with whom the poet is infatuated, and a woman who steals the young man away. The first 125 sonnets concern the 'better angel', the young man, and most are addressed to him directly.

This young man has been identified as Southampton, but before we examine the claim in more detail, we must first establish the relationship between this 'man right fair' and the author. The modern reader does not have to read far before the impression of homosexuality presents itself. Is the author's love for the youth a gay infatuation? The poet certainly uses many descriptions that today would infer sexual appreciation: 'the beauty of your eyes . . . such heavenly touches ne'er touch'd earthly faces'. But this was a time well before the moral revolution of the Victorian era, when male friendships were often expressed without inhibition. Much of the second series of sonnets is addressed to the woman, which seem equally passionate. The first seventeen sonnets all urge the youth to take a wife, which hardly suggests a gay relationship with the author. Even his anger at the woman in the second series is directed at her corrupting influence on his behaviour, not necessarily on his sexuality.

The passionate language can be explained without inference to Shakespeare's sexual preference if the youth is identified as the Earl of Southampton. Southampton was one of the Queen's favourites and extremely vain; and around 1594, when the first series is thought to have been written, Southampton's patronage was sought by many poets. In the early 1590s Southampton was widely acknowledged as the most handsome nobleman at Court, and the poet George Peele wrote of him in identical terms to Shakespeare in his *Anglorum Feriae*. In 1594 Thomas Nashe dedicated his *Jack Wilton* to Southampton, calling him 'a dear lover and cherisher as well of lovers of poets as of the poets themselves'. The language used by Shakespeare may therefore simply reflect his bid to secure patronage. Indeed, the notion that Southampton was the subject of the *Sonnets* is further supported by the similar terms in which Shakespeare writes to him in his *Lucrece* dedication that very year: 'The love I dedicate to your Lordship is without end.'

Returning to the theme of the *Sonnets*, after the youth refuses to take a wife, Sonnet 18 (which begins with the famous line, 'Shall I compare thee to a summer's day?') initiates a series on the tribulations of his relationship with the poet. The threat to their friendship comes from a rival poet, and also the woman of wiles who has designs on the youth. If we compare what is known of Southampton's life, it becomes patently clear that he is indeed the youth in the *Sonnets*.

Southampton's father died two days before his eighth birthday, thus in 1581, at the age of seven, he became the Third Earl of Southampton. Fatherless, he was made ward of State Secretary William Cecil, together with his friend-to-be, Robert Devereux, the Earl of Essex. Southampton was educated at St John's College, Cambridge, where he received an MA, graduating to law school at Gray's Inn. His education also involved a foreign language tutor, the Italian poet John Florio. In 1594 Cecil tried to persuade Southampton to marry his granddaughter Elizabeth Vere, but Southampton refused, and Elizabeth eventually married Lord Strange's brother, the Sixth Earl of Derby.

By 1598 Southampton was working for William Cecil's son Robert in the British embassy in Paris, secretly returning to marry the Queen's lady in waiting, Elizabeth Vernon of Hodnet in Shropshire. As with Ralegh, a few years earlier, the Queen was furious about her favourite's marriage, and ordered the couple arrested. Before long they were released, but Southampton was refused at Court. Embittered, he became closely associated with the Earl of Essex, a relationship that eventually led to his involvement with the abortive Essex rebellion of 1601. Southampton was arrested along with Essex, and narrowly avoided execution through the intervention of William Cecil. The Queen agreed to commute his sentence to life imprisonment, although in 1603 he was set free by the new King, James I.

The *Sonnets* appear to sit with Southampton's life. The series urging him to marry could relate to the proposed marriage to Elizabeth Vere, which would have been an advantageous political manoeuvre. The rival poet may be Barnabe Barnes, a youthful protégé of the earl; Shakespeare even seems to paraphrase Barnes's description of Southampton's eyes. And the temptress, the so-called Dark Lady, could be Elizabeth Vernon. From what is known of her, the description would certainly appear to fit:

> My mistress' eyes are nothing like the sun;
> Coral is far more red than her lips' red
> If snow be white, why then her breasts are dun;
> If hairs be wires, black wires grow on her head.

Elizabeth Vernon had wiry black hair and a deathly pale complexion. If she was the Dark Lady, then she may also have been Shakespeare's mistress for a time; indeed, he addresses her as such in the above passage. Many scholars of literature believe that in his writing Shakespeare is implying that he was in love with the Dark Lady.

Returning to the Thorpe dedication: if the subject of the poem is Southampton, as it certainly seems to be, and if begetter means inspirer, then Mr W.H. is indeed Henry Wriothesley, the Earl of Southampton. But the unanswered question remains – why reverse the initials and why call a lord 'Mr'? There may well be another explanation for the dedication, which has nothing to do with the subject of the *Sonnets*, even if it is Southampton.

Thomas Thorpe's dedication on the cover of the 1609 Shakespeare's
Sonnets. Who is the mysterious 'Mr W.H.'?

TO.THE.ONLIE.BEGETTER.OF.
THESE.INSVING.SONNETS.
Mr.W.H. ALL.HAPPINESSE.
AND.THAT.ETERNITIE.
PROMISED.

BY.

OVR.EVER-LIVING.POET.

WISHETH.

THE.WELL-WISHING.
ADVENTVRER.IN.
SETTING.
FORTH.

T. T.

It is known that Elizabethan writers made considerable use of
double entendre. Greene's 'shake-scene' is a good example, or
Ben Jonson's similar pun on Shakespeare's name in the First
Folio 'shake a stage'. Perhaps Thorpe's word begetter has a similar double meaning, the creator *and* the procurer. However,
since it seems odd to dedicate the works to the man who obtained
them, rather than the poet who wrote them, the obvious solution
is that the begetter is the one who begot the *Sonnets*, in other
words the author. If so, then Mr W.H. *is* the author and hence
William Shakespeare. The begetter in this sense is the parent, as
one who begets a child. An excellent example of Shakespeare

being described as the parent of his works is in the dedication in the First Folio in 1623. In the introduction the dedicatees are reminded that they had shown favour to William Shakespeare in life, and are asked to indulge the plays as they 'have done unto their parent'.

Either way, we come back to Mr W.H. being one and the same as William Shakespeare. If we look again at the dedication, examining the precise way in which it was printed, we may discover what Thorpe is really saying. The lettering is reproduced below exactly as it appeared on Thorpe's original imprint:

TO.THE.ONLIE.BEGGETTER.OF.

THESE.INSVING.SONNETS.

MɼW.H. ALL.HAPPINESSE.

AND.THAT.ETERNITIE.

PROMISED.

BY.

OVR.EVER-LIVING.POET.

WISHETH.

THE.WELL-WISHING.

ADVENTVRER.IN.

SETTING.

FORTH.

T.T.

The use of the initials 'Mr W.H.' seems to suggest that Thomas Thorpe was dedicating the *Sonnets* to someone whose identity he wished to conceal. But perhaps he is also revealing the identity to those who have eyes to see. Setting aside the spelling, which was not yet uniform in Elizabethan times, the first point of note is the odd use of the stop marks. Why insert a full stop (period) after each word? Could this be drawing our attention to some peculiarity, the spaces between the words perhaps? If so, the stop mark is being employed as a space. Yet in one instance Thorpe has also used a genuine space, after the initial H.

MɼW.H. ALL.HAPPINESSE.

There is a genuine space between the H. and ALL and it only

occurs here. Using inverse logic, often employed in cryptography, inferring that Thorpe is telling us that there should really be no space here at all, then the name is MR W.HALL.

Could Thorpe be dedicating the *Sonnets* to the author, William Shakespeare, also known as Mr W. Hall? Is it coincidence that the Cecil agent whom we have suggested as William Shakespeare was using the name William Hall?

Such a suggestion could lead to the accusation of Baconian logic, akin to the supposed cipher on the Shakespeare tomb. However, in that example the resultant anagram could be read in many different ways. As explained earlier, a cipher, to be a cipher, must have only one reading. If our hypothesis is correct, the Thorpe dedication is a straightforward reading, with no further anagrams of replacement of letters.

Indeed, when we look at the dedication, absolutely nothing is lost from the message by removing the word 'all':

> To the only begetter of these ensuing sonnets, Mr
> W.Hall, happiness and that eternity promised by our
> ever-living poet, wisheth the well-wishing adventurer in
> setting forth.

'To the begetter . . . all happiness' or 'To the begetter . . . happiness'. The text still flows, while losing nothing from the meaning. The argument could be taken further to suggest that Thorpe is referring to Mr W.H. as both 'an ever-living poet' and 'the well-wishing adventurer'. This would certainly be true if Shakespeare doubled as an agent for the Secret Service.

Moreover, a very similar inversion cipher – using dots to indicate spaces, and spaces to indicate a close-up of letters – appeared in a pamphlet published by Thorpe's printer George Eld in 1608. Written by Thomas Hariot, it included the description of a cipher message sent by Galileo to the astronomer Kepler, concerning his telescope observation that Venus has phases similar to the moon. The cipher message, plus its solution, is almost certain to have been known to Thorpe. Surely it is no coincidence that a cipher printed on one of Thorpe's partner's publications just a year before should provide us with the name W. HALL when applied to the dedication in the *Sonnets*.

It is quite possible that Hariot's paper gave Thorpe the idea of using this simple cryptogram. Furthermore, it had become something of a fad for writers of dedications and epigraphs to allude to the dedicatee in cipher. For example, an anonymous poem appeared in 1590, containing an interesting acrostic:

> Shall honour, fame, and titles of renown,
> In clods of clay be thus inclosed still?
> Rather will I, though wiser wits may frown,
> For to enlarge his frame extend my skill.
> Right, gentle reader, be it known to thee,
> A famous knight doth here interred lie,
> Noble by birth, renowned for policy,
> Confounding foes, which wrought our jeopardy.
> In foreign countries their intents he knew,
> Such was his zeal to do his country good,
> When dangers would by enemies ensure,
> As well as they themselves he understood.
> Launch forth ye muses into streams of praise,
> Sing, and sound forth praise-worthy harmony;
> In England death cut off his dismal days,
> Not wronged by death, but by false treachery.
> Grudge not at this imperfect epitaph;
> Herein I have expressed my simple skill,
> As first-fruits proceeding from a graffe:
> Make then a better whosoever will.

This was written in memory of someone apparently unnamed, but the name of the person to whom it referred was hidden in the poem. The first letter in each line, read from top to bottom, SIR FRANCIS WALSINGHAM.

If Thorpe's dedication is an allusion to Shakespeare's alias, how could he have known of this alias? One possibility is via Ben Jonson, who, as we shall see, appears to have become Shakespeare's close friend. Thorpe was already Jonson's publisher, with whom he spent considerable time. Jonson has long been suspected of being a Secret Service agent. It is also known from contemporary accounts that Jonson was a man who had a loose tongue.

Having established that Shakespeare's strange double life could be explained by activities as a Secret Service agent, we now turn to the possibility that he became embroiled in a conspiracy to defeat Sir Walter Ralegh.

Summary

A Secret Service agent known as William Hall appears a number of times in the Secretary of State's records of the 1590s. Each time the name occurs there is a link to William Shakespeare. Was William Hall a cover name used by Shakespeare as a Secret Service operative?

1. On 28 August 1593, a Secret Service communique was despatched from William Cecil to his agent Edward Kelly in Prague. The contents of the letter are unknown, although the payment for the messenger was recorded by the Chamber Treasurer at the time. Cecil's clerk's record of this letter names the courier as William Hall. Under various spellings, the same name occurs in association with the Secret Service on a number of occasions, and each time there is a connection to Shakespeare. Was William Hall a cover name used by William Shakespeare as a Secret Service agent?

2. On 17 June 1592 a 'Will Hall' was paid £10 for spying with Anthony Munday, and on 19 March 1596 the Chamber Treasurer paid £15 to 'Hall and Wayte' for 'messages' conveyed from the Netherlands to the Secretary of State. If this is the same Hall, there are two associations with colleagues of Shakespeare. First, it is known that Shakespeare was working with Munday around 1592 – the *Sir Thomas More* play dates from around that time, and Munday's troupe, The Lord Admiral's Men, had already amalgamated with Lord Strange's Men. Second, Shakespeare *was* associated with a man named Wayte in 1596, which is exactly the year in which the rolls of the Queen's Bench record that a William Wayte craved sureties of the peace against William Shakespeare.

3. Shakespeare working as a courier might explain the apparent knowledge of foreign culture exhibited in many of his plays. Indeed, on one occasion when the agent Hall surfaces, he has just

returned from Denmark. On 2 October 1601 a 'Willm Halle' is mentioned by the Secretary of State's clerk as having returned with intelligence from Denmark. This presents another possible link with Shakespeare. *Hamlet* was written around 1601 (it was registered in 1602), the same time that Halle returned from Denmark. Could Shakespeare have acquired a first-hand experience of the Danish Court, which inspired him to write the play, because he had recently travelled there incognito?

4. If Shakespeare was using an alias to cover Secret Service activities, he would not have been the only dramatist to do so. Anthony Munday, for example, used the name George Grimes as a Secret Service agent. As a popular playwright, Munday was a well-known figure, so was obviously not attempting to conceal his identity. Rather the name Grimes was used as a false account, a name for the records of payment. A further case for Hall being Shakespeare is the choice of name. Munday, for instance, seems to have used the name Grimes as his godfather was called Matthew Grimes. Shakespeare's family in Stratford seems to have been closely attached to a local family called Hall. Indeed, Shakespeare's daughter eventually married one of this family, physician John Hall. Moreover, the Christian name is the same – William.

5. Evidence that Shakespeare actually used such a cover name appears in the dedication of the 1609 edition of the Shakespeare *Sonnets*. The cover dedication by the publisher Thomas Thorpe reads: 'To the only begetter of these ensuing sonnets, Mr W.H., all happiness and that eternity promised by our ever-living poet, wisheth the well-wishing adventurer in setting forth.' Here Thorpe appears to be dedicating the *Sonnets* to the author, a Mr W.H. But we know from the prefatory note that they are 'Shakespears sonnets', and two of them bearing Shakespeare's name had already appeared in 1599. Thorpe appears to be referring to Shakespeare as Mr W.H. Could W.H. be William Hall?

6. An unusual spacing between the 'W.H.' and the word 'all' in the dedication's original printing suggests that the second initial and the following word should be read together – Mr W.Hall. An

identical procedure to conceal information appeared in a pamphlet published by Thorpe's printer George Eld in 1608. Written by Thomas Hariot, it included the description of a cipher message sent by Galileo to the astronomer Kepler, concerning his telescope observation that Venus has phases similar to the moon. The cipher message, plus its solution, is almost certain to have been known to Thorpe. Surely it is no coincidence that a cipher printed in one of Thorpe's partner's publications just the year before should produce the name W. Hall when applied to the dedication in the *Sonnets*.

Chapter 15

The Bye Plot

Elizabeth I died on 24 March 1603 and King James of Scotland became King of England. William Cecil had died in 1598 and his son Robert had already taken his place as Secretary of State. It was largely because of Robert's influence that James had become King. Elizabeth had no children and, as the son of Mary Queen of Scots, James was the next in line of succession. But as king of a foreign country, few believed that the accession would be a smooth transition. However, although James had been brought up as a Calvinist Protestant, his wife Anne was a Catholic, and he was eventually accepted in the hope that he would unite both religious factions. But Cecil had other plans. Like his father before him, Robert Cecil was vehemently anti-Catholic.

Although James was both learned and intelligent, he was easily manipulated, a process to which he had long been accustomed. He was only a year old when his mother was deposed in Scotland and he became King. Now, at thirty-seven, he had become James I of England and, for the first time, the whole of mainland Britain was ruled by one person. Cecil, however, intended the real power to remain in his own hands, and he was able to achieve this aim, serving as James's chief minister until his death in 1612. Under Cecil's influence, James reversed any surviving policies of leniency towards Catholicism.

When the new King did not act as expected and repeal the anti-Catholic laws (in particular the recusancy fines, which were imposed on Catholics who failed to attend Church of England services) there were widespread fears of an uprising. Cecil's initial priority was to cement his own position, and the first step was to rid himself of his father's old rival Walter Ralegh. Ralegh had a popular following and, as a religious liberal, he was the natural focus for many potential rebels.

On Cecil's advice, Ralegh was called before the King at Cecil's home at Burghley House, where tradition holds that James greeted him with the words 'I have heard rawly of thee'. Ralegh was dismissed as Captain of the Guard, Warden of the Mines, and Governor of Jersey. He was even evicted from his London home, Durham House, and shortly afterwards his Sherborne estate was seized and given to the King's favourite Robert Carr.

Cecil's other priority was to discredit the Catholics, and in the summer of 1603 an opportunity arose for him to kill two birds with one stone. In July Cecil received intelligence regarding a conspiracy to assassinate the King and his sons, and place on the throne James's daughter Princess Elizabeth. Elizabeth was only seven years old, and evidently the plan was to use her as puppet for a Catholic regime.

Known as the Bye Plot, it seems to have been the brainchild of the Catholic priest Father Watson, who hired two assassins, the experienced soldier Sir Griffin Markham and a mysterious Mr Copley. Another conspirator was the Catholic landowner George Brooke, recently returned from France with news that a Catholic army was prepared to invade once the King was dead. Brooke's brother Henry, Lord Cobham, was also recruited into the plot, and through him Walter Ralegh became involved. At his trial Ralegh vigorously denied the charges, but the evidence weighs against him.

Cobham was on intimate terms with both Ralegh and Henry Percy, and Ralegh certainly had reasons for wanting the King and the present government removed. Although Ralegh was no Catholic, many of his associates were, including Henry Percy and Lord Cobham. If the various allegations are to be believed, Ralegh intended to transform a Catholic plot into a secular plot, benefiting all religious groups by removing an intolerant regime. There were certainly many intellectuals, including Percy and Hariot, to whom the notion would appeal. Yet it is the plan to enthrone Princess Elizabeth which suggests more than simply Catholic interest. Elizabeth had become the focus of attention for wealthy Protestants at the heart of Europe.

Around 1600 the Wittenberg theologian Simon Studion

Genealogy showing Shakespeare's relationship to the Gunpowder Plotters.

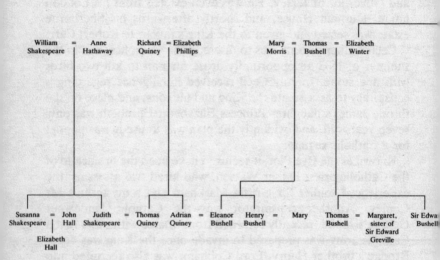

The Bye Plot

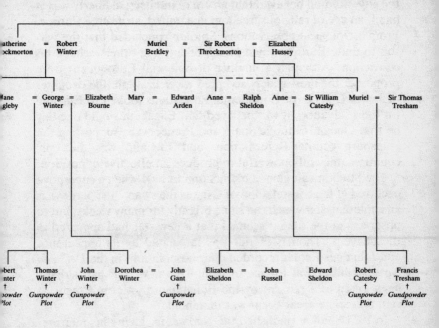

attracted a mass of cult followers with his ideas of a new age of enlightenment. His work circulated widely, particularly in Prague, having considerable influence among the intelligentsia of the city. Studion believed that an era of intellectual liberty was at hand, an age of religious freedom in a united, strife-free Europe. From astrological observations, Studion concluded that the person to unite Europe would be a woman, and others echoed his conviction. Although a number of potential Euroqueens were proposed, the most widely accepted was Elizabeth, the daughter of James I. As most Continental Protestants looked to England for their salvation, it was believed that Elizabeth would one day be that Queen. Catholic Spain and France were supporting the Hapsburg counter-Reformation, and England was the only country sufficiently powerful to produce an effective opposition.

The Studion cult gained momentum in 1604 when a supernova occurred in the constellation of Cygnus the swan. A supernova is an exploding star which can shine brightly for many weeks, but to observers at the time it seemed that a new star had appeared in the heavens. Thomas Hariot was fascinated by its appearance and Johannes Kepler recorded their observations in the *De Stella Nove*, published at Prague in 1606. The 'new star' had already been taken as a portent by the Bohemian mystics in Prague, a sign that some great event was imminent.

In 1605 Studion published the *Naometria*, giving his interpretation of what the star foretold – the new age was at hand. Indeed, the belief in Princess Elizabeth as the European unifier continued for over a decade. In 1613, when Elizabeth married Frederick V of the Palatinate, Studion's followers urged the couple to invade Bohemia. Fascinated by mysticism, Frederick rashly agreed, only to initiate a futile war which lasted for thirty years. After 1604 a number of mystical and occult texts followed Studion's original, announcing that the new age had finally arrived. Like the *Naometria*, these pamphlets often included illustrations depicting Elizabeth riding on horseback to oppose tyranny.

The Bye Plot to enthrone Elizabeth in 1603 would therefore have appealed to many influential academics in the German and Central European states. Both Ralegh and Cobham were aware of the *Naometria* and its popularity in Prague; indeed, Cobham's brother, George Brooke, had recently been in Prague attempting to secure finance for the plot. Evidently the money was found and was to be channelled through what had been Ralegh's island of Jersey.

Some time in June Robert Cecil became aware of the plot, and a few weeks later Brooke was arrested, followed closely by Cobham. Under interrogation Cobham denounced Ralegh and he, too, was arrested. At Ralegh's trial in mid-July Cobham confessed his guilt, but Ralegh pleaded innocence. Besides Cobham's confession, obtained under torture, there was no real evidence against Ralegh but, according to contemporary legal practice in a treason trial, the onus was on the accused to prove his innocence.

To this day it remains a mystery exactly how the plot was discovered. The official explanation was that a Jesuit priest, Father Blackwell, betrayed Father Watson to the Bishop of London, believing that the plot would jeopardise a proposed peace with Spain. The truth is probably alluded to in a letter of 3 July, a communiqué sent to Robert Cecil from a Secret Service operative named Parrot, assuring the Secretary of State that the information he (Cecil) had received was genuine. In the letter, now preserved in the Cecil papers at Hatfield House, Parrot states, 'I believe in all truth that you may proceed'. Proceed with what? Since the next action Cecil takes is to arrest Brooke, it seems safe to assume there is a connection.

Although next to nothing is known about Parrot, his name does appear on other occasions as an informant. In one instance, he is working for Cecil in the summer of 1597 as an agent planted in Marshalsea Prison to spy on the imprisoned Jesuit Father Barkworth. Interestingly, he ends up spying on Shakespeare's friend Ben Jonson. In that year Jonson was imprisoned in Marshalsea for writing the seditious comedy *The Isle of Dogs*. According to Jonson's friend, the Scottish poet William Drummond, Jonson recounted that they placed in his cell 'two damned villains, to catch advantage of him', that is to spy on him. Jonson had been forewarned by one of the jailers, whom he seems to have befriended. According to Drummond, Jonson referred to these two spies as 'Pooly and Parrot'.

Is this man another familiar agent? Could Pooly have been

Robert Poley? It is certainly known that he worked for the Cecils around 1597, and had previously worked for Francis Walsingham in a similar capacity as a prison informant, in the Tower of London following the Babington Plot.

A number of historians have suggested that Jonson may himself have been recruited into the Secret Service. For some reason, Jonson claimed to have been converted to Catholicism during his imprisonment, although after his release his new-found pretensions were ignored by the Privy Council, implying that he may have been working on their behalf. There were even rumours that he befriended the Gunpowder Plot's Robert Catesby in order to spy on him. As it is quite possible that Jonson was recruited by Parrot and/or Poley at some time after his imprisonment, was Jonson also embroiled in the Bye Plot?

Jonson certainly knew Ralegh, as he enjoyed his patronage for a time and he also worked with another School of Night man, George Chapman. (Together, Chapman and Jonson wrote *Eastward Ho*.) Could Jonson have been the informant to whom Parrot refers in his letters? It is unlikely that the depth of Jonson's association with Ralegh would have been sufficient to have brought him knowledge of any conspiracy against the government. However, the inside man may have been Jonson's friend William Shakespeare – if, that is, Shakespeare was the spy William Hall. Hall had already worked with Parrot before.

On the occasion that William Hall received payment for a trip to Denmark in 1601, Parrot is recorded in the Chamber Treasurer's account as receiving the sum of £10 for 'a message conveyed'. It therefore seems that Hall and Parrot had travelled to Denmark together. The only other mention of Parrot as a courier is also in association with William Hall. On 19 March 1596 Parrot was paid £15 for his services, along with Hall and Wayte.

Returning to the Bye Plot, we know that Parrot advised Cecil to proceed with what can be surmised as the arrest of the conspirators. He also confirms that the information conveyed to Cecil by someone else was trustworthy. Could this someone else have been William Hall? Not only had Parrot and Hall worked together on two previous occasions, but the final mention of Hall was on 29 June, just five days before the Parrot message to Cecil.

In a despatch from Cecil to Ralegh's sworn enemy, the King's favourite Lord Henry Howard, Cecil assured Howard that he need not worry about Ralegh gaining influence with the new monarch. He also states that 'Ralegh's man' informed him that Ralegh would be his own undoing through 'some untimely interest'. In other words, Cecil had someone close to Ralegh informing him of some scheme in which Ralegh was involved. This must surely be the same informant referred to in the Parrot message.

On the very day Cecil wrote to Howard, he ordered the Chamber treasurer to pay £20 to 'Will Halle'. Usual payments for courier work were registered as such, and payments made for 'other business' – usually for supplying information – were not specified. Hall being paid for unspecified 'other business', on exactly the same day that Cecil admits to receiving information from 'Walter Ralegh's man', is persuasive evidence that Hall was indeed that man. But if, as we have argued, William Hall was really Shakespeare, how would he have learned of the Bye Plot?

We have already examined the possible links between Shakespeare and Ralegh, but what of the other Bye Plot conspirators? Shakespeare almost certainly knew Lord Cobham. When the Burbage company's patron Lord Hunsdon died on 22 July 1596, Cobham's father (William, the Eleventh Earl Cobham) had for a time replaced him as Lord Chamberlain until his death in March 1597.) Cobham had closely overseen a Court performance of the Burbage players in December 1596. There is also a strong possibility that Henry Percy was involved in the Bye Plot, again someone with whom Shakespeare may have been associated in the School of Night.

The argument for Percy's involvement in the Bye Plot is the similarity of the conspiracy to the Gunpowder Plot the following year, a conspiracy for which he was eventually convicted. Not only was the planned uprising almost identical, but both plots had the unusual idea of placing Elizabeth on the throne.

The Gunpowder Plot of 1605 was led by Robert Catesby, a country squire from Ashby St Ledgers in Northamptonshire. Catesby had convinced a number of close friends that his plan to blow up the King and his ministers at the State opening of Parliament in November was feasible. Eventually, a storage cellar was rented beneath the House of Lords, and barrel-loads of gunpowder were smuggled in. One of the plotters, Guy Fawkes, volunteered to remain behind to light the fuses and make his escape at the last moment.

Catesby and a group of some forty others met at Dunchurch in Warwickshire, where they planned to ride to Coombe Abbey, near Coventry, and seize the Princess Elizabeth who was staying there with her tutor William Craven. But the plan went disastrously wrong. On the night before the opening of Parliament on 5 November, the King's soldiers broke in and arrested Fawkes. Learning of the plot's discovery, Catesby tried in vain to incite a rebellion among the Catholics of the Midlands. Having failed, the conspirators were eventually surrounded at Holbeach House near Wolverhampton, the home of fellow conspirator Stephen Lyttleton, where Catesby was gunned down and others arrested.

Cecil seems to have known of the plot all along. Seeing a chance to discredit the Catholics irreparably, he appears to have secretly encouraged it. If Catholics were discovered about to murder the entire government, it would outrage the whole nation. It is remarkable how the plotters failed to recognise the warning signs. Originally they were attempting to dig a tunnel under Parliament from a nearby building, but when this proved impossible the conspiracy was abandoned. At that precise moment a cellar directly below the House of Lords was up for rent. Cecil almost certainly arranged for the cellar to be made available, wishing to foil the conspirators at the eleventh hour.

If, as many historians suspect, the Gunpowder Plot was orchestrated by Cecil, his plan worked. The public outrage was such that resultant reprisals against the Catholics caused them to lose basic human rights for the next two centuries. Moreover, the annual burning of a Guy Fawkes effigy survives to this day. Initially, however, it had been an effigy of the Pope that was thrown on to the bonfire, accompanied by the famous chant that ends with the promise Cecil made to the nation on the day the conspirators were hanged: 'Gunpowder treason will *never* be forgot.'

The Bye Plot was virtually a blueprint for the Gunpowder Plot. Except for the drastic plan to murder the entire government, the main details are identical: a rebellion in Warwickshire and the capture of Princess Elizabeth. It has even been argued that there was method in such apparent madness. Who would expect exactly the same plot twice? Since one is so similar to the other, historians have suggested that both were the brainchild of one man, some proposing Henry Percy. Percy was certainly implicated in the Gunpowder Plot and, if Ralegh really was involved in the Bye Plot, then Percy may also have been. If so, it is very possible that Catesby and the known Gunpowder Plotters would also have been linked to the Bye Plot, standing ready for the planned uprising in the Midlands and the seizure of Elizabeth.

There were probably many involved in the Bye Plot who were allowed to remain at large. Cecil's investigations following the plot were almost non-existent. Once he had Ralegh in the dock, he seemed to lose interest in following up any further accusations made by Brooke and Cobham. Cecil probably wanted the conspirators free until he could manipulate them into his master-plan, the Gunpowder Plot the following year.

Returning to Shakespeare's possible involvement, he may well have known the key participants. In the Bye Plot, there were two main conspirators, Ralegh and Cobham, and a third possible, Percy. As we have argued, Shakespeare seems to have been close to both Ralegh and Percy, and Cobham appears to have been his patron for a time. If the Gunpowder Plotters were also involved, he probably knew them as well. In the Gunpowder Plot the chief conspirators included Midlanders Robert Catesby, Robert and Thomas Winter, Francis Tresham and members of the Throckmorton family, relatives of Ralegh's wife Elizabeth. Incredibly, Shakespeare was eventually related, through the marriages of his daughters, to all of these men. Since these families were so closely connected, Shakespeare could well have been on intimate terms with all the major Gunpowder conspirators.

One point is certain. Following James's accession, Shakespeare and his company received unparalleled royal favour. Like his father, in the early 1590s, Robert Cecil would have been in a unique position to influence the King's favour in payment for services rendered. In May 1603 the Burbage players were given royal patronage, and thereafter performed as The King's Men, making them the premier company of the day. Later that year, following the Bye Plot, they were invited to appear before the King at Wilton in Wiltshire, the home of William, Earl of Pembroke. Pembroke was a close friend of the King and supposedly the richest man in England; and along with his brother, the Earl of Montgomery, he became one of the dedicatees of Shakespeare's First Folio in 1623. Pembroke and Shakespeare must have become close because the dedication reads:

> Since your lordships have been pleased to think these trifles something, heretofore; and have prosecuted both them, and their author living, with so much favour; we hope, that . . . you will use the like indulgence toward them, you have done unto their parent.

The Burbage players became the King's favourites. In the winter of 1603–4 they were called upon for eight royal performances, the following year eleven, and by 1611 an astonishing twenty times. As for Walter Ralegh, after his trial at Winchester in 1603 he was imprisoned in the Tower of London for thirteen years.

In conclusion, the agent responsible for the betrayal of the Bye Plot was almost certainly William Hall, a man of whom nothing is known – not his home town, his age, his occupation or any significant detail. The name therefore is almost certainly an alias. As everyone Hall seems to be involved with was associated with Shakespeare, and the printer Thorpe seems to refer to Shakespeare as W. Hall, it seems likely that William Hall was an alias for William Shakespeare. If so, Shakespeare was the man seemingly responsible for Ralegh's imprisonment, a responsibility for which he may ultimately have paid with his life.

Summary

In 1603, when James I succeeded to the throne, Walter Ralegh was convicted of a plot to murder the King. The chief informant against the conspirators appears to have been the agent William Hall.

1. Elizabeth I died on 24 March 1603 and King James of Scotland became King of England. William Cecil had died in 1598 and his son Robert had already taken his place as Secretary of State. It was largely because of Robert's influence that James had become King. Under Cecil's influence, James reversed any surviving policies of leniency towards the Roman Catholics.

2. Cecil's initial priority was to cement his own position, the first step being to rid himself of his father's old rival Walter Ralegh. Ralegh had a popular following and, as a religious liberal, was the natural focus for many potential rebels. On Cecil's advice, Ralegh was dismissed as Captain of the Guard, Warden of the Mines, and Governor of Jersey.

3. Cecil's other priority was to discredit the Catholics, and in the summer of 1603 an opportunity arose for him to kill two birds with one stone. In June Cecil received intelligence pertaining to a conspiracy to assassinate the King and his sons, and enthrone James's daughter Princess Elizabeth. Elizabeth was only seven years old and the plan was evidently to use her as puppet for a Catholic regime.

4. Known as the Bye Plot, the plan seems to have been contrived by the Jesuit priest Father Watson and the Catholic landowner George Brooke. Brooke's brother Henry, Lord Cobham, was also recruited into the plot, and through him Walter Ralegh became involved. At his trial Ralegh vigorously denied the charges, but the evidence weighs against him.

5. Sometime in July Robert Cecil became aware of the plot. A few weeks later Brooke was arrested, followed closely by Cobham. Under interrogation, Cobham denounced Ralegh and he too was arrested. It has remained a mystery exactly how the plot was discovered. However, the answer is probably contained in a letter of 3 July, sent to Robert Cecil from a Secret Service operative named Parrot, assuring the Secretary of State that the information he (Cecil) had received was genuine. In the letter Parrot states 'I believe in all truth that you may proceed.' Since Cecil then arrests Brooke, the letter probably referred to the Bye Plot.

6. Parrot seems to have worked with William Hall. On the occasion that Hall received payment for a trip to Denmark in 1601, Parrot is recorded in the Chamber Treasurer's account as receiving the sum of £10 for 'a message conveyed'. It therefore seems that Hall and Parrot had travelled to Denmark together. The

only other mention of Parrot as a courier is also in association with William Hall. On 19 March 1596 Parrot was paid £15 for his services, along with Hall and Wayte.

7. Parrot advised Cecil to proceed with what was seemingly the arrest of the Bye Plot conspirators. He also confirms that the information conveyed to Cecil by someone else was trustworthy. Could this someone else have been William Hall? Not only had Parrot and Hall worked together on two previous occasions, but the final mention of Hall was just five days before the Parrot message to Cecil.

8. In a despatch from Cecil to Ralegh's sworn enemy, the King's favourite Lord Henry Howard, Cecil assured Howard that he need not worry about Ralegh gaining influence with the new monarch. He also states that 'Ralegh's man' informed him that Ralegh would be his own undoing through 'some untimely interest'. In other words, Cecil had someone close to Ralegh informing him of some scheme in which Ralegh was involved. This must surely be the same informant referred to in the Parrot message.

9. On the very day Cecil wrote to Howard, he ordered the Chamber treasurer to pay £20 to 'Will Halle'. Usual payments for courier work were registered as such, and payments made for 'other business' – usually for supplying information – were not specified. Hall being paid for unspecified 'other business' on exactly the same day that Cecil admits to receiving information from 'Walter Ralegh's man' is persuasive evidence that Hall was indeed that man.

10. Following James's accession, Shakespeare and his company received unparalleled royal favour. In May 1603 the Burbage players were given royal patronage, and thereafter performed as The King's Men, making them the premier company of the day. Later that year, following the Bye Plot, they were invited to appear before the King at Wilton in Wiltshire, the home of William, Earl of Pembroke. Like his father, in the early 1590s, Robert Cecil would have been in a unique position to influence the King's favour in payment for services rendered.

11. The Burbage players became the King's favourites. In the winter of 1603–4 they were called upon for eight royal performances, the following year eleven, and by 1611 an astonishing twenty times. As for Walter Ralegh, after his trial at Winchester in 1603 he was imprisoned in the Tower of London for thirteen years.

Chapter 16

The Final Years

We now arrive at the mystery of Shakespeare's final years. Although Secret Service activities might explain the non-awareness in Stratford of Shakespeare's accomplishments during his career, it would not account for the same situation when he returned there permanently in the last years of his life. Why is there still a complete lack of visible recognition? An investigation into this enigma may also provide a solution to three further Shakespeare mysteries: why there is no contemporary portrait, a lack of literary references in his will, and the writing difficulty apparent from his signature.

Shakespeare's illustrious career seems to have ended abruptly with the burning down of the Globe Theatre on 29 June 1613. The play was a historical drama on the life of Henry VIII, and during the final act an attempt at special effects went disastrously wrong. Theatre-goer Sir Henry Wotton provides us with the only surviving eyewitness account:

> Now, King Henry making a masque at the Cardinal Wolsey's house, and certain chambers being shot off at his entry, some of the paper, or other stuff, wherewith one of them was stopped, did light on the thatch, where being thought at first but an idle smoke, and their eyes more attentive to the show, it kindled inwardly, and ran round like a train, consuming within less than an hour the whole house to the very ground.

After the Globe was gutted, the shareholders all paid around £60 each for the rebuilding, except Shakespeare. Since there is no record of Shakespeare's contribution, he probably sold his interest in the theatre at this time, accounting for the absence of the shares in his will. As the will makes no reference to the Blackfriars shares, it must be assumed that he also sold these shares. But why should Shakespeare suddenly relinquish his stake in both theatres, especially when he had recently bought a new house in London?

Three months before the fire, on 10 March, Shakespeare purchased a house at Puddle Wharf, near the Blackfriars Theatre, for £140. It had belonged to a Henry Walker. Described as a minstrel, he was probably a theatre colleague. Evidently this was the first time Shakespeare had bought his own home in London, indicating his intention to spend more time in the proximity of the theatre. But he failed to move in and rented the building to a John Robinson. Shakespeare still owned the property, as he eventually bequeathed it to his daughter Susanna. Why the apparent change of mind? Since Shakespeare apparently wrote no more plays, left the theatre scene and moved from London after the Globe burned down, the fire seems to have been a pivotal turning point in his life.

The destruction of the Globe was undoubtedly a tragedy, but does it satisfactorily account for Shakespeare's immediate retirement? It seems unlikely. It was not the end of the world for the Burbage company, nor its playwrights. The Globe was rebuilt and the Blackfriars Theatre continued to prosper. That Shakespeare bought a house on the north bank of the Thames, near the Blackfriars Theatre, and not on the south bank, closer to the Globe, suggests that he himself considered Blackfriars the more lucrative of the two. Yet the Globe fire, coinciding precisely with Shakespeare's sudden retirement, seems to indicate an interrelationship between the two events. Perhaps a life's work perished in the blaze. This would certainly explain the lack of manuscripts in Shakespeare's will. But thirty-seven of his plays survived, and all but one, *Pericles*, were later preserved in the First Folio. As far as is known, this accounts for all the works. It seems likely that there is another explanation for Shakespeare's retirement, one that may be alluded to in the introductions of the 1623 First Folio.

In their prefatory introduction, Shakespeare's fellow actors Heminge and Condell write:

It has been a thing, we confess, worthy to have been wished, that the author himself had lived to have set forth, and overseen his own writings. But since it hath been ordained otherwise, and he, by death, departed from that right, we pray you do not envy his friends, the office of their care, and pain, to have collected and published them. And so to have published them, as where before you were abused with diverse, stolen, and surreptitious copies; maimed, and deformed by the frauds and stealths of injurious impostors that exposed them. Even those, are now offered to your view cured, and perfect of their limbs; and all the rest, absolute in their numbers, as he conceived them. Who as he was a happy imitator of nature, was a most gentle expresser of it. His mind and hand went together: and what he thought, he uttered with that easiness, that we have scarce received from him a blot in his papers. But it is not our province, who only gathers his works, and give them to you, to praise him. It is yours that read him. And there we hope, to your divers capacities, you will find enough, both to draw, and hold you: for his wit can no more lie hid, than it could be lost. Read him therefore; and again, and again. And if then you do not like him, surely you are in some danger, not to understand him. And so we leave you to other of his friends, whom if you need, can be your guides: if you need them not, you can lead yourselves, and others. And such readers we wish him.

Here we learn that Shakespeare had been defrauded, that his plays were stolen, and that he had been the victim of some grave injustice. The sense is one of sorrow for an unhappy Shakespeare, having been abused and misunderstood. This hardly appears to resemble the Shakespeare who had, two decades earlier, entertained the King and won the praise of England's wealthiest man. Since he appears to have been phenomenally successful before the second decade of the seventeenth century, the passage must be alluding to later events. It certainly implies that his retirement was sullen and miserable. Perhaps some legal injustice following the Globe fire had resulted in Shakespeare's disenchantment with the theatre scene. But his will indicates that he was anything but poor, and no one is known to have stolen the rights to his works.

Two words are employed in an unusual context in the above passage, which may provide a clue to Shakespeare's predicament. Heminge and Condell say that Shakespeare was 'maimed and deformed by the frauds and stealths of injurious impostors'. What is their meaning of 'maimed and deformed'? The phrase appears an odd way of describing the alteration of his works – seemingly the meaning implied. Also, there is no surviving evidence that Shakespeare's works were ever published or performed in any way other than they appear in the First Folio. Were Heminge and Condell making an oblique reference to something about Shakespeare and not the plays? Could the playwright himself have been maimed and deformed? Had Shakespeare been seriously injured in the Globe fire? Perhaps he had rushed into the flaming theatre, in a desperate attempt to save his precious manuscripts, and instead been terribly burned.

If Shakespeare was disabled it might have compelled him to withdraw from public life. He certainly seems to have kept to himself in Stratford after 1612. Aside from some minor involvement in the matter of land enclosures in 1614, there is no longer any record of his usual business transactions.

A further indication that Shakespeare had been injured in (or around the time of) the fire is fuelled by the mystery of his will. The will was drawn up by Shakespeare's executor Thomas Russell, stepfather of the poet Leonard Digges. It is difficult to imagine Shakespeare not writing his own will unless, for some reason, he was unable to do so. Was there some physical restraint that made writing almost impossible? We have seen how his surviving signatures, all post-1612, appear to be written by an incompetent and unsteady hand. Some disability seems a rational explanation for Shakespeare's weak and inconsistent signature. Having lost the ability to write would certainly explain Shakespeare's complete departure from the theatre, as cruel an infliction as Beethoven's eventual deafness.

But Shakespeare may have sustained even greater injury. Heminge and Condell speak of Shakespeare being maimed *and* deformed. Indeed, some manner of facial deformity is hinted at by Ben Jonson in his eulogy on Shakespeare in the First Folio. For some reason, Jonson draws attention to Shakespeare's portrait, reproduced on the cover:

> This Figure, that thou here seest put
> It was for gentle Shakespeare cut.

In Elizabethan context the word 'figure' means 'feign'. Accordingly, Jonson is telling us that this is not Shakespeare's true appearance. Admittedly, the picture appears to be a crude caricature, but Jonson seems to imply much more when he continues:

> Wherein the Graver had a strife
> With Nature, to out-do the life.

The engraver of the portrait had a strife with nature, he had not portrayed what he saw. He had outdone life, made it better than life. There can be no doubt that this is exactly what Jonson means, as these two lines are taken from Shakespeare's *Venus and Adonis*. In Shakespeare's poem, the author is speaking of a painter of a horse who seeks to improve on nature. So why should the engraver try to improve on Shakespeare, unless he was in some way unusual in appearance or disfigured?

As if to ensure his readership fully understands Shakespeare's cruel affliction, Jonson continues to labour the point:

> O, could he but have drawn his wit
> As in brass, as he hath hit
> His face; the print would then surpass
> All that was ever writ in brass.
> But, since he cannot, Reader, look
> Not on his picture, but his book.

Here Jonson is further suggesting that we should not look upon Shakespeare's face, literally that we should not judge a book by its cover.

Shakespeare's disfigurement may also address another mystery of his life. Why is there no authentic portrait, when portraits have survived of many comparable dramatists of the time? Perhaps Shakespeare destroyed all record of his former appearance in a fit of depression, as Thomas Hariot had done when afflicted with cancer of the nose in the 1620s.

This brings us to the crucial point: why no one in Stratford appears to have known of Shakespeare's poetry, his plays and his former glory, on his return home. If he had been disfigured or otherwise deformed, he might have refused to socialise, confining himself to a sullen, hermit-like existence. Moreover, if he could no longer write, he may have decried his own work, even eradicated whatever original material he still possessed. Although this is pure speculation, few logical alternatives present themselves. Something along these lines must have occurred. Only those who had known him in London later praised him, whilst Stratford completely ignored him.

It seems certain that Shakespeare was inflicted by some physical ailment after 1612, even if this was not a result of the Globe fire. Regardless of the fire, he already appears to have been suffering in some way. Many critics believe that Shakespeare's last plays exhibited symptoms of a nervous breakdown, drawing attention to the loose and long-winded style of his writing. In his final play *The Tempest*, written around 1611, there is evidence that Shakespeare was already preoccupied with thoughts of retirement. The principal character, the magician Prospero, hopes to avoid damnation by destroying his magic staff and his book of spells:

> I'll break my staff,
> Bury it certain fathoms in the earth.
> And deeper than did ever plummet sound,
> I'll drown my book.

Shakespeare seems to have been haunted by the words of Christopher Marlowe. In Marlowe's play *Doctor Faustus*, Faustus renounces his occult life in the hope of salvation. He also promises to burn his books of magic:

> Ugly Hell, gape not! Come not, Lucifer!
> I'll burn my books.

But it is too late for Faustus, for these are his last lines before his descent into hell.

Had Shakespeare burned his books, perhaps cast them into the River Thames or the Avon? As the near-final words of the principal character in his last play concern the destruction of books, this must at least indicate that Shakespeare was considering downing his pen once and for all; or breaking it, if this is the symbolism of the staff. There is evidence of paranoia in Shakespeare's last days. His tomb inscription, for instance:

> Cursed be he that moves my bones.

All the above points, coupled with Heminge and Condell's reference to Shakespeare's misery, certainly suggest substantial problems in the playwright's final years. But however Shakespeare perceived himself by the time he died, his closest surviving colleagues finally came out of the closet and openly praised him. In the First Folio Ben Jonson writes:

> Oh sweet swan of Avon, what a sight it were
> To see thee in our waters yet appear,
> And make those flights upon the banks of Thames
> That so did take Eliza, and our James.

In fact, Jonson immortalised Shakespeare as the first person in the world of entertainment ever to be called a star:

> But stay, I see thee in the hemisphere
> Advance, and make a constellation there.
> Shine forth, thou star of poets.

We come finally to Shakespeare's death. In the spring of 1616, for the first time in his life, Shakespeare drew up his will. On 25 March he had it finalised, and within a month, on 23 April, he died. The proximity of the will-making to his death suggests that Shakespeare knew he was dying. However, from the only account of his death, written by John Ward, the vicar of Stratford in the 1660s – within living memory of the event – Shakespeare did not die after a lengthy illness. According to Ward, Shakespeare suddenly fell violently sick in the early hours of the morning and died before sunrise. Such an acute sickness could have resulted from poisoning, accidental or otherwise. Indeed, Reverend Ward actually says that Shakespeare's death had been attributed to food or drink taken the previous evening. If this was the true manner of Shakespeare's death, then it could hardly have been foreseen, unless it had been deliberate. Shakespeare's apparent foresight of his own death could therefore suggest that he believed his life to be in danger. Recalling the suspicious circumstances surrounding the deaths of Christopher Marlowe and Lord Strange, and the sinister world of intrigue that appears to have surrounded Shakespeare's life, it is tempting to speculate whether the past had finally caught up with him.

If Shakespeare was murdered, who had the motive, means and opportunity? Many of those with whom he may have been involved in the world of espionage were already dead or imprisoned, while others had conveniently disappeared. Richard Baines was arrested for murder and hanged on 6 December 1594. Richard Cholmeley disappeared in 1593, as did Parrot ten years later. Nicholas Skeres was imprisoned at Bridewell in July 1601 and was never heard of again. Thomas Kyd died from the torture he received in 1594 and Robert Poley ran his final government errand in 1601, vanishing without trace. Others settled for the quiet life. Anthony Munday gave up persecuting Catholics and became a recluse, Thomas Walsingham was content to live as a country squire, Matthew Roydon joined the entourage of William Hamilton, a Scottish favourite of James I, and Ingram Frizer retired to Eltham in Kent, where he became a church-warden.

As for the Gunpowder Plotters, those directly implicated were all dead, while Henry Percy had been in the Tower since 1606, where he would remain until 1621.

The man who may have had the strongest motive was still alive, free and certainly aggrieved: Sir Walter Ralegh. If Shakespeare was William Hall, Ralegh had rotted in prison for thirteen long years as a consequence of Hall's actions. Ralegh also had the means and had previously evidenced a ruthless and violent streak. But most importantly, he had the opportunity. After spending thirteen years in the Tower of London, Ralegh was finally released on 19 March 1616, just six days before Shakespeare made his will. Is this merely coincidence? Or did Shakespeare know of Ralegh's release and consider himself in danger?

The evidence for William Hall being Shakespeare is compelling, the evidence for Hall betraying the Bye Plot is overwhelming, and that Ralegh was involved in the Bye Plot is beyond reasonable doubt. After thirteen years Ralegh is released from prison. Within only a few weeks the man most likely to have caused his incarceration dies, seemingly from some form of poisoning. Although the pattern of circumstances seems suspicious, without further evidence this must remain an unsolved mystery in the strange life of William Shakespeare.

* * *

The turbulent years of the Elizabethan era saw the end of William Shakespeare, the man, but marked only the beginning of the world's most famous literary figure. The mythical image of Shakespeare will doubtless continue to flourish. We have concerned ourselves with an investigation into Shakespeare's true role in Elizabethan history. Whatever the extent of his involvement in the machinations of the period to which he has given his name, nothing can detract from the brilliance of the man or his work. Perhaps in the future new material will be discovered, enabling us to know still more about Shakespeare's life and character. It is hoped that the speculations and discoveries in this examination may encourage new lines of investigation into the true history of the genius whose work continues to inspire millions across the world.

Summary

An investigation into the enigma of Shakespeare's sudden retirement in 1613 may provide the solution to three further mysteries. Why there is no contemporary portrait, the lack of literary references in his will and the writing difficulty apparent from Shakespeare's signatures.

1. Shakespeare's theatrical career seems to have ended abruptly

with the burning down of the Globe Theatre on 29 June 1613. After the fire the shareholders paid around £60 each for the re-building, except for Shakespeare. As there is no record of Shakespeare's contribution, he must have sold his interest in the theatre at this time, accounting for the absence of the shares in his will. Since the will makes no reference to the Blackfriars Theatre shares it must be assumed that he also sold these.

2. The Globe fire, coinciding precisely with Shakespeare's sud-den retirement, appears to indicate an inter-relationship. Perhaps a life's work perished in the blaze. This would certainly explain the lack of manuscripts in Shakespeare's will. But thirty-seven of his plays survived, and all but one, *Pericles*, were later preserved in the First Folio. As far as is known, this accounts for them all. There has to be an additional explanation for Shake-speare's retirement.

3. In their prefatory introduction in the 1623 First Folio, Shake-speare's fellow actors Heminge and Condell say that Shakespeare was 'maimed and deformed by the frauds and stealths of injurious impostors'. As 'maimed and deformed' seems an odd way of describing the alteration of his works, seem-ingly the meaning implied, Heminge and Condell may be referring to something about Shakespeare himself. Had Shake-speare been seriously injured in the Globe fire?

4. Shakespeare's disablement might have compelled him to with-draw from public life. He certainly seems to have kept to himself in Stratford after 1612. Aside from some minor involvement in the matter of land enclosures in 1614, there is no longer any record of his usual business transactions.

5. Further suspicion that Shakespeare had been injured in the fire is fuelled by the mystery of his will. It was drawn up by Shakespeare's executor Thomas Russell. It is difficult to imagine Shakespeare not writing his own will unless, for some reason, he was unable to do so. Was there some physical restraint, making writing almost impossible? We have seen how his surviving signa-tures, all post-1612, appear to be written by an incompetent and

unsteady hand. Some disability seems to be the only rational explanation for Shakespeare's weak and inconsistent signature.

6. Shakespeare may have sustained even greater injury. Some manner of facial deformity is hinted at by Ben Jonson in his eulogy on Shakespeare in the First Folio. For some reason, Jonson draws attention to Shakespeare's portrait, suggesting that it is not Shakespeare's true appearance. He also says that the engraver had been forced to improve upon Shakespeare's features. Why should the engraver have to improve on Shakespeare, unless he was in some way unusual in appearance or disfigured?

7. Shakespeare's disfigurement may also answer another mystery of his life. Why is there no authentic portrait, when portraits have survived of many comparable dramatists of the time? Perhaps Shakespeare destroyed all record of his former appearance in a fit of depression, as Thomas Hariot had done when afflicted with cancer of the nose in the 1620s.

8. Why did no one in Stratford appear to have known of Shakespeare's poetry, his plays and his former glory, when he returned home? If he had been disfigured or otherwise deformed, he might have refused to socialise, confining himself to a sullen, hermit-like existence. Moreover, if he could no longer write, he may have decried his own work, even eradicated whatever original material he still possessed.

9. In the spring of 1616, for the first time in his life, Shakespeare drew up his will. On 25 March it was finalised and within a month, on 23 April, he died. Such proximity suggests that Shakespeare knew he was dying. However, from the only account of his death, written by John Ward, the vicar of Stratford in the 1660s, Shakespeare suddenly fell violently sick in the early hours of the morning and died before sunrise. Such an acute sickness could have resulted from poisoning. Indeed, Reverend Ward actually says that Shakespeare's death had been attributed to food or drink taken the previous evening.

10. If Shakespeare was murdered, the man who may have been

responsible was Sir Walter Ralegh. If Shakespeare was William Hall, then it seems that Ralegh had spent years in prison as a result of Hall's work. After spending thirteen years in the Tower of London, Ralegh was released on 19 March 1616, just six days before Shakespeare made his will. Did Shakespeare know of Ralegh's release and consider himself in danger?

Chronology

1564   26 April: William Shakespeare baptised at Holy Trinity Church, Stratford.

1567   Mary Queen of Scots seeks asylum in Britain. She is confined to house arrest for the next nineteen years.

1571   Shakespeare's father John appointed chief alderman of Stratford.

1573   Warrant issued for John Shakespeare's arrest for the non-payment of £30.

1576   The opening of James Burbage's Theatre in Shoreditch, the first purpose-built theatre in England since Roman times.

1577   John Shakespeare forced to mortgage a property inherited by his wife Mary.

1579   John Shakespeare unable to pay the town levies.

1580   John Shakespeare arrested for disorderly conduct and fined £20.
       Richard Baines and Anthony Munday working as spies in Rheims.
       Lord Strange befriends Edward Kelly in Lancashire.

1581   William Shakespeare included in the will of Alexander Hoghton of Lea Hall near Preston.
       Thomas Watson first associated with the Walsinghams in Paris.

1582   Kelly and Strange meet regularly with astrologer John Dee.
       John Shakespeare ceases attending church 'for fear of process for debt'.
       January: Matthew Roydon signs a bond to repay £40 to

a London goldsmith. The bond is co-signed by Nicholas Skeres.

27 November: Licence issued for William Shakespeare to marry Anne Whatley of Temple Grafton.

28 November: Marriage of William Shakespeare to Anne Hathaway of Stratford.

1583 Robert Poley working for Philip Sidney at Barn Elms.

26 May: Baptism of Shakespeare's daughter Susanna.

1584 Francis Bacon enters Parliament.

1585 The Ralegh group meets at the home of Fulke Greville in Whitehall.

2 February: Baptism of Shakespeare's twins Hamnet and Judith.

1586 The Privy Council endorse an unspecified annual grant of £1,000 to Lord Oxford.

Matthew Roydon writes for Philip Sidney.

May: The Babington Plot to enthrone Mary Queen of Scots is hatched at the Plough in London's Temple Bar. Robert Poley infiltrates the conspiracy.

6 July: Anthony Babington writes to Mary Queen of Scots, informing her of the aims of the conspiracy and seeking her consent.

4 August: Walsingham's agents surround the Babington Plotters at the house of Anthony Hall.

14 August: Anthony Babington arrested.

20 September: Babington Plotters executed.

1587 John Shakespeare suspended from Stratford council. Richard Field inherits the Blackfriars publishing concern.

8 February: Mary Queen of Scots beheaded at Fotheringay Castle.

13 June: The Queen's Men perform in Stratford.

2 October: Christopher Marlowe mentioned as a courier in despatches to the Secretary of State from Utrecht in Holland.

1588 The defeat of the Spanish Armada.

Anthony Munday working for the Archbishop of Canterbury arresting religious extremists.

1589 Lord Strange first patronises his company of players.

William Shakespeare named in legal proceedings regarding an unpaid mortgage on his mother's property in Wilmcote.

July: Robert Poley working for Francis Walsingham.

18 September: Marlowe arrested for fighting a duel in Finsbury.

3 December: Marlowe acquitted of murder.

1590 Death of Sir Francis Walsingham.

Publication of Thomas Watson's *Meliboeus*.

Lord Strange's Men temporarily amalgamate with The Lord Admiral's Men.

Publication of Edmund Spenser's *The Fairy Queen*.

Shakespeare working with Anthony Munday on *Sir Thomas More*.

Completion of *Titus Andronicus*, most likely Shakespeare's first play.

Marlowe and Shakespeare working together in Lord Strange's company and at the Burbage Theatre in Shoreditch.

1591 Ralegh banned from Court.

William Cecil recruits Edward Kelly to work as an informant in Prague.

May: Matthew Roydon working for William Cecil as a courier.

1592 Henry Field dies and Shakespeare's father values his estate.

Thomas Watson includes Roydon's poems, together with personal praise, in his *Ekatompathia*.

Marlowe referred to as a messenger between the government and the British Ambassador in Paris.

Father Robert Parsons, in his *Responsio ad Elizabethae Edictum*, writes of 'the popular school of atheism of Walter Ralegh'.

The *Advertisement* mounts an attack on Ralegh's atheism.

Giordano Bruno refers to 'Ralegh's School of Atheism' from first-hand experience.

Robert Greene's *Groat's-worth of Wit* warns other writers about the arrogant 'upstart crow', possibly referring to William Shakespeare.

January: Marlowe's *Doctor Faustus* performed at the Theatre.

26 February: Marlowe's *The Jew of Malta* first performed by Lord Strange's Men at the Theatre.

23 April: Last performance at the Shoreditch Theatre of Marlowe's *Doctor Faustus*.

17 June: 'Will Hall' paid for services to the Archbishop's Pursuivant Anthony Munday.

1593   Amalgamation of Lord Strange's Men and the Burbage players.

The printer Henry Chettle takes offence at Greene for his criticism of various writers, one of which may by the 'upstart crow'.

January: Lord Strange's Men perform the premiere of Marlowe's *Massacre at Paris*.

10 March: George Chapman writes to Walter Warner concerning the Ralegh group, implicating Marlowe, Hariot and Strange.

18 April: Shakespeare's *Venus and Adonis* registered in the Stationers' Register and published later in the year.

22 April: Thomas Kyd arrested by the Privy Council.

18 May: Marlowe summoned for questioning by the Privy Council.

20 May: Marlowe appears before the Privy Council.

21 May: Richard Cholmeley instructed to spy on Marlowe.

Late May: Richard Baines's Marlowe report sent to the Privy Council.

30 May: Death of Christopher Marlowe.

1 June: Coroner's report on the Marlowe killing.

12 June: Robert Poley paid as a government courier.

28 June: Ingram Frizer acquitted of the Marlowe killing.

29 June: Frizer working for Thomas Walsingham.

28 August: William Hall travels to Prague with a despatch from William Cecil to Edward Kelly, probably concerning the Hesketh Plot.

25 September: Lord Strange becomes the Earl of

Derby.

27 September: Richard Hesketh tries to involve Lord Strange in his plan to overthrow the government. Strange informs William Cecil.

10 October: Hesketh arrested and later executed.

October: Gabriel Harvey writes the poem *Gorgon*.

1594 Poley working for William Cecil in the Netherlands, Scotland and France.

March: The Cerne Abbas commission to investigate Ralegh's alleged atheism.

10 March: Strange summoned to the Privy Council, supposedly to answer allegations of blasphemy.

29 March: William Cecil receives letter from Strange, informing him of a conspiracy. The conspiracy seemingly involves Thomas Walsingham and/or Walter Ralegh, and a plan to assassinate Cecil.

1 April: Strange returns to his country home at Lathom House, near Ormskirk in Lancashire. Soon after his arrival he falls violently ill.

9 April: Cecil seems unaware of Strange's condition, as a new summons is issued for him to attend the Privy Council.

16 April: Death of Lord Strange. Lord Strange's Men patronised by the Lord Chamberlain Lord Hunsdon.

22 April: Ralegh writes to the Queen, requesting permission to return to sea.

19 May: Registration of William Shakespeare's second published poem, *The Rape of Lucrece*.

6 December: Richard Baines hanged for murder.

December: 'Will Kempe, Will Shakespeare, and Richard Burbage, servants to the lord chamberlain' are paid £20 for 'several comedies' acted before the Queen.

1594–8 *Henry VI: Parts I & II, Richard III, Titus Andronicus, Romeo and Juliet* and *Richard II* published anonymously in London.

1596 Richard Field's name appears on a document proposing the building of the Globe.

Joseph Hall, in his *Hall's Satires Book IV*, suggests that Bacon is the author of the Shakespeare poems.

19 March: The Chamber Treasurer pays £15 to 'Hall and Wayte' for 'messages' conveyed from the Netherlands to the Secretary of State. Agent Parrot paid £15 for unspecified services.

22 July: Death of Lord Hunsdon. William, Eleventh Earl Cobham, replaces him as Lord Chamberlain.

August: Shakespeare's son Hamnet dies and is buried in Stratford.

29 November: Rolls of the Queen's Bench in London record that a William Wayte craves sureties of the peace against William Shakespeare 'for fear of death and so forth'.

1597 Secret Service agent Parrot working with Robert Poley in Marshalsea Prison, spying on the imprisoned Jesuit Father Barkworth.

Death of James Burbage.

Publication of Thomas Beard's *Theatre of God's Judgements*.

Bacon writes a collection of ten essays on political behaviour.

17 March: Hunsdon's son, George Carey, becomes Lord Chamberlain.

4 May: Shakespeare buys New Place, the second largest house in Stratford.

November: Tax collectors for the ward of Bishopsgate in London list Shakespeare as failing to pay a tax of five shillings (25p) before leaving the area.

1598 Building of the Globe at Southwark.

Field publishes Philip Sidney's collected works.

In his *Pigmalion's Image*, John Marston suggests that Bacon is the author of the Shakespeare poems.

A passage from George Puttenham's *Arte of English Poesie* refers to Lord Oxford as the leader of a group of courtly poets.

Francis Meres, in his *Palladis Tamia*, considers Shakespeare to be among 'the most excellent' English playwrights. Meres also praises Shakespeare's poems, and names twelve of Shakespeare's plays. This list, coupled with the known existence of the six already printed, brings the total number of known Shakespeare plays to fourteen by this year.

Ben Jonson lists Shakespeare as an actor in his play *Every Man in his Humour*.

24 January: Abraham Sturley of Stratford writes to a Richard Quiney, saying that Shakespeare may decide 'to deal in the matter of our tithes'.

4 February: Shakespeare is listed in Stratford as holding 80 bushels of grain.

4 August: Death of William Cecil. His son Robert replaces him as Secretary of State.

1 October: Shakespeare wanted for tax evasion in the London Parish of St Helen's.

25 October: Richard Quiney of Stratford writes to Shakespeare asking for a loan of £30.

December: Stratford Civic Chamber records ten pence paid to Shakespeare for one load of stone.

1599   William Jaggard publishes *The Passionate Pilgrim*, a collection of poems he attributes to Shakespeare. Included are two of the 154 *Sonnets* (138 and 144) published in full ten years later.

21 February: Shakespeare holds a 10 per cent shareholding in the Globe, along with Heminge, Condell, Augustine Phillips and 'other partners'.

May: Shakespeare occupies a house in St Saviour's parish, London.

30 June: The Jesuit George Fenner writes two letters naming Lord Derby as a playwright.

6 October: Shakespeare again wanted for tax evasion in London's St Helen's parish, traced to Sussex by the authorities.

1600   John Bodenham's *Garden of Muses* contains poems composed by Lord Strange.

Publication of William Vaughan's *The Golden Grove*.

October: The tax owed by Shakespeare is referred to the Bishop of Winchester for collection. Later the bishop records that the sum is paid in full by unnamed persons referred to him by the sheriff.

1601   7 February: The Lord Chamberlain's Men stage

Richard II at the globe.

8 February: The abortive Essex rebellion.

19 February: Lord Southampton sentenced to death, later commuted to life imprisonment.

25 February: Lord Essex executed.

July: Nicholas Skeres imprisoned at Bridewell.

8 September: John Shakespeare buried at Holy Trinity Church.

2 October: 'Willm Halle' recorded by the Secretary of State's clerk as having returned with intelligence from Denmark. Agent Parrot also mentioned in the Chamber Treasurer's account as receiving the sum of £10 for 'a message conveyed'.

*c*1601   Students of St John's College, Cambridge, stage the play *Pilgrimage to Parnassus*, which includes a speech by the actor William Kempe. During his speech Kempe mentions his 'fellow' Shakespeare.

1602   Stratford legal proceedings regarding New Place use the words 'generous gentleman', referring to Shakespeare.

13 March: John Manningham writes in his diary of the joke between actor Richard Burbage and William Shakespeare.

1 May: Shakespeare pays William and John Combe £320 for 107 acres of land north of Stratford.

28 September: Shakespeare buys a cottage on 'Walkers Street alias Dead Lane' in Stratford for an undisclosed amount.

1603   24 March: Death of Elizabeth. King James of Scotland becomes James I of England. Ralegh dismissed as Captain of the Guard and Governor of Jersey.

Francis Bacon knighted.

Bacon writes *The Advancement of Learning*, hoping to persuade James I to support the development of physical science.

A lease for a property east of New Place in Stratford mentions that it adjoins the land of Mr William Shakespeare.

19 May: Shakespeare's company granted a King's licence to continue to perform. The licence names

Lawrence Fletcher, William Shakespeare, Richard Burbage, Augustine Phillips, John Heminge, Henry Condell, William Sly, Robert Armin, Richard Cowly 'and the rest of their associates'.

29 June: Robert Cecil assures Lord Howard that he has an informant working close to Ralegh. Cecil indicates he has proof to implicate Ralegh in conspiracy. The same day he orders the Chamber Treasurer to pay £20 to a 'Will Halle' for information supplied.

3 July: A despatch sent to Robert Cecil from Secret Service operative Parrot, assures the Secretary that the intelligence he has received is trustworthy.

Ralegh implicated in the Bye Plot and arrested. He is sentenced to death, commuted to life imprisonment.

2 September: The King's Men appear before the King at Wilton in Wiltshire, the home of William, Earl of Pembroke.

1604   Supernova occurs in the constellation of Cygnus.

Publication of Thomas Middleton's *Black Book*.

Shakespeare lodging with Christopher Mountjoy, a maker of women's headdresses in Cripplegate.

March: The King's Men, with William Shakespeare heading the list, are given red cloth to prepare for King James's tour of the city of London.

July: Shakespeare takes legal action to collect a debt of £1.15s.10d (£1.80) from a Stratford apothecary, Philip Rogers. The money owed is for malt supplied the previous March.

1605   William Camden, antiquary and headmaster of Westminster School, in his *Remaines*, calls Shakespeare one of the 'most pregnant wits of our times'.

Simon Studion publishes the *Naometria*, in which he predicts a new age of enlightenment.

May: Augustine Phillips's will names William Shakespeare.

24 July: Shakespeare purchases half the corn and hay tithes in three Stratford hamlets. The price paid is £440.

November: The Gunpowder Plot.

1606   Henry Percy implicated in the Gunpowder Plot and

imprisoned in the Tower of London.

Johannes Kepler records the 1604 supernova in his *De Stella Nove*.

1607 Francis Bacon appointed Solicitor General.

5 June: Marriage of Shakespeare's daughter Susanna to local physician John Hall.

9 September: Shakespeare's mother Mary is buried at Holy Trinity Church.

1608 The Blackfriars Theatre erected.

Thorpe's printer George Eld publishes Thomas Hariot's pamphlet, which includes the coded message sent by Galileo to the astronomer Kepler.

9 August: The Blackfriars Theatre is leased by seven men, including Richard and Cuthbert Burbage, John Heminge, William Shakespeare and Henry Condell.

December: Shakespeare sues John Addenbrooke of Stratford for a debt of £6 plus £1.15s (£1.75) costs. Addenbrooke arrested.

1609 Publication of Bacon's *On the Wisdom of the Ancients*.

Printer Thomas Thorpe publishes the 154 *Shake-speare's Sonnets*.

1610 Shakespeare involved in legal proceedings regarding New Place, and buys a further twenty acres of land.

8 October: John Davies's poem entered in the Stationers' Register. A few lines refer to Shakespeare as an actor, while comparing his work as a dramatist to the Roman playwright Terence.

*c***1611** Shakespeare writes his last play, *The Tempest*.

1611 Shakespeare involved in legal proceedings regarding his tithe holding.

September: Shakespeare's name appears on a list of Stratford citizens contributing to a fund to persuade Parliament to pass a bill for the better repair of highways.

1612 John Webster writes in complementary terms about seven of his fellow playwrights, including Shakespeare.

Playwright Thomas Heywood refers to Shakespeare's works in passing.

11 May: Shakespeare's signature appears on a

deposition regarding a legal suit being brought against Christopher Mountjoy.

24 May: Death of Robert Cecil.

1613 Francis Bacon appointed Attorney General.

28 January: John Combe, a Stratford pawnbroker, draws up a will in which he leaves Shakespeare £5.

10 March: William Shakespeare buys a house in Blackfriars near the Blackfriars Theatre for £140. Both the deed and mortgage documents are signed by Shakespeare.

29 June: The Globe burns down. Although the theatre is rebuilt, Shakespeare seems to have relinquished his shares in the company.

1614 The King's Men appeal to James I to allow them to establish their theatre on a new location. Francis Bacon opposes the move.

A number of Stratford landowners attempt to enclose land belonging to the town corporation. Shakespeare is involved as both the owner of 107 acres and as part-owner of tithes from adjoining land.

1615 Francis Beaumont writes a poetical letter to Ben Jonson including the words, 'And from all learning keep these lines as clear as Shakespeare's are'.

May: Shakespeare is named in a suit involving his Blackfriars property.

1616 Bacon appointed to the Privy Council.

10 February: Shakespeare's daughter Judith marries Thomas Quiney.

19 March: Ralegh released from the Tower of London.

25 March: Shakespeare makes his will. Daughter Susanna gets most of the property, nearly all goods and household effects go to son-in-law John, daughter Judith receives a yearly allowance of around £150, and wife Anne gets the 'second best bed'.

The will, drawn up by Shakespeare's executor but signed by Shakespeare himself, contains nothing to link Shakespeare with any literary activities. There is no reference to books, manuscripts or the shares in the Globe and Blackfriars theatres.

25 April: The burial register of Stratford's Holy Trinity Church records the burial of 'Will Shakspere gent'.

1618 29 October: After displeasing the King and failing to return with gold from Guyana, Walter Ralegh is beheaded.

1619 13 March: Death of Richard Burbage.

1620 Bacon's *The Great Instauration* includes an encyclopedia of natural phenomena.

1621 Ben Jonson is a guest of honour at Bacon's birthday celebrations at York House on the Strand. After being made Viscount St Albans, Bacon is convicted for accepting bribes. During and after his imprisonment, Bacon completes a number of historical, scientific and philosophical works, including *De Augmentis Scientiarum* which contains the AB code.

1623 8 August: Burial of Shakespeare's wife Anne in Holy Trinity Church.
8 November: Shakespeare's First Folio is registered for publication. It contains thirty-six plays, including eighteen never before printed. The Folio is prefaced by dedications from John Heminge and Henry Condell, and four poems praising Shakespeare by Ben Jonson, Hugh Holland, Leonard Digges and a mysterious I.M.

1624 A letter written to Bacon by his friend Sir Tobie Mathew suggests that Bacon is a dramatist using a pseudonym.

1626 9 April: Death of Francis Bacon.

1634 Lieutenant Hammond proposes that the Shakespeare tomb in Stratford's Holy Trinity Church is the final resting place of the playwright William Shakespeare.

1656 An engraving in Sir William Dugdale's *Antiquities of Warwickshire* shows the original Shakespeare bust in Holy Trinity Church.

1662 John Ward becomes vicar of Stratford. In his diaries Ward records the little he has discovered about Shakespeare's life in his parish.

1663 Thomas Fuller writes a few lines on the Shakespeare of Stratford in his *Worthies of England*. He finds little to couple the Stratfordian with the Shakespeare plays.

1681 Antiquarian John Aubrey includes William Shakespeare in his *Minutes of Lives*.

1709 Publication of Nicholas Rowe's Shakespeare biography, *Some Account of the Life of Mr William Shakespeare*. One illustration shows a Shakespeare tomb bust similar to Dugdale's drawing.

1725 Alexander Pope's Shakespeare biography is published.

1748 Theatrical manager John Hall restores the Shakespeare bust in Holy Trinity Church.

1755 Publication of Samuel Johnson's *Dictionary*.

1781 English clergyman Reverend Wilmot concludes that Shakespeare had not possessed the necessary education nor experience to have written the plays accredited to him. He proposes Francis Bacon as the true author.

1785 Editor George Stevens describes Shakespeare's original tomb slab in Holy Trinity Church.

1821 An illustration of Shakespeare's original tomb inscription is published in Edmund Malone's edition of Shakespeare's plays.

1830 Shakespeare's tomb slab in Holy Trinity Church is replaced.

1857 In his pamphlet *Bacon and Shakespeare*, William Henry Smith makes the first substantial claim for Bacon's authorship of the Shakespeare plays.

1859 Lord Chief Justice Campbell discredits the Baconian legal argument.

1871 Richard Simpson suggests that Shakespeare had helped edit Anthony Munday's *Sir Thomas More* around 1590.

1887 In an article in the October issue of the *North American Review*, Hugh Black proposes a Bacon confession code in the Shakespeare tomb inscription.

1888 American lawyer Ignatius Donnelly publishes *The Great Cryptogram* proposing that Francis Bacon had left concealed messages in the Shakespeare plays admitting authorship.

1889 W.C. Devecmon's *Re Shakespeare's Legal Acquirements* advances a strong case against the plays being written by an important lawyer such as Bacon.

1913 J.M. Robertson's *The Baconian Heresy* further

discredits the Baconian case. He demonstrates that other contemporary playwrights used precisely the same legal phraseology as Shakespeare.

1916 Sir E. Maunde Thompson, the British Museum's Principal Librarian, publishes a series of essays, *Shakespeare's Handwriting*, arguing that the six known examples of Shakespeare's signature match the handwriting of the editor of Munday's *Sir Thomas More*.

1919 The French professor Abel Lefranc proposes William Stanley, Earl of Derby, as the author of the Shakespeare plays.

1920 Gateshead schoolmaster John Looney proposes Edward de Vere, Earl of Oxford, as the author of the Shakespeare plays.

1925 Discovery of the original coroner's report on Marlowe's death in the archives of the London Record Office by Leslie Hotson.

1952 Publication of A.W. Titherley's *Shakespeare's Identity*, proposing Lord Derby's handwriting matches Shakespeare's amendments to Munday's *Sir Thomas More* play.

1955 Canadian journalist Calvin Hoffman proposes Christopher Marlowe as the author of the Shakespeare plays.

1956 Hoffman opens the Walsingham tomb in Chislehurst.

1985 In his *Shakespeare: The Lost Years*, Ernst Honigmann proposes the Lancashire tutor William Shakeshafte as William Shakespeare.

Bibliography

Abbreviations for Manuscript Collections, etc.

BL – British Library. CRS – Catholic Records Society. CSP – Calendar of State Papers. HMC – Historical Manuscripts Commission. LP – Lambeth Palace Library. PRO – Public Records Office. SP – State Papers. APC – Acts of the Privy Council (1542-1604).

Source Material in the Original

Babington Plot: PRO SP 53. Bodleian Rawlinson D264. BL Lansdowne 49. Plough Meeting: CSP Scottish 8. Babington Letter: PRO SP53/19. Queen Mary's Reply: CSP Scottish 9. Babington & Poley: CSP Scottish 8. Skeres & Babington: CSP Scottish 8.

Baines, Richard: Marlowe Report: BL Harley 6848. Queen's Copy: BL Harley 6853. In Rheims: PRO SP 12/155.

Bruno, Giordana: CSP Foreign.

Catholic Activities Abroad: CRS 52.

Cecil, William: BL MS Lansdowne PRO E351/542. HMC Cecil 4 & 5. Cecil Diary: HMC Cecil 13.

Chamber Treasurer Accounts: PRO E351/542.

Chapman, George: APC 23 & 24.

Cholmeley, Richard: BL Harley 6848.

Elizabethan Secret Service: PRO E351/542. CSP Scottish 8. BL Lansdowne MSS. HMC Cecil 5. Accounts: PRO E351/542. Cecil Diary: HMC Cecil 13. Secret Service Activities: 1591: PRO SP12/238. 1592: PRO SP12/243. 1593: PRO SP12 245.

1594: LP MS 650. 1595: HMC Cecil 5. Secret Service
Couriers: PRO SP 106/2. PRO E351/542.

Frizer, Ingram: PRO Close Rolls 1339. PRO Exchequer Plea
Rolls 381 & 396. Pardon for Marlowe Killing: PRO Patent
Rolls 1401.

Hall, Anthony: CSP Scottish 8.

Hall, William: Hesketh Plot: HMC Cecil 4. SP Hamburg III.
As Courier: PRO SP 106/2. Bye Plot: HMC Cecil 20.

Hesketh Plot: HMC Cecil 4. HMC Cecil 5.

Kelly, Edward: Kelly & Dee: BL Sloane 3188. CRS 52. As
Secret Service Agent: Bodleian Ashmole 1420. HMC Cecil
4. PRO SP 12/239.

Kyd, Thomas: Testimony of: BL Harley 247 & 6448. CRS 52.

Marlowe, Christopher: As Secret Service Agent: PRO E351/
542. Arrest: APC 24. Death Inquest: PRO C260/174. And
Thomas Walsingham: APC 24.

Munday, Anthony: CRS 2. CRS 5.

Parrot: PRO SP12/170. CRS 2.

Parsons, Robert: CRS 52. CRS 2.

Percy, Henry: CRS 21. BL Hargrave 226. Percy & Watson:
Bodleian Northumberland 1928. Petworth Library: BL
Harley 1879.

Poley, Robert: PRO SP 12/222. PRO SP 78/17. PRO SP12,
SP84 & SP106. CSP Scottish 8. Chamber accounts: PRO
E351/542. Cecil 4 & 5. Poley and Babington: CSP Scottish 8.
Poley & Southwell: CRS 52. In Marshalsea: PRO SP12/170.
CRS 2.

Roydon, Matthew: PRO Close Rolls 1144/24.

School of Night: BL Harley 6849.

Sidney Philip: CSP Scottish 8. HMC Cecil 3. PRO SP84/43.

Skeres, Nicholas: HMC Cecil 5. PRO 5 S9/8. Skeres &
Babington: CSP Scottish 8. As Secret Service Agent: PRO
E351/542.

Strange, Lord: HMC Cecil 4. PRO SP12/243. CRS 5. PRO
SP12/249. CSP Domestic 4. HMC Cecil 13.

Walsingham, Francis: CSP Foreign 1581–2. CSP Scottish 8.

Warner, Walter: HMC I 277.

Watson, Thomas: PRO Chancery Misc 68. PRO Patent Rolls
32 C66/1340. CSP Domestic 3. Watson's Daughter: PRO
SP12/222.

Woodleff, Drew: PRO Chancery Proceedings W 25.

Selected Bibliography

Acheson, Arthur. *Shakespeare's Lost Years in London*. Quaritch, London 1920.

Adams, John. *The Globe Playhouse*. Cambridge Univ. Press 1942.

Adams, Joseph. *Shakespearean Playhouses*. Mifflin, Boston 1917.

Akrigg, G. *Shakespeare and the Earl of Southampton*. Hamish Hamilton, London 1962.

Amphlett, Hilda. *Who Was Shakespeare?* Heinemann, London 1955.

Arber, Edward (ed). *A Transcript of the Registers of the Company of Stationers of London 1554–1640*. London 1875.

Aubrey, John. *Aubrey's Brief Lives*. Clarendon, Oxford 1898.

Bagley, J. *The Earls of Derby*. Sidgwick & Jackson, London 1985.

Barnard, E.A.B. *New Links with Shakespeare*. Cambridge Univ. Press 1910.

Bentley, Gerald Eades. *Shakespeare: A Biographical Handbook*. Yale Univ. Press, New Haven 1961.

– *The Profession of Dramatist in Shakespeare's Time*. Princeton Univ. Press 1971.

– *The Profession of Player in Shakespeare's Time*. Princeton Univ. Press 1984.

Bindhoff, S.T. *Tudor England*. Penguin, Harmondsworth 1950.

Boas, Frederick. *University Drama in the Tudor Age*. Clarendon Press, Oxford 1914.

– *Christopher Marlowe*. Clarendon, Oxford 1940.

Bradbrook, Muriel. *The Rise of the Common Player*. Chatto & Windus, London 1962.

Brown, Ivor. *Shakespeare*. Collins, London 1949.

Burgess, Anthony. *Shakespeare*. Cape, London 1970.

Camden, William. *Annales*. Fisher, London 1625.

– *Remaines*. Russell Smith, London 1870.

Chambers, E. *The Elizabethan Stage*. Clarendon Press, Oxford 1923.

– *Oxford Book of Sixteenth-Century Verse*. Clarendon, Oxford 1961.

Chute, Marchette. *Shakespeare of London*. Souvenir, London 1977.

Condell, Charles. *They Gave us Shakespeare*. Oriel Press, Stockfield 1982.

Courthope, W.J. *A History of English Poetry*. Macmillan, London 1920.

Cunningham, Peter. *Extracts from the Accounts of the Revels at Court in the Reigns of Queen Elizabeth and King James I*. Shakespeare Society, London 1842.

Dasent, John (ed). *Acts of the Privy Council of England*. Eyre & Spottiswoode, London 1907.

Davies, Michael Justin. *The Landscape of William Shakespeare*. Webb & Bower, Exeter 1987.

Donnelly, Ignatius. *The Great Cryptogram*. New York 1888.

Dugdale, William. *Antiquities of Warwickshire*. Warren, London 1656.

Durning-Lawrence, Edwin. *Bacon Is Shakespeare*. London 1910.

Dutton, Richard. *William Shakespeare: A Literary Life*. Macmillan, London 1989.

Eccles, Mark. *Shakespeare in Warwickshire*. Univ. of Wisconsin Press, Madison 1961.

– *Christopher Marlowe in London*. Cambridge Univ. Press 1934.

Fido, Martin. *Shakespeare*. Hamlyn, London 1978.

Fripp, Edgar. *Shakespeare's Stratford*. Oxford Univ. Press, London 1928.

– (ed) *Minutes and Accounts of the Corporation of Stratford-upon-Avon*. Dugdale Society, Oxford 1921.

Friedman, William & Elizabeth. *The Shakespeare Ciphers Examined*. Cambridge Univ. Press 1957.

Fuller, Thomas. *The History of the Worthies of England*. London 1662.

Gibson H.N. *The Shakespeare Claimants*. Methuen, London 1962.

Goadby, Edwin. *The England of Shakespeare*. Cassell, London 1981.

Gordon, George. *Shakespeare's English*. Clarendon, Oxford 1928.

Gray, Joseph. *Shakespeare's Marriage*. Chapman & Hall, London 1905.

Greene, Robert. *Greene's Groat's-worth of Wit*. W. Wright, London 1592.

Gurr, Andrew. *The Shakespeare Stage*. Cambridge Univ. Press, 1970.

Hamilton, Charles. *In Search of Shakespeare: A Study of the Poet's Life and Handwriting*. Robert Hale, London 1986.

Harbage, Alfred. *Conceptions of Shakespeare*. Harvard Univ. Press 1966.

Harsnett, Samuel. *A Declaration of Egregious Popish Impostures*. 1603.

Herford, C.H. *The Works of Ben Jonson*. Clarendon, Oxford 1947.

Hilton, Delia. *Who Was Kit Marlowe?* Weidenfeld, London 1977.

Hinman, Charlton. *The First Folio*. Norton, New York 1968.

Hoffman, Calvin. *The Man Who Was Shakespeare*. 1955.

Honigmann, E.A.J. *Shakespeare: The Lost Years*. Manchester Univ. Press, 1985.

Hosking, G.L. *The Life and Times of Edward Alleyn*. Cape, London 1952.

Hotson, Leslie. *The Death of Christopher Marlowe*. London 1925.

Hubler, Edward. *The Riddle of Shakespeare's Sonnets*. Basic Books, New York 1962.

Jenkins, Simon. *The Companion Guide to Outer London*. Collins, London 1981.

Jones, Emrys. *The Origins of Shakespeare*. Clarendon, Oxford 1971.

Kay, Dennis. *Shakespeare: His Life, His Works and Era*. Sidgwick & Jackson, London 1992.

Kennedy, W.P.M. *Elizabethan Episcopal Administration*. Mowbray, London 1924.

Kittredge, George. *The Complete Works of Shakespeare*. Ginn, Boston 1936.

Leftwich, Ralph. *The Evidence of Disease in Shakespeare's Handwriting*. Proceedings RSM, London 1919.

Leishman, James. *The Three Parnassus Plays*. Nicholson & Watson, London 1949.

Levi, Peter. *The Life and Times of William Shakespeare*.
Macmillan, London 1988.

Lewis, B. Roland. *The Shakespeare Documents*. Stanford
Univ. Press, 1940.

Looney, Thomas. *Shakespeare Identified as Edward de Vere,
the 17th Earl of Oxford*. Palmer, London 1920.

McGrath, Patrick. *Papists and Puritans under Elizabeth I*.
Blandford, London 1967.

Malone, Edward. *Shakespeare's Plays*. George Stevens,
London 1790.

Manningham, John. *Manningham's Diary*. John Bruce,
Westminster 1868.

Martin, Milward. *Was Shakespeare Shakespeare? A Lawyer
Reviews the Evidence*. Cooper, New York 1965.

Meres, Francis. *Palladis Tamia*. Triphook, London 1815.

Milward, Peter. *Shakespeare's Religious Background*. Sidgwick
& Jackson, London 1973.

Moryson, Fynes. *Shakespeare's Europe*. Sherratt & Hughes,
London 1903.

Muir, Kenneth. *The Sources of Shakespeare's Plays*. Methuen,
London 1977.

Nashe, Thomas. *Works of Thomas Nashe*. Blackwell, Oxford
1958.

Nicholl, Charles. *The Reckoning*. Cape, London 1992.

Notestein, Wallace. *The English People on the Eve of
Colonization*. Harper, New York 1954.

Nungezer, Edwin. *A Dictionary of Actors and of Other
Persons Associated with the Public Representation of Plays in
England Before 1642*. Yale Univ. Press, New Haven 1929.

O'Connor, Gary. *William Shakespeare: A Life*. Hodder &
Stoughton, London 1991.

Ogburn, Charlton. *The Mystery of William Shakespeare*.
Sphere, London 1988.

Payne, Robert. *By Me, William Shakespeare*. Everest, New
York 1980.

Pearson, H. *A Life of Shakespeare*. Carroll & Nicholson,
London 1949.

Piper, David. *The Companion Guide to London*. Collins,
London 1977.

Plowden, Alison. *The Elizabethan Secret Service*. London 1991.

Prockter, Adrian and Taylor, Robert. *The A to Z of Elizabethan London*. London Topographical Society 1979.

Ralegh, Sir Walter. *The Works of Sir Walter Ralegh*. Oxford Univ. Press, London 1929.

Rutter, Carol. *Documents of the Rose Playhouse*. Manchester Univ. Press 1984.

Read, Conyers. *Lord Burghley and Queen Elizabeth*. Cape, London 1960.

Rowe, Nicholas. *Some Account of the Life of Mr William Shakespeare*. Tonson, London 1709.

Rowse, A.L. *William Shakespeare: A Biography*. Harper & Row, New York 1963.

Sampson, George. *The Concise Cambridge History of English Literature*. Cambridge Univ. Press, 1961.

Schoenbaum, Samuel. *William Shakespeare: A Documentary Life*. Clarendon, Oxford 1975.

Shakespeare, William. *Mr William Shakespeare's Comedies, Histories and Tragedies*. Blount, London 1623.

Sheavyn, Phoebe. *The Literary Profession in the Elizabethan Age*. Manchester Univ. Press.

Smith, Alan. *William Cecil: The Power Behind Elizabeth*. RKP, London 1934.

Smith, William Henry. *Bacon and Shakespeare*. Smith, London 1857.

Speaight, Robert. *Shakespeare: The Man and his Achievements*. Dent, London 1977.

Spielmann, M.H. *The Title Page of the First Folio of Shakespeare's Plays*. Oxford Univ. Press. London 1924.

Stopes, Charlotte. *The Life and History of Henry, Third Earl of Southampton, Shakespeare's Patron*. Cambridge Univ. Press, 1922.

Strong, Roy. *The Cult of Elizabeth*. Thames & Hudson, London 1977.

Titherley, A.W. *Shakespeare's Identity: William Stanley, Sixth Earl of Derby*. Warren, Winchester 1952.

Thomas, David. *Shakespeare in the Public Records*. HMSO, London 1985.

Tillyard, E.M.W. *Shakespeare's History Plays*. Macmillan, New York 1946.

Wallace, Willard, *Sir Walter Ralegh*. Princeton Univ. Press
  1959.
Williamson, Hugh. *The Gunpowder Plot*. Faber & Faber,
  London 1951.
Wilson, Frank. *Marlowe and the Early Shakespeare*.
  Clarendon, Oxford 1953.

Index

222

Coming soon from Century

THE SEARCH FOR THE GRAIL

Astonishing new proof of the existence of the Grail in Britain

BY GRAHAM PHILLIPS

In *The Search for the Grail*, historical detective Graham Phillips describes his quest to locate the true Holy Grail.

In 1993, the discovery of a hitherto overlooked Arthurian story, buried in a longer poem, gave the author a precise geographical location for the Grail's original hiding place in Britain – the White Abbey, an Augustan priory in Shropshire. Further research revealed that the Grail was one of several treasures taken in 410 AD from Rome to the safety of Viroconium (near Shrewsbury) – virtually the last remaining vestige of Roman civilisation. But what happened to the Grail afterwards? Did it remain in the White Abbey until it was secretly discovered there in the late 16th century? Early in 1994, Phillips read a 17th century poem by Lord Vernon, who had been responsible for renovating the Abbey ruins. This describes how Sir Gawain retrieves the Grail after it had been stolen from the monks of the White Abbey, hiding it away in an unspecified location. But then the author discovers a secret code in the poem, envisaging the local landscape as a giant chessboard, which does specify the hiding place . . .

Now available in Arrow paperback

KING ARTHUR – THE TRUE STORY

BY GRAHAM PHILLIPS AND MARTIN KEATMAN

For fifteen hundred years, King Arthur has remained a mystery. For the first time, *King Arthur – The True Story* discovers the historical King Arthur, his Camelot, and his final resting place. As the authors uncover their vital evidence, centuries of myth are peeled away to reveal the truth behind the romance, and the Grail and Excalibur legends.

The search for Arthur's Camelot leads to ancient ruins in the heart of Britain – an incredible Dark Age city recently unearthed by archaeology. A mediaeval manuscript in Oxford's Bodleian Library finally identifies King Arthur's burial site: the real Avalon.

'Amazing book . . . brilliantly presented thesis' *Daily Mail*

'The popular myths fall like ninepins' *Sunday Express*

'As in all good detective stories, they save up their revelation to the denouement in the last chapter' *The Times*

OTHER TITLES AVAILABLE IN ARROW

☐ *King Arthur – The True Story*	Graham Phillips & Martin Keatman	£5.99
☐ *Novacosm – The Original Zodiac*	Melissa Marshall with Graham Phillips	£4.99
☐ *The Princes in the Tower*	Alison Weir	£6.99
☐ *The Six Wives of Henry VIII*	Alison Weir	£8.99
☐ *JFK – Reckless Youth*	Nigel Hamilton	£9.99

ALL ARROW BOOKS ARE AVAILABLE THROUGH MAIL ORDER OR FROM YOUR LOCAL BOOKSHOP AND NEWSAGENT.

PLEASE SEND CHEQUE/EUROCHEQUE/POSTAL ORDER (STERLING ONLY) ACCESS, VISA OR MASTERCARD

☐☐☐☐☐☐☐☐☐☐☐☐☐☐☐☐☐☐

EXPIRY DATE.......................... SIGNATURE..................................

PLEASE ALLOW 75 PENCE PER BOOK FOR POST AND PACKING U.K. OVERSEAS CUSTOMERS PLEASE ALLOW £1.00 PER COPY FOR POST AND PACKING.

ALL ORDERS TO:
ARROW BOOKS, BOOK SERVICE BY POST, P.O. BOX 29, DOUGLAS, ISLE OF MAN, IM99 1BQ. TEL: 01624 675137 FAX: 01624 670 923

NAME..

ADDRESS ....

....

Please allow 28 days for delivery. Please tick box if you do not wish to receive any additional information ☐

Prices and availability subject to change without notice.